In a Great and Noble Tradition

Pastel portrait of Dom Guéranger in 1840 by Victor Galland (conserved in the Abbey of Solesmes).

In a Great and Noble Tradition

The Autobiography of
Dom Prosper Guéranger (1805–1875),
Founder of the Solesmes Congregation
of Benedictine Monks and Nuns

Translated and edited by
Br David Hayes, OSB
and
Sr Hyacinthe Defos du Rau, OP

I burn with zeal for your house (Ps 68 [69]:10)

*The Holy Spirit is exhibited to us under the symbols of a dove
and of fire, because all whom he fills he makes both meek with
the simplicity of the dove and glowing with the fire of zeal.*
(St Gregory the Great, *The Pastoral Rule,* 16.17)

GRACEWING

First published in 2009

Gracewing
2 Southern Avenue
Leominster
Herefordshire HR6 0QF

The right of David Hayes and Hyacinthe Defos du Rau to be identified as
the authors of this work has been asserted in accordance with the Copy-
right, Designs and Patents Act 1988.

ISBN 978 0 85244 309 5

Typeset by Action Publishing Technology Ltd
Gloucester GL1 5SR

Contents

Acknowledgements

In presenting this translation of Guéranger's autobiography, we wish to record our gratitude to the following individuals for their kind assistance, advice and encouragement: Monsignor Bernard Ardura (secretary of the Pontifical Council for Culture); Père Robert Bonfils (archivist of the Jesuit archives at Vanves); Frère Lucien-Jean Bord (archivist and librarian of the abbey of Ligugé); Monsieur J. Bottin (archivist of the diocese of Versailles); Mr Brian Butler; Père Bernard Causin (chancellor of the diocese of Langres); Monsieur L. de Chassy (historical archivist of the archdiocese of Tours); Dom Loïc de Courville (sub-archivist of the abbey of Saint-Pierre de Solesmes); Soeur Maryvonne Duclaux (archivist of the French province of the Sacred Heart sisters); Madame Claire Gurvil (historical archivist of the diocese of Nantes); Dom Patrick Hala (abbey of Saint-Pierre de Solesmes); Rev. Dom Benedict Hardy (Pluscarden Abbey), who translated the Latin appendix; Père Herman Janssens (archivist of the Norbertine monastery of Averbode); Frère Gérard Landron (abbey of Saint-Pierre de Solesmes); Père Georges Lavalade; Madame Catherine Lefour (historical archivist of the diocese of Angers); Monsieur François-Xavier Lemercier and Madame Marie-Thérèse Berthelot (historical archivists of the diocese of Rennes); Père M. Longère (archivist of the 'Compagnie de Saint-Sulpice'); Père André Mark (archivist of the French province of the Picpus Congregation); Père Camille Moulin (historical archivist of the diocese of Le Mans); Monsieur Benoît Pedretti (director of the departmental archives of La Sarthe); Soeur Marie-Pierre (archivist of the Visitation monastery, Nantes); Monsieur Philippe Ploix (historical archivist of the archdiocese of Paris); Abbot Edmund Power (Abbey of Saint Paul-outside-the-walls); Dom Joachim Salzgeber (archivist of the abbey of Einsiedeln); Monsieur Philippe de Scorbiac; Abbot Geoffrey Scott (Douai Abbey); Dom Louis Soltner (archivist of the abbey of Saint-Pierre de Solesmes); Rev. Dom Hugh Somerville-Knapman (Douai Abbey); Professor Robert Tombs (University of Cambridge). For this English edition, we have provided extensive footnotes in order to facilitate understanding of the events and persons recounted. Nevertheless, the obscurity of certain people mentioned by Guéranger has made it impossible to find bibliographical material for all of the more than 250 persons cited. Finally, we owe an immense debt of gratitude to Dr Judith Bowen for her introduction, which serves to situate the text in the social, religious and historical context to which it refers.[1] We hope that this book will promote a renewed appreciation of Guéranger among Anglophone readers, for whom he does not yet enjoy the popular recognition that he deserves.

Br David Hayes, OSB
Sr Hyacinthe Defos du Rau, OP
4 April 2009
(Anniversary of the birth of Dom Prosper Guéranger)

---

[1] For further information, see J. M. Bowen, *Serving the Greater Cause: Aspects of the Religious Thinking of Prosper Guéranger (1805–1875)*, PhD thesis, University of York, 2005.

Introduction

The Context

Prosper Guéranger (1805–1875) was a French monk and writer best known for his work in arguing for the restoration of the Roman liturgy.[2] He was also the founder and first abbot of the Benedictine monastery, Saint-Pierre de Solesmes, in the Sarthe valley, some thirty miles from Le Mans. Towards the end of his life, in the 1860s, he wrote an account of his experiences from childhood up to 1833, when the first five monks and four lay brothers restored communal life in the deserted buildings of a former priory that had been closed during the Revolution. The monastic community which still thrives there is on the French, if not the English, tourist circuit, but the true extent of what Guéranger achieved is probably not appreciated by the casual visitor. Many will come to hear the Mass sung in Latin and some to view the famous sculptures in the abbey church, but the situation in which he initiated the community in 1833 is less familiar. This translation of Guéranger's autobiography, first published in French in 2005 to commemorate the 200th anniversary of his birth, is welcome not only because it describes the conditions surrounding the restoration, but also because it affords insights into the origins of other, less familiar aspects of his religious thinking, notably his respect for the mystical and monastic traditions of the Church.[3]

---

[2] *Institutions liturgiques*, vols 1–4, (Revised Edition), Le Mans, 1878–85.
[3] P. Guéranger, *Mémoires autobiographiques*, Preface by L. Soltner, Solesmes, 2005.

The date of the foundation is important. The Gallican Church (the Catholic Church in France which, from early medieval times, felt herself to have a special status among the daughter churches of Rome) was in a particularly vulnerable position. The constitutional reforms arising from the French Revolution and the Napoleonic regime had created what was, in effect, a State Church subject to the politics of whichever government was in power.[4] The Restoration of the monarchy (1815–1830) had given false hopes to the Legitimists in the Church, but the failure of the senior branch of the Orleans dynasty to provide effective leadership meant that these hopes were dashed, especially after the succession to the throne of Louis-Philippe in 1830. Louis declared himself to be king of the French people rather than king of France. In the early years of his reign there was initial popular resistance to the Church, but this was followed by a period of relative liberty of religious expression, which provided the opportunity for Guéranger and his supporters to renew the monastic tradition, even though the institution was still technically illegal.[5] It is in this political context that Guéranger's early years must be viewed, and it is important to recognize that he was only twenty-eight when, in 1833, he and his companions first began to live in the abandoned buildings of the former priory. Although as a child and adolescent he could not have been fully aware of the significance of the events, it is clear that the sporadic outbreaks of unrest in his home town and the situation with which his family had to deal (his father was a teacher during the Napoleonic period and the Restoration) may partly account for his reluctance to submit formally to any government. He was equally determined to retain a certain distance from the diocesan authority in Le Mans, something that was to cause him problems throughout his life. His early attachment to

---

[4] The Concordat (1801) was the agreement signed between Pius VII and Napoleon Bonaparte whereby the Church became, in effect, an arm of the State. Some of the clergy refused to take the oath of allegiance or did not return from exile.

[5] The organic articles (1804) required all religious associations to obtain approval from the government, something that Solesmes never sought.

Mennaisian ideas on papal supremacy never wavered and, after the establishment of Solesmes as an independent abbey in 1837, he continued to argue that only the papacy could rally Catholics to the renewal of faith. It is for this reason that he can be seen as a true Ultramontane. His idealism was not infrequently challenged, and the legal status of the monastic community remained ambiguous; events after his death meant that the monks had to leave France in 1901, and they did not return until the 1920s.[6]

The geographical location of Solesmes may also have helped in the early days of the foundation. The region was sufficiently close to the Vendée to be affected by the religious wars that followed the Revolution, and by the persistence of support for the remnants of the Chouan resistance as late as 1826. A section of the community in La Sarthe and in neighbouring La Mayenne was deeply religious and only belatedly gave up hope for a return to the 'Old Church'. In 1830, Solesmes was sufficiently distant from Paris to avoid attracting attention from the new government, a fact noted by Guéranger in his autobiography (p. 227). At the same time Sablé began to develop as a small industrial town.[7] There was a shift from agricultural-based technologies to the expansion of the marble industry, and the extension of the railway line from Le Mans brought in new residents. This occurred after the period described in the autobiography, but some of the trends were already apparent, for example the various proposals to use the disused priory buildings for industrial purposes. Although Guéranger acknowledges his debt to the Cosnard family, he was dismissive of much of the local bourgeoisie. Later on he was to benefit from the support of some of the newer incomers and, perhaps more significantly, of their wives. Guéranger's influence with these

---

[6] The Law of Association (1901) required religious associations that had not requested authorization from the government to do so. This was applied with particular severity after 1902, and the anti-clerical climate in the first part of the twentieth century in France continued to disrupt the life of all French monastic communities.

[7] T. Greffier, *Une petite ville du Maine au 19è siècle*, Université de Rennes, 1960.

people was considerable and led to the establishment of a sister house of enclosed nuns in 1866. He also developed good relationships with the mayor of Solesmes, Léon Landeau.

The local tensions were particularly strong earlier on; for example Guéranger records the lack of support on his visit to Nantes to gain the approval of the Church hierarchy to raise funds, no doubt in part because of the different loyalties of the clergy in that diocese. He also suffered, especially during the period 1826–1833, from his known association with Lamennais and the journal *Mémorial*. Although Guéranger is at pains to point out the limited extent of his agreement with this writer (the importance of papal authority and the need to return to ecclesiastical tradition), it is clear that he was generally frustrated by the lack of intellectual understanding of his ideas among both the clergy and lay people, which may explain the urge he seems to have felt from very early on to write down and publicize his ideas.

This frustration seems to have its origins in his experiences at the seminary in Le Mans. Although he glosses over his time spent at the college in Angers, this does seem to have been for him a period of intellectual stimulus. His experience in the first year of the seminary at Le Mans, in contrast, was disappointing and, together with his own efforts to educate himself through private reading, brought about the breakdown that he describes. His illness was followed by the mystical experience in 1823 concerning the meaning of the Immaculate Conception. This experience was to inspire him for the rest of his life, and it underpins and explains his theological positions. This section of the work is interesting since it demonstrates the poverty of the curriculum in the seminary at the time; it must be remembered that the Church was still struggling in 1820 to recover from the effects of the Revolution and the loss of ecclesiastical leadership, not to say of competent and intellectually stimulating teachers. Guéranger's future diatribes against the Jansenists and Gallicans in the Church surely derive in part from his disappointment with the aridity of the curriculum in the seminary and with its failure to teach ecclesiastical history.[8]

From a more sociological perspective, it is possible that he was experiencing a syndrome common to many of his contemporaries in the later Romantic Movement. This generation (the men and women born at the beginning of the century) had experienced during their youth three changes of constitutional arrangements, contradictory policies concerning both education and culture, and a lack of career opportunities; innovation was not welcomed and eighteenth-century styles in music, architecture and even literature were the norm.[9] In this climate the government of Louis-Philippe offered a new challenge and, although not primarily aiming at religious revival, the relative religious tolerance in its early days did provide a climate in which renewal of the patrimony was a legitimate concern.[10] It was Guéranger's insight that a revival of physical heritage must be accompanied by a revival of religious heritage, and in the 1840s this led him to write his most famous work, *Institutions liturgiques*.

The autobiography reveals the feelings of a young man, caught up in the general uncertainty of the period and disillusioned with the leadership offered by both secular and religious hierarchies. For Guéranger, the dilemma expresses itself as a desire to return to the 'Old Church' without the associated baggage; this baggage included Legitimist nostalgia and the *indifférence* in the Gallican Church, which was epitomized for him by the fragmentation of liturgies, the emphasis on a rigid moralism, suspicion of papal authority, the denial of mystical experiences and the undervaluing of the Marian tradition.[11]

---

[8] Ernest Renan, who was a generation younger than Guéranger, was still disillusioned with the curriculum in the seminary. In his case this resulted in his leaving the priesthood in 1845. See E. Renan, *Souvenirs d'enfance et de jeunesse*, Paris, 1883.

[9] A. Spitzer, *The French Generation of 1820*, Princeton, 1987. Some examples are Berlioz in music, Viollet-le-Duc in architecture and George Sand in fiction. The careers of all these people took a distinctly secular route.

[10] P. Rosenvallon, *Le moment Guizot*, Paris, 1955.

[11] F. Lamennais, *Essai sur l'indifférence en matière de la religion*, (4 vols), Paris, 1817–23. The term applies to doctrine and not to people.

Whether or not Guéranger was correct in attributing these features of contemporary worship to the Jansenist tendencies of the seventeenth- and eighteenth-century Church is not relevant. It was his perception of the problems which drove him to seek a return to the earlier traditions of the Church; his decision to set up a monastic community had ecclesiastical precedent and provided him with the independence to put his beliefs into practice.

Guéranger's religious understanding, as the auto-biography recounts, had been influenced by his readings of the early Fathers in the editions published by the Bene-dictines of Saint-Maur, mainly produced between 1660 and 1750. These works form an important link in the history of the diffusion of the Fathers in the West, and copies were held in the seminary library at Le Mans. The superiors responsible for the reform of Saint-Maur placed special emphasis on patristic and medieval monastic literature; they regarded reading of these texts as a crucial part of the monastic timetable, and scholarly skills were initially devoted to the production of editions for the edification of the Congrega-tion itself. The fate of the monasteries during the Revolution brought an end to this work. Guéranger describes his visit to the virtually abandoned abbey at Saint-Vincent in Senlis, and explains his reasons for not taking up the offer of the site for his own purposes (p. 209). It is interesting to speculate on why he did not see scholarly production as the main focus of the Solesmes revival. Although he initially obtained commis-sions to continue the *Gallia christiana* from Guizot, minis-ter of culture in the government of Louis-Philippe, and, along with Dom Pitra, a request to edit some of the early *Patrolo-gies* for J.-P. Migne, Guéranger did not pursue this activity after 1860. The pressures of editing and the difficulty he encountered in recruiting scholars with the necessary skills played a part in this, but his focus was always on the divine office and its significant role in embodying the fundamentals of the Catholic faith. As he saw it, this was the contribution made by the early Benedictines, and one that would best foster a reform of the Church at the time.

Guéranger is often criticized, not least by musical

scholars, for perpetuating an outdated and conservative form of divine office in his insistence on returning to Gregorian chant and the adoption of the Roman breviary. A close reading of his defence of the *Institutions liturgiques,* however, shows that he considered the liturgy to embody Christian doctrine and practice. Over the course of the liturgical year, a narrative of the life of Christ draws the participant into a celebration of the festivals commemorating his life, death and resurrection. The monastic community undertakes this celebration as its daily task, demonstrating the critical place of prayer in kindling and sustaining belief (*lex orandi, lex credendi*). It is in this sense that a monastery can serve as an exemplar, a point to which I return at the end of this introduction.

The Text

On Guéranger's own admission, the autobiography was written for the members of the community when he was older and, hence, distanced from the events that he describes. It was written largely in the 1860s, when Guéranger must have felt the approach of old age. It is incomplete and was not intended for publication, which may account for the harshness of some of his judgements of certain individuals.[12] His request for privacy, I think, must be taken at face value since he wrote a commentary on the Rule of St Benedict for publication during the same period, and he translated and edited the exercises of St Gertrude, the thirteenth-century German nun.[13]

This suggests a deliberate focus on the monastic community, away from liturgical revival, although it is always difficult to separate the strands in Guéranger's writing. Perhaps it is

---

[12] *Mémoires autobiographiques*, Préface, p. 4.

[13] *Les Exercices de Sainte-Gertrude*, Poitiers, 1863. Gertrude's mystical experiences were associated with the divine office. She was a choir nun from a very early age, and the exercises are a set of prescriptions that describe how to obtain the same communion with Christ that she herself experienced.

best to say that, with the arguments for the Roman liturgy
largely won, Guéranger was concerned both to set the historical record straight and to describe what is involved in
embracing a monastic vocation. His aim was to show the
hand of God in events, and he emphasizes the obstacles that
were overcome without rational explanation and the appar-
ently desperate situations, especially financial, which beset
the aspirant community. He is also concerned to show that
the development of a monastic vocation is a slow process,
and one that should not be undertaken without an understanding of what is involved. The fairly large number of
people he writes about who thought of coming to Solesmes
but who then gave up are perhaps a testimony to this, and he
is quite often harsh in his comments on those who let him
down, including the secular clergy who were reluctant to
offer verbal or written support to the enterprise. In contrast,
he stresses the contributions of Bishop Carron of Le Mans
and Canon Ménochet, who had suffered under the Revolu-
tionary regime.

Several historiographical concerns are raised. Unlike the
original document, the translation offered here contains
references to people and events, which are important for the
modern lay reader if he or she is to understand and have
confidence in the account. Bearing in mind that Guéranger
was writing thirty years after the events, and that several of
these events were controversial, the omissions and errors do
not seem significant; much of what he writes can be cross-
checked with other evidence from contemporary publications and correspondence. Perhaps the most obvious case of
his benefiting from hindsight is his gloss on the critical visit
to the Vatican in 1832 by Lamennais, Lacordaire and
Montalembert (pp. 145–8). The early biographers of
Guéranger tended to underplay his attachment to
Mennaisian ideas and the letter printed in the appendix
(p. 245), which can be seen as a way of Guéranger distancing
himself from the project. The earlier correspondence
between Lamennais and Guéranger, however, reveals the
difference in priorities of the two men, and the fact that
Montalembert later spent time amicably at Solesmes suggests

that any rancour had been dissipated long before the autobiography was composed.[14]

The interest of the autobiography lies in viewing it as a piece of reflective writing that gives insights into Guéranger's character, and into the motivations that drove him in later life. What emerges is his clear attachment to Solesmes and the Sarthe region, and his dislike of being away from both for too long. He never seems to have been happy in Paris, although his time in Bishop de La Myre's household gave him the valuable experience of meeting people from a very different social class. He was always willing to travel in order to sort out monastic problems or to raise funds, and he seems to have had no difficulty in attracting the friendship of such people as Madame Swetchine, no doubt because she sensed the extent of his commitment (p. 201).[15] Guéranger's account of the journey back to Solesmes from Le Mans on two inadequate horses is a reminder of the discomfort and hazards of travel before the building of the railway line. His later life was to see him visiting Rome, Paris and even England, but he was always anxious to return to his abbey. His combative instincts were to remain with him all his life and frequently got him into deep water in intellectual debates, as did his unfashionable support for the supernatural in an age of positivism and naturalism.[16]

The autobiography also shows the emergence of what we

---

[14] A. Roussell, *Lamennais et ses correspondants inconnus*, Paris, 1912, pp. 189–231.

[15] A Russian *émigrée* who converted to Catholicism in 1815, and whose salon in rue Saint-Dominique became a focus for the young Catholic elite in the 1820s. An early benefactor of Solesmes, she was something of a mystic herself and subsequently sought advice from Guéranger until her death in 1857.

[16] Perhaps the best example of this are his articles about Mary of Agreda, a seventeenth-century Spanish mystic, which were published in *L'Univers* from 1855–1859. Mary's biography of the Blessed Virgin Mary had been banned in France since 1695. These articles have been largely ignored by Guéranger's biographers or treated as an example of his whimsicality. On closer examination, they support his arguments about Jansenist undercurrents which persisted in nineteenth-century Gallicanism.

would today call management skills, and the ability to identify and bring out the best in others, a crucial quality needed for the leadership of a monastic community. Dom Pitra, patristic scholar and later cardinal, and Dom Pothier, editor and composer of Gregorian chant, are just two of his famous protégés. This ability to recognize and encourage talent was also very evident in his support for the early efforts of G.-B. de Rossi during his excavations in the Roman catacombs. The correspondence between these two men reveals a close friendship, which survived intellectual disagreements over dating, a lack of interest in France in catacomb archaeology as opposed to saintly relics, as well as the Italian wars of unification.[17] Guéranger's relationships with the outside world remained stormy to the end and his achievements went largely unrecognized by writers of the new Catholicism in the later nineteenth century.[18]

English Connections

One possible reason why Guéranger's work is so little known in England is a similar failure by nineteenth-century British church historians to become interested in the Roman Catholic renewal. Neither did his later writing on saints and the criticism of naturalistic trends in ecclesiastical history find favour with their Roman Catholic peers, such as Baron Acton (1834–1902). Guéranger did, however, come to England in 1860 on the invitation of Lawrence Shepherd, a great admirer of his monastic and liturgical innovations who

---

[17] C. Johnson, *Liturgie et archéologie*, Rome, 2003.

[18] For example, Louis Duchesnes (1843–1922), church historian and professor at the *Institut Catholique* in Paris until 1885. Those who knew Guéranger well were much more appreciative of his qualities. See, for example, Mgr Pie, *Funeral oration of the Right Reverend Father Dom Prosper Guéranger, Abbot of Solesmes*, delivered by Mgr Pie in the abbatial church of Saint-Pierre de Solesmes, 4 March, 1875, Dublin, 1875.

[19] Lawrence Shepherd (1825–1885) was a monk of Ampleforth Abbey, Yorkshire. He translated eleven volumes of Guéranger's *L'Année liturgique* between 1867 and 1883. For further information, see F. Sandeman, 'Lawrence Shepherd, 1825–85, Apostle of Guéranger', in *The Ampleforth Journal*, LXXX (1975): 38–47.

had spent time at Solesmes.[19] At Shepherd's invitation, Guéranger attended the consecration of St Michael's abbey church at Belmont and also visited Westminster Abbey, Ely Cathedral, the Birmingham Oratory (where he met Newman) and the London Oratory (where he met Faber). Perhaps unsurprisingly, Guéranger got on better with the latter than with the former, although the inability of either Newman or Guéranger to communicate in each other's language probably did not help. More seriously, the aims of the two men clearly diverged. Newman had left the Anglican Communion in 1845, and one of the disappointments of the Tractarian Movement, of which he had been a leading member, was its failure to found any enduring male monastic communities. This failure is unsurprising in the context of the history of monasticism in the United Kingdom since the Reformation. Although attracted to the monastic ideal, Newman was above all a scholar and an intellectual, and his writings are a model of systematic historical research and analysis. In the debates surrounding Mary, the two men were to reach not dissimilar conclusions, although their style of writing and their strategies for change could not have been more different.[20]

Perhaps Guéranger can best be understood in the context of the widespread movement in Europe for religious revival in the first half of the nineteenth century.[21] He embarked on his project when there was an urgent need to renew commitment to the faith among Christian congregations, and to restore enthusiasm for Christian traditions and Christian heroes after nearly two centuries of Enlightenment scepticism. The routes to the renewal of commitment to faith among congregations were many and varied in the nineteenth-century French Catholic Church, but what emerges from all Guéranger's writing and actions is the importance of prayer and its public forms if people are to be fully engaged with faith. It is this insight which underpins

---

[20] For Newman's position, see J. H. Newman, *An essay on the development of Christian doctrine,* London, 1900, pp. 137–42, 415–18.

[21] R. W. Franklin, *Nineteenth-century churches: The history of a new Catholicism in Wurtemberg, England and France,* New York, 1987.

Guéranger's work, and the autobiography reveals his early appreciation that a monastic community can act as an exemplar for Christian belief. The notion of exemplarity is important for an understanding of Guéranger's writing and explains his belief that, in the aftermath of the Revolution, monastic life could offer to his contemporaries a mirror that would reflect all of the traditions of the Church – a commitment to obedience and to collective prayer, daily reminders of saintly lives, a reaffirmation of mystical experience and the discipline required to observe the liturgical calendar.

From as early as 1850, the emphasis in theology was to shift to a more rigorous historical scholarship, aided by the new disciplines of philology and archaeology, and to a new professionalism among its practitioners. This led, in some respects, to a divergence of doctrinal emphasis among the various Christian confessions. The centrality of worship, however, remained a concern for all and the image of the monastery as a microcosm of the Church has retained its power right up to the present time.

Dr Judith Bowen
Emeritus lecturer, Leeds Metropolitan University

9 February 1860[22]

I have agreed to write down some memoirs about the history of the Congregation. Several of my brethren have often urged me to do this, and I too have often realized the need for this work, considering how the true account of the finer details is liable to be altered or even lost. I am now surrendering to this task, with the sole aim of serving the religious family whose direction has been entrusted to me by God. I pray that God will help me with his truth in everything that I shall recount, and that he will preserve me from any kind of introspection and self-glorification, whether by recounting personal faults that I must not conceal, or by telling of some particular good that it has pleased God's divine majesty to bring about through my unworthy hands. In beginning this task, I implore the help of the most Holy and Immaculate Mary, Mother of God, of the Holy Guardian Angel of this monastery, of St Peter our patron, of St Benedict our great patriarch and of St Scholastica, whose solemnity is already upon us, asking them humbly to assist me in this work that I dedicate to their glory.

---

[22] This is the date when Guéranger began his account, but the narrative indicates that he was still writing after 1868. The original manuscript, which is preserved in the archives of the abbey of Saint-Pierre de Solesmes, comprises nineteen notebooks of around twelve pages each. These notebooks are not bound together, and the text is generally written on one side only. The page numbering runs from 1 to 197. This translation has been made from the following edition of the manuscript published by Solesmes: *Dom Guéranger – Mémoires autobiographiques (1805–1833)*, Solesmes, 2005, which corrects and modernizes Guéranger's original spelling and accentuation. Guéranger's errors in the recording of proper names have been corrected in our translation.

Childhood and Initial Studies

I must begin these memoirs with my birth, in order to correct the more than inaccurate stories that have been circulating in the monastery concerning my life before the restoration of Solesmes.[23] This account is after all entirely personal and is not intended for any official use. Firstly, I was born in Sablé[24] on 4 April 1805. My father[25] worked as a teacher in this town, a position he took up in 1799 when Sablé was deprived of teachers due to the destruction wrought there, as everywhere, by the Revolution. My father had rented the former convent[26] of third order sisters of St Francis, and it was in this former religious house that I entered the world. I had the good fortune to be baptized on

---

[23] The priory of Solesmes was founded by Geoffroi de Sablé in 1010 and became affiliated to the Congregation of Saint-Maur in 1664. It was rebuilt in 1773, suppressed at the Revolution, and re-founded by Guéranger in 1833. See L.-H. Cottineau, *Répertoire Topo-Bibliographique des Abbayes et Prieurés*, Macon, 1935, v. 2, pp. 3055–7.

[24] A commune in the arrondissement of La Flèche, 49km from Le Mans. Its name changed to Sablé-sur-Sarthe in 1894. For further information, see R. Charles, *Guide illustré du tourisme au Mans et dans La Sarthe*, Le Mans, 1880, pp. 170–6.

[25] Pierre Guéranger (1775–1849). He married Françoise Jarry (1773–1829) on 27 January 1798. For further information, see A. des Mazis, 'La Vocation Monastique de Dom Guéranger – milieu et influences', in *Revue Bénédictine*, 83 (1973): 119–80, esp. 122.

[26] The Franciscan convent of 'Our Lady of the Crib' was founded in 1632 and dissolved in 1792. For further information, see G.-M. Oury, 'Le couvent des Cordelières de Sablé', in *La Province du Maine*, 76 (1974): 329–44.

the very day of my natural birth. I was my parents' fifth child: two of my brothers born before me did not survive, and one of them could not even be baptized. My brother[27] who is a parish priest is my parents' last child and the sixth of us children.[28]

I was entering my third year of age when the municipal authorities of Sablé invited my father to come and live in the former college and thus take up an official position in the city. This house had previously been the property of the monks of Solesmes, who had withdrawn to it during times of war. When the town of Sablé offered it to my father, the building was being used by the gendarmerie. A complete reversal then occurred: my father moved into the college, and the gendarmerie took his place in the former Elizabethine convent.[29] Later, when Solesmes was re-established, a former religious sister of this convent, Mother Agatha,[30] was still living in the town of Solesmes. She played a great part in the foundation through her prayers and her kindness. For about ten years we saw her joining in at our offices with her Roman breviary, which we used until 1846.

I was given the name Prosper at my baptism, which was the name of one of my brothers who did not survive. I do not know the reason for the choice of this name, or for the name

---

[27] Constantin Guéranger (1807–1862), ordained priest in 1830; became parish priest of the Chapelle Saint-Aubin near Le Mans in 1832. See the archives of the diocese of Le Mans.

[28] Apart from two sons who died as infants, Pierre Guéranger's sons were as follows: Fréderic (1799–1858), a school teacher; Édouard (1801–1895), a pharmacist, amateur chemist, paleontologist and botanist; Prosper (1805–1875), the future abbot of Solesmes; and Constantin (1807–1862), a parish priest.

[29] In 1229 St Elizabeth of Hungary (1207–1231) established a community of women at Marberg, Germany which became a Congregation of third order hospitallers. They were variously called the 'Grey Sisters', the 'Daughters of St Elizabeth', the 'Elizabethines' or even 'Franciscans', and formed the oldest branch of the third orders. For further information on St Elizabeth of Hungary, see D. Farmer, *Oxford Dictionary of Saints* (fifth edition), Oxford, 2003, p. 169.

[30] Person currently unidentified.

Louis.[31] As for Pascal, that was given to me because my birth took place in the days close to the solemnity of Easter.[32] It was only later that I learnt of the providential reason that had led me to be born on 4 April rather than on another day. When I was going to catechism classes, I was on several occasions given some pictures of St Ambrose as a prize. I remember being extremely moved by them. As I got older, I became ever fonder of this saint's character until I learnt, but much later, that St Ambrose died on 4 April (his true *natalis*[33]) and that 7 December was only the day of the translation of his relics.[34] This love for such a great and attractive saint has grown in me ever since, and if God lets me live long enough I have planned a small tribute in honour of this beloved patron.[35]

My early childhood passed without incident, but at the age of four I nearly died through my own mischievousness and that of the devil. I have always had a very sweet tooth. I had noticed a small phial containing green ink in my father's medical cabinet, and for several days I was seized with a burning desire to taste its contents. One Sunday, when my parents had gone to the High Mass, I made the most of an odd moment, when the nanny keeping an eye on me had disappeared, to climb up on a chair and grab the phial. It took me only a second to uncork it and swallow the liquid. A blind force, or rather an impulse from the devil, drove me to do this and, if the green liquid had not tasted so vile, I would have drunk the lot. In no time at all I felt the effects of this harmful brew, and even before my parents had returned

---

[31] This name was probably given in honour of Guéranger's godfather, Louis-Guillaume Gazeau (1748–1805), who was a family friend and a priest of the Sablé region. See G.-M. Oury, *Dom Guéranger – moine au cœur de l'Église*, Solesmes, 2000, p. 13.

[32] The name Pascal is derived from the French word for Easter, *Pâques*.

[33] The date of St Ambrose's death in 397 (his birth into heaven).

[34] Guéranger is mistaken here since 7 December is the anniversary of St Ambrose's episcopal consecration in 374.

[35] This tribute appears not to have been written. For a complete bibliography of Guéranger's published works, see *Bibliographie des Bénédictins de la Congrégation de France*, Solesmes, 1889, pp. 3–33.

from Mass I had already vomited several times. Despite my efforts to conceal the state I was in from my nanny, she finally noticed that some sudden and very serious illness had got hold of me. When my parents came back, she told them what she had seen and, upon being interrogated by them, I admitted everything, telling them naively that if the liquid had tasted good I would have drunk it all. While I was talking to them, I had violent convulsions and a ghastly stomach ache. The taste of this nasty liquor remains to this day an ever vivid memory to my palate. I vomited several times in front of my parents, and the green-coloured contents bore witness to the terrible cause of the accident.

The doctor, an old septuagenarian called Dr Pavet,[36] was called at once. He announced that I was suffering from poisoning and, after assessing my symptoms and examining the liquid, he recognized that the ink in the phial was based on copper-oxide. He decided to treat me quite simply with milk. I swallowed several bowls of it, with the proviso that a large lump of sugar should be placed at the bottom of each bowl. Every time I took a dose, the milk was vomited back up at once, completely congealed and green in colour. With time, however, this infernal colour faded, indicating the diminution of its poisonous element. At last, towards 2 or 3 o'clock in the afternoon, I was no longer vomiting but was exhausted. I got a little better during the night. The following day, I was made to take some creamy syrup or other that completely restored my stomach. I thank God for allowing me to be saved in time, and for ensuring that I did not leave this world at the age of four due to an act of gluttony.

Soon afterwards, my mother taught me to read, and I was soon able to do so by myself. By the age of six or seven, reading had become a passion for me. I used to read everything I came across, but I only ever found pious books. I started to become clearly aware of the gift of faith that God

---

[36] This may have been Bernard-Charles Pavet de La Clementière, who qualified as a medical doctor in 1775. See A. Angot, *Dictionnaire historique, topographique et biographique de La Mayenne,* Laval, 1902, v. III, p. 240.

had placed within me, and which has governed all my perceptions ever since. I am mentioning this here in order to express my gratitude to the Lord, and I do so with trembling because I know that he will ask me to account for it.

As soon as I could express in words what I would one day like to become, I began to say that I wanted to be a priest. The sight of priests had a surprising effect on me; I did not consider them to be like other men. The ceremonies and chants of the liturgy had an extraordinary effect on me, and I felt drawn to replicate them. From the age of five or six, I used to say Mass, sing Vespers, as well as conduct processions and even burials. I carried on these liturgical experiments under one form or another until I was about twelve. Around the age of ten, I came across a missal, which I was able to browse through for several days. I could not describe the joy I felt in holding and leafing through this mysterious book which, until then, I had only seen from afar on the altar.

Every evening we used to read the life of a saint with my parents from the collection made by Mésenguy.[37] I used to listen eagerly to this reading, and I often reread it afterwards. What struck me most were the acts of the martyrs, and I cried a great deal when I heard them. The lives of the Eastern solitaries also made a great impression on me. I often began to daydream about this subject. I sought my own desert among the picturesque rocks mingled with greenery, which have since been spoilt by what are called the *Folies-Vielle*.[38] I also frequently thought about settling on the *poulie*[39] of

---

[37] François-Philippe Mésenguy (1677–1763), Jansenist ecclesiastical writer. He received minor orders and taught humanities, first in Beauvais and then in Paris. His six-volume *Vie des Saints*, was published in 1730, although the work was completed by the Oratorian Claude-Pierre Goujet (1697–1767). See G. Vapereau, *Dictionnaire Universel des Littératures,* Paris, 1876, pp. 914, 1386.

[38] The name of a park in Sablé situated next to the river Sarthe. It owes its name to Michel Vielle, who was its former owner.

[39] In the west of France (a weaving region) the *poulies* were areas of non-cultivated land exposed to the sun, where cloth was spread out to be bleached.

Solesmes, whose spiky rocks and uneven terrain attracted me greatly. I wanted to take with me only a few books that I intended to read slowly, which was not my usual practice. As for the monastery of Solesmes itself, I never dreamt about it. I was looking for solitude, not buildings. I had been taken to see the 'Saints'[40] from an early age, and I was happy whenever I returned there. All these statues made a vivid impression on me, but I never felt within me any premonition that I would one day live in the former Benedictine priory.

My secular reading consisted of *Robinson Crusoé*,[41] *Télémaque*,[42] the *Veillées du château* by Madame de Genlis,[43] *Don Quijote*,[44] the works of Florian,[45] etc., but I was always drawn back to my favourite theme: religion. I was particularly

[40] The 'Saints of Solesmes' are the two groups of sculptures found in the transepts of the abbey church of Saint-Pierre de Solesmes. There are about forty statues in all.

[41] The principal character of a famous novel by the English writer Daniel Defoe (1661–1731) entitled, *The life and surprising adventures of Robinson Crusoe*, which portrayed the hero's adventures on a desert island. The first part of this work was published in 1719, although Guéranger would have read it in a later French translation. See Vapereau, *op. cit.*, pp. 592–3.

[42] *Les Aventures de Télémaque* is a prose poem written by François de Salignac de La Mothe Fenelon (1651–1715), archbishop of Cambrai (1694–1715), who was appointed private tutor to the royal children in 1689. The work was originally written as a private manuscript for the amusement and education of the duc de Bourgogne. It was published as an anonymous manuscript in 1699 and as a book in 1717. See Vapereau, *op. cit.*, pp. 775–80, esp. pp. 777–8.

[43] Stéphanie-Félicité Ducrest de Saint-Jean, comtesse de Genlis (1746–1830), woman of letters and governess to the children of the duc d'Orléans. Her prodigious literary output included her three-volume collection of readings and tales entitled, *Les Veillées du château, ou Cours de morale à l'usage des enfants*, Paris, 1784. See Vapereau, *op. cit.*, pp. 868–9.

[44] A famous novel by the Spanish writer Miguel de Cervantes Saavedra (1547–1616). *El Ingeniosa Don Quijote de la Mancha* was published in 1605, although Guéranger would have read it in a later French translation. See Vapereau, *op. cit.*, pp. 407–8.

[45] Jean-Pierre Claris, chevalier de Florian (1755–1794), poet and prose writer. The name 'Florian' is derived from a childhood nickname given to the author by his uncle. He published comedies, novels, plays, poems and several translations, one of which was Cervantes' *Don Quijote*. See Vapereau, *op. cit.*, pp. 805–6.

attracted to an odd volume of Sacy's Bible[46] containing the books of Exodus and Leviticus. I read and reread this Bible continually. Between the age of eight or nine, I briefly came across a volume of the *Génie du Christianisme*.[47] The impression made on me by the pages that I read has never faded. It is the passage where Chateaubriand describes a village funeral.[48] The book was taken from me at once, but I had an instinct that no other author would have such a powerful hold on me if I had been able to read this book straight through.[49]

I began to study Latin at the age of eight. I was quite good at it, but a certain amount of laziness on my part, as well as my reading programme, prevented me from making as much progress as possible. I soon had to go to catechism classes. We

[46] This rather vague reference could apply to several versions of the Bible that would then have been available. Two of the most likely editions are, *La Sainte Bible traduite sur la Vulgate par M. Le Maistre de Sacy,* Paris, 1730 (10 vols), or *La Sainte Bible contenant l'Ancien et le Nouveau Testament* translated by Isaac Le Maistre de Sacy, Paris, 1731.

[47] *Génie du christianisme ou les beautés de la religion chrétienne* was published as a five-volume work in 1802 by François-René Chateaubriand (1768–1848). It was written as an apology for Catholicism, which had been denigrated in France during the eighteenth century and attacked during the French Revolution. This apology was situated mainly at the level of aesthetics, and sought to bring modern man to the Christian religion via his heart and imagination more than via scientific, historical or dogmatic arguments. See Vapereau, *op. cit.,* pp. 436–9, esp. p. 437.

[48] *Génie du christianisme*, II, IV, XI in Chateaubriand, *Oeuvres complètes*, Paris, 1836, v. 12, p. 301.

[49] Guéranger would have been eight or nine years old in 1813–1814. By this time, Chateaubriand's relationship with Napoleon, which was always difficult, had deteriorated into open hostility. Following Napoleon's first abdication in April 1814, Chateaubriand wrote a pamphlet celebrating his decline and then went on to support the Bourbon cause. It is therefore likely that his *Génie du christianisme* was taken from Guéranger at this time in order to avoid giving the appearance that his family supported Chateaubriand rather than Napoleon. In view of the position of Guéranger's father as principal of the local college, the family's public conformity to the established regime would have been important. For further information, see *Encyclopaedia Universalis,* v. 5, pp. 414–418, esp. p. 415.

were taught the catechism of the Empire, with its great lesson about Napoleon.[50] I was once rewarded with the picture that was given to whoever could recite this lesson without making any mistakes. At that time, everything was full of Napoleon and the war. Troops were constantly marching through Sablé, and my parents often put up soldiers. At other times, Spanish and Austrian prisoners of war came to stay. There were unending announcements of new victories in church. In the grounds of the château, splendid feasts were given by the town to mark the Emperor's marriage,[51] and for the birth of the king of Rome.[52] All this made me think slightly of the army, but I was not really smitten with the idea. Indeed, I became aware of a stronger and deeper desire to be a priest.

Until 1813 I did not know that the pope was in captivity.[53] We never spoke about this in my parents' home, and still less at church. A curate from Sablé (Fr Poirier[54]) let it slip one day when I was present. When he left I wanted to ask all sorts of

---

[50] Napoleon Bonaparte I (1769–1821), first consul for life (1802–1804) and then emperor of France (1804–1815). For further information, see Jean-Louis Voisin, *Dictionnaire des Personnages Historiques,* Paris, 1995, pp. 761–7. The imperial catechism was approved by Cardinal Capara (the papal nuncio) in Paris on 30 May 1806. Its lesson about Napoleon taught that: 'In particular, we owe Napoleon I, our Emperor, love, respect, obedience, fidelity, military service, the prescribed contributions for the preservation and defence of the Empire, as well as fervent prayers for his salvation and for the spiritual and temporal prosperity of the State.' Quoted (in French) in P. Levillain (ed.), *Dictionnaire historique de la papauté* (2nd ed.), Paris, 2003, p. 1338.

[51] Following the declaration of nullity of his first marriage to Joséphine, Napoleon I married Marie-Louise, the daughter of the emperor of Austria, on 2 April 1810. See Voisin, *op. cit.,* p. 765.

[52] François-Charles-Joseph Napoleon Bonaparte (1811–1832), the son of Napoleon I and Marie-Louise, and who was nicknamed 'The Eaglet'. He was declared king of Rome at birth, but was educated in Austria. He died prematurely from consumption. See Voisin, *op. cit.,* p. 768.

[53] Pius VII (1742–1823), pope from 1800–1823, was arrested on the orders of Napoleon I in 1809 after he excommunicated the emperor as a punishment for the capture of the Papal States. He was held in captivity until 1814, initially at Savona until 1812 and then at Fontainebleau in France. For further information, see Levillain, *op. cit.,* pp. 1334–42.

[54] Person currently unidentified.

questions, but was quickly told to keep my mouth shut.[55] The news made a very strong impression on me, however, and all the more so since I had always heard it said that the pope lived in Rome. Shortly before this, I had heard read out from the pulpit a circular letter that contained the famous Concordat of 1813 declaring peace with the Church.[56] I did not realize how unhappy the priests seemed to feel about it. Neither was I aware of some unsettling albeit rather vague words that my father had said about this subject. All this was quite intriguing for the Catholicism of a seven-year-old.

Political events soon gained pace. With the return of the Bourbons,[57] the face of Sablé changed. There was nothing but feasts, bright lights, garlands, coloured paper lanterns and dances in the streets. I learnt to recognize the 'fleur de lys',[58] which I had often seen but did not know about. Then the hundred days[59] were upon us. Since there were

---

[55] The reluctance of Guéranger's family to discuss this affair may again be due to his father's position as principal of the college in Sablé: 'Holding such a position of significance in the public life of the small town of Sablé would imply that the Guéranger family accepted without apparent difficulty the political situation of the "Nouveau regime" and the "Église concordataire" of Napoleon Bonaparte. Consequently, the subject of the captivity of Pius VII was something of an embarrassment to this family and was not a matter for discussion.' C. Johnson, *Prosper Guéranger (1805–1875): A Liturgical Theologian – An introduction to his liturgical writings and work* (Studia Anselmiana 89, Analecta Liturgica 9), Rome, 1984, p. 51.

[56] On 25 January 1813, Pius VII, held in captivity at Fontainebleau, approved the Concordat demanded by Napoleon I, in which he conceded the alienation of the Papal States, accepted the principle of a metropolitan archbishop canonically instituting a bishop to a vacant see on his own authority rather than that of Rome, and accepted an imperial endowment. The pope later retracted this agreement on 24 March 1813. For further information, see Levillain, *op. cit.*, pp. 1334–42.

[57] Following Napoleon's first abdication in 1814, Louis XVIII (1755–1824), king of France (1814–1815) and (1815–1824), returned to Paris on 3 May 1814, having made a declaration at Saint-Ouen the previous day in which he promised to create a constitutional monarchy. For further information, see Voisin, *op. cit.*, pp. 651–2.

[58] The lily, the royal symbol.

[59] The name given to Napoleon's final government that ruled from 20 March until 22 June 1815, a period of 97 days that is rounded up to 100

Chouans[60] in the region, a large garrison was sent to Sablé, which was made ready for siege and fortified. All this was very interesting for me and for the other children. The defeat at Waterloo[61] opened up Sablé to the Chouans, who took possession of it without any difficulty since the troops had withdrawn two hours previously. Then the Prussian and Saxon allies arrived. These latter were hussars of death, and they had the head of a dead man on their shako.[62]

The children of Sablé divided into two camps. I was more than ten years old, and declared myself to be a Bonapartist. This made me quarrel with Fr de Lucé,[63] the curate of Sablé, who had been in the army and who was my confessor. He

---

for ease of reference. During this government, Napoleon tried to adopt a less authoritarian manner in a bid for survival. His defeat at Waterloo on 18 June, however, forced his second and final abdication. See Robinet, Robert and Le Chaplain, *Dictionnaire Historique et Biographique de la Révolution et de l'Empire 1789–1815,* Paris, v. 1, p. 356. For further information on the hundred days in this region, see M.-H. Berranger, 'Les Cent-Jours dans La Sarthe et la Chouannerie de 1815 dans Le Maine' in *Bulletin de la Société d'Agriculture, Sciences et arts de La Sarthe,* 7 (1937): 49–96; *Ibid.* (1938): 204–25.

[60] The name of the Royalist guerrillas opposed to the Revolution, whose name originates from their rallying cry during nocturnal forays, which was an imitation owl cry (the zoological term for an owl in French is *chouette*); the Chouannerie was very active in the Sablé region. See Robinet et al., *op. cit.,* v. 1, p. 412.

[61] The defeat of Napoleon I at Waterloo by the allies of the sixth coalition (Austria, England, Russia, Prussia, Germany and Sweden) on 18 June 1815 ended the Hundred Days, and forced Napoleon to abdicate a second time. See *Les 2000 Dates qui ont fait la France, 987–1987,* Paris, 1988, p. 154 (hereafter, *Les Dates*).

[62] That is, a military headdress of Hungarian origin. It is still worn in France today by the Saint-Cyriens and by the infantry of the Republican Guard of Paris.

[63] Pierre-Ambroise Gougeon de Lucé (1771–1830), was driven out of seminary by the Revolution and joined the Republican army, but later deserted when he learnt that his father had been guillotined. He then became a lieutenant in the Bourmont dragoons, and a Chouan in the Sablé region. After the Revolution he was ordained priest, serving as a curate in Sablé (1803); hospital chaplain (1816); and parish priest of Sablé from 1821 until his death. See Angot, *op. cit.,* v. IV, p. 413.

was a Royalist like Charette[64] and reproached me in the confessional about this subject. Nevertheless, however much of a 'pataud'[65] I was, I did not cease to think that my future lay in an ecclesiastical vocation.

The time came for my first communion, which I made in 1816 when I was eleven. This communion made a great impression on me, but its effects were minimal. Mésenguy's ideas in his *Vie des saints*, and the several books of Jansenist piety that I had read, had not contributed to the formation within me of a very rich and broad devotion. Moreover, since I felt drawn effortlessly towards religious matters, I had done almost nothing to cultivate my devotion. I was very glad to enjoy this lively faith through which God was drawing me to himself. I had little inclination to perform good works, however, since they would have cost me dear in terms of personal effort. Hence I barely drew any nourishment from either my first communion or from my second, which I made in 1817. This was followed by confirmation, which I received along with other children from Sablé in Moranne, where Bishop Montault,[66] the bishop of Angers, was carrying out a pastoral visitation. The parish priest of Sablé had arranged this event with Bishop de Pidoll,[67] the bishop of Le Mans,

---

[64] François-Athanase Charette de La Contrie (1773–1796), an officer in the Vendéen Royalists. He was initially a naval officer and came to the defence of the Tuileries in 1792. His Royalist sympathies meant that he played a leading role in the Vendéen insurrection. In 1795 he received the title of 'General of the Catholic and Royal army' from Louis XVIII, but was captured and shot in 1796. See Voisin, *op. cit.*, pp. 205–6.

[65] The name given to Bonapartists and Republicans by the Vendéen Royalists.

[66] Charles Montault des Isles (1755–1839), a lawyer in the parliament of Paris who was ordained priest in 1783. He was curate in Loudun, elected constitutional bishop of Vienne in 1791, and appointed bishop of Angers in 1802. For further information, see A. Maupoint, *Vie de Mgr Charles Montault des Isles,* Angers, 1844.

[67] Michel-Joseph de Pidoll von Quintenbach (1734–1819), bishop of Le Mans (1802–1819). For further information, see A. Sifflet, *Les Évêques Concordataires du Mans – I Monseigneur de Pidoll, 1802–1819,* Le Mans, 1914.

whose infirmities had for a long time prevented him from visiting the diocese.

When I had reached my twelfth year, I felt a growing desire to expand my knowledge of religion, something to which I felt ever more drawn. This desire prompted me to ask if I could read Fleury's *Ecclesiastical History*.[68] I had been prepared for this by the lives of the saints, by the liturgy (which I already understood in Latin) and by various readings. I was therefore able to tackle this work and read it with enough understanding. The analyses of the Fathers interested me greatly, and a certain unity was established in my mind into which I could associate facts, understand doctrines and deduce practical implications. Unfortunately, I began with historical and doctrinal errors; Fleury had literally poisoned my mind. I took his words to be so many oracles and found his own false notions pervading his historical accounts. Taken in by both the facts and the doctrines, I could not escape his influence. My views on the decadence of the Church in the seventh century, the usurpations of papal power, the inferiority of the modern discipline, along with a profound contempt for the Middle Ages were all the result of this reading, and these prejudices remained with me for many years. I ask the Queen of Heaven to forgive me for the fact that her Immaculate Conception was to my eyes an unfounded prejudice that I felt bound to resist. At thirteen I was a Gallican[69] in the manner of the eighteenth century, armed for combat and inclined to think admirable in every respect the Gallican liturgical innovations against which the Lord later gave me the grace to fight.

[68] Claude Fleury (1640–1723), writer and cleric. He was successively sub-tutor to the princes des Conti (1672), tutor to the comte de Vermandois (1680), and sub-tutor to the king's grandsons, the ducs de Borgongne, d'Anjou and de Berry (1689). His twenty-volume *Histoire ecclésiastique* appeared from 1691 and was his principal work. Another sixteen volumes were later added to this work by the Oratorian Fr Fabre, who took the account up to the year 1594. See Vapereau, *op. cit.*, p. 804.

[69] A supporter of the French church conceived of as existing in isolation from Rome and independent of papal authority. For further information, see P. Larousse, *Le Grand Dictionnaire du Dix-Neuvième Siècle* (24 vols), Paris, 1866, v. 7, p. 247.

With all this going on, my literary education did not make much progress. I needed a large college and also to get out of Sablé in order to acquire the intellectual development that I lacked. My father obtained a full grant for me to go to school in Angers, and I started there in October 1818 in order to repeat my third year.

The change of diocese and liturgy was something with which I was very much preoccupied. Passionate about the liturgy of the diocese of Le Mans (which I knew largely by heart), I had a preconceived contempt for the liturgy of Angers, which had been portrayed to me as having much in common with the Roman liturgy. This Angevian liturgy gave way to the Parisian rite a few years later.[70] Nevertheless, I happened to attend a Requiem Mass in the church of Notre-Dame a few days before starting school. I must say that the chants, especially the offertory, made a great impression on me, and made me feel that Gregorian chant could move the innermost recesses of the human heart even more effectively than the melodies of Fr Lebeuf.[71] The cathedral of Angers, the organ and the sight of a bishop surrounded by his canons, all greatly moved this child from Sablé who was hardly paying attention to anything else. Besides, my imagination had been prepared by the numerous stories that I had heard and the numerous questions I had asked since reaching the age of reason. I used to listen to and interrogate old people and those who were well-travelled about

---

[70] For a discussion of the local diocesan liturgies in France at this time, see Johnson, *op. cit.,* pp. 147–89.

[71] Jean Lebeuf (1687–1760), a historian and a canon and sub-chanter of Auxerre cathedral. He had been entrusted with composing chants for the new Parisian liturgies. For an example of his scholarly work, see his *Traité historique et pratique sur le Chant ecclésiastique,* Paris, 1741. Guéranger had no kind words for him: 'Having spent ten years placing notes upon lines and lines upon notes, he presented the clergy of our capital city with a monstrous composition, almost all of whose parts are as tiring to execute as they are to listen to...', in 'Considérations sur la Liturgie Catholique', *Mémorial catholique* (28 février 1830): 49–57, esp. 57. Reproduced in *Mélanges de liturgie, d'histoire et de théologie 1. 1830–1837,* Solesmes, 1887, pp. 5–110 (hereafter *Mélanges*).

anything that could give me some idea of the Church in times gone by.

College life was completely new to me since I had until then been educated at home. I soon became accustomed to it. The principal was the old Fr Tardy,[72] an academic at heart. The vice-principal was a tall, hard man called Collet[73] whom I never liked, a feeling that was mutual. The chaplain, Fr Pasquier,[74] was a young priest who was full of warmth and intelligence, and who took an interest in my studies. He lent me many helpful books, and sent me up to the sacred table of the Lord five or six times a year.[75] The school was very immoral in terms of its pupils' conduct, and several of its teachers were known to live rather dissolute lives. I owe it to the Holy Virgin to have never had the least cause for reproach in this respect throughout the whole of my school years. I am all the more indebted to her for this since, due to the poorly chosen reading of my childhood, I only ever had a very lukewarm devotion towards her.

I did not do much work in this third-year class, no more than in those that I would attend until the completion of my studies. I was top of the class from time to time, but was not diligent enough to maintain this position for a whole term. On the other hand, I read a lot. It was in this year that I was finally able to read the *Génie du Christianisme*. This reading had a great effect on me, hastening the development of my

---

[72] Marie-Joachim Tardy (b. 1755), appointed principal in 1817. See the archives of the diocese of Angers.

[73] Person currently unidentified.

[74] Jacques Pasquier (1790–1861), ordained priest in 1814 and appointed curate at the cathedral. He became chaplain of the college in Angers from 1818–30, after which he resumed his curacy at the cathedral. He was appointed parish priest of Maulévrier (1831), and of Notre-Dame d'Angers (1837). See F. Uzereau, 'Les treize aumôniers du lycée d'Angers (1806–1935)', in *Andegaviana*, 31 (1936): 280–8, esp. 282.

[75] At this time infrequent communion was the norm for Catholics. It was not until the pontificate of Pius X (1835–1914), pope from 1903–1914, that more frequent communion was encouraged. Furthermore, Pius X brought forward the age for reception of first Holy Communion to the age of seven in his decree *Quam singulari* of 11 August 1911. See Levillain, *op. cit.*, pp. 1349–51.

poetic instinct in religious matters. I was working hard at everything in spite of my previous reading, and was in no position to pass judgement on Chateaubriand, for whose work I had complete admiration. Nevertheless, the overall result was extremely valuable; I began to gain a sense of myself, albeit vaguely. All this was not making me devout, but increasingly I valued my faith and always kept to my decision to be a priest, even though I never spoke about this to anyone. I had a few close friends, and we spoke to one another about religion all the time. I was trying to share my enthusiasm for the *Génie du Christianisme* with my friends. The teacher, called Blottin,[76] who was truly the most infamous loud-mouth I have ever seen, had given me the task of leading the prayer at the beginning and end of class, which made the pupils call me the chaplain. Fr Jules Morel[77] was in my class, but as a day pupil. He already embodied what he has now become: a perfect wit.

The holidays of 1819 (spent in Sablé) which followed this first year of school were very significant for my future due to the death of Fr Lefebvre,[78] the parish priest of Solesmes. I went to his burial, and I still remember the profound, obvious impression that this funeral ceremony made on the parishioners, all of whom attended. He had been the parish priest of Solesmes from the time of the Benedictines and, after ten years of exile in Spain, had come to reclaim his parish. This octogenarian was the most venerable, lovely old man I had ever seen in my life. He was replaced by Fr

---

[76] Person currently unidentified.

[77] Jules-Pierre-Joseph Morel (1807–1890), ordained priest in 1830, after first spending some time with de La Mennais and his companions from 1829. He returned to the diocese of Angers in 1831, where he worked until 1843. He collaborated in the founding of the journal *L'Union de l'Ouest* in 1845, and also worked on *L'Univers* from 1850 until 1886. He published numerous works attacking liberal Catholicism and was appointed a Consultor to the Congregation of the Index in 1875. See the archives of the diocese of Angers.

[78] Jacques Lefebvre (1735–1820), parish priest of Solesmes (1803–1820). See G.-M. Oury, 'La paroisse de Solesmes au XIXe Siècle', in *La Province du Maine,* 4 (1975): 198–211, esp. 199. Guéranger is mistaken in recounting that this funeral occurred in 1819.

Jousse,[79] the curate in Auvers, whom these memoirs will mention on more than one occasion.

I soon returned to my school to attend the fourth-year courses. I found that my principal was Monsieur Laborie,[80] an old officer who had been in the war of independence in Spain[81] and who had fought against the French. He was about as Spanish as his predecessor, Fr Tardy, was English. This was a very turbulent year and a revolt almost broke out. This agitation was caused by the exasperation provoked by certain schoolmasters. The plot was halted by expelling seven pupils from the senior recreation ground. The assassination of the duc de Berry on 13 February caused a great sensation.[82] For my part, I became extremely Legitimist, especially after reading the life of the prince by Chateaubriand.[83] It was in this same year that I read the *Martyrs*,[84] and with such enthusiasm that I more or less knew by heart the twenty-four books of this prose poem. I also read the *Lettres édifiantes* with great interest and often surprised myself by feeling something of a vocation for the foreign missions. I then started to read the principal landmarks of French and foreign literature, and became familiar

---

[79] Jean-Baptist Jousse (1796–1868), ordained priest in 1819; curate of Auvers-le-Hamon; parish priest of Solesmes from 1821–1860. See the archives of the diocese of Le Mans.

[80] Laurent Laborie, appointed principal in 1819. See M.-C. Port, *Dictionnaire Historique, Géographique et Biographique de Maine-et-Loire*, Paris-Angers, 1878, v. 1, p. 81.

[81] This war occurred in 1808.

[82] Charles-Ferdinand de Bourbon, duc de Berry (1778–1820), the second son of Charles X. He was assassinated by a fanatic on 13 February 1820 upon leaving the opera in Paris with his wife, Marie-Caroline de Bourbon-Sicile (1753–1821). See *Les Dates*, p. 155.

[83] *Mémoires, lettres, et pièces authentiques touchant la vie et la mort de S.A.R. Monseigneur Charles-Ferdinand d'Artois, fils de France, duc de Berry*, Paris, 1820. In this period of his life, Chateaubriand was an ardent Royalist.

[84] A five-volume work published in 1809, also by Chateaubriand. It is a prose poem set at the end of the third century and which leads the reader on journeys through many regions of the Roman Empire. See Vapereau, *op. cit.*, p. 438.

with the *Cours de Littérature*[85] by La Harpe. I was not doing
much in class since I had a teacher whom I did not like, and
who liked me still less: Monsieur de Condren,[86] the great-
nephew of the former superior general of the Oratory. This
same year I also had to begin mathematics. I was not really
taken with it and was never able to get the method for doing
division into my head. On the other hand, we had a special
teacher for history. This course was very useful to me and I
devoted myself to it diligently. Also in this fourth year, I read
and soon knew by heart the first *Méditations poétiques* by
Lamartine,[87] which delighted me. God had given me such a
Catholic sensibility, however, that I did not fall victim to the
prejudice of so many others, who had taken Lamartine, at
least in this first phase, for a Christian poet. On the contrary,
I was both upset and worried by his naturalism, which I
recognized beneath the gloss that had duped so many
others. The biblical imitations in this volume made me want
to read the Sacred Scriptures. Fr Pasquier lent me the translation by Genoude,[88] which I devoured.

From a literary perspective, my fifth year was better. The
teacher was a respectable man called Monsieur Mazure,[89]
the father of the Monsieur Mazure[90] who, like me, writes in
L'Univers.[91] He was very good at playing the flute but quite
a mediocre humanist; among other limitations he knew

---

[85] Jean-François de La Harpe (1739–1803), literary critic and writer. From
    1786 he gave a course on literature in Paris for twelve years, which met
    with great success. His great work *Lycée ou Cours de littérature anci-
    enne et moderne,* 1799, was an anthology of the lessons he gave in
    Paris. See Vapereau, *op. cit.,* pp. 1167–9, esp. p. 1168.

[86] Person currently unidentified.

[87] Alphonse-Marie-Louis Prat de Lamartine (1790–1869), poet. The *Médi-
    tations poétiques* (1820), a collection of separate pieces characterized
    by emotional intimacy and of religious inspiration, launched his literary
    career and became the poetic accompaniment to Chateaubriand's
    Génie du christianisme. See Vapereau, *op. cit.,* pp. 1171–3, esp. p. 1171.

[88] Eugène de Genoude, *La Sainte Bible traduite d'après les textes sacrés.*

[89] Person currently unidentified.

[90] Person currently unidentified.

[91] A Catholic daily newspaper with Ultramontane leanings founded in
    1833. It ceased publication in 1914.

Greek no better than anyone else. We did not have a Hellenist among our teachers, and they made us work in proportion to their very limited knowledge. This is the reason why I have never really mastered the essentials of the Greek language and, left to my own devices, I have neglected to learn by myself what I was not taught at my school desk. I have always felt the effects of this deprivation, having continual need to enquire into the traditions of the Greek Church and having only translations at my disposal, and not always even these. Be that as it may, I devoted myself with gusto to French composition in my fifth year, and was quite good at it.

As for my own reading, whose purpose was to broaden my outlook and lead me forwards, I was very fortunate in this year (1821) to become acquainted with the book entitled *Du Pape,* which had just been published by Joseph de Maistre.[92] This work opened up for me a number of perspectives on the Middle Ages and the role of the popes at this time, and I began to mistrust Fleury. Many things went over my head, however, and I was still too far from a sound understanding of the Church's constitution to understand the wide-ranging projects of the great publicist. I felt overawed, but was sorely lacking in a systematic overview that would have made things clearer for me. In the previous year I had read the *Histoire de Bossuet* by Cardinal de Bausset,[93] and the claims of this historian had confirmed my prejudices; there was therefore much that still needed to be done in my understanding. I

---

[92] Joseph-Marie, comte de Maistre (1754–1821), a lawyer who later turned to a literary career. His two-volume work *Du Pape* was first published in 1819. It is an apology for the spiritual and temporal power of the papacy, arguing that only a supreme sovereign power can provide the protection for which modern man longs against the abuses of sovereignty, and that this supreme sovereign power is found only in the papacy. See Vapereau, *op. cit.,* pp. 1309–10.

[93] Louis-François de Bausset (1748–1824), educated at the seminary of Saint-Sulpice, Paris; vicar general of Aix and of Digne; ordained bishop of Alais in 1784; canon of Saint-Denis in 1806; made a cardinal in 1817. His four-volume *Histoire de Bossuet* was published in 1814. See Vapereau, *op. cit.,* pp. 212–13.

read the *Considérations sur la France*[94] by the comte de Maistre, and *La Monarchie selon la Charte*[95] by Chateaubriand. The complete lack of intermediary concepts was the reason why I understood these books very imperfectly. I was also busy with the *Législation primitive* by Bonald[96] but was in no position to judge this work, which did nevertheless suit my rather absolutist turn of mind quite well. It is true that I was reading the *Considérations sur la Révolution française* by Madame de Staël[97] at the same time, which is why I began to greatly admire Necker.[98] It must also be said, however, that the author of *Corinne*[99] could have

---

[94] *Considérations sur la France* was published in London in 1796. It was prohibited in France, although was still sold clandestinely. The book claimed that France is God's chosen instrument for good and evil. The Revolution was a divine chastisement, by means of human terrorists, on the French royalty, clergy and aristocracy as a punishment for allowing the spread of harmful doctrines from eighteenth-century philosophy. He predicted a restoration of these institutions, but without the past abuses. See Vapereau, *op. cit.,* p. 1309.

[95] *De la Monarchie selon la Charte,* Paris, 1816.

[96] Louis-Gabriel-Ambroise, vicomte de Bonald (1754–1840), publicist for the Bourbon royalty and philosopher. He was a *député* under the restored Bourbon regime from 1815 until 1822, and a member of the Chamber of the Peers from 1823. He refused to take the oath after the July Revolution in 1830 and retired from the Chamber. The second edition of his three-volume *Législation primitive* was published in 1821. See Vapereau, *op. cit.,* pp. 292–3.

[97] Anne-Louise-Germaine Necker, baronne de Staël-Holstein (1766–1817), a famous author whose collected works run to more than seventeen volumes: *Oeuvres complètes de Mme de Staël* (1820–21). This was followed by a two-volume collection of her unpublished works: *Oeuvres inédites* (1836). Her *Considérations sur les principaux événements de la Révolution française* first appeared in 1818 and enjoyed critical acclaim. See Vapereau, *op. cit.,* p. 1911–13.

[98] Jacques Necker (1732–1804), a banker and statesman who wrote in his spare time. Madame de Staël was especially impressed with his work *De l'importance des opinions religieuses* (1788), which defended the concept of God against prevalent materialism. Madame de Staël wrote *Vie privée de M. Necker,* which appeared at the front of the *Manuscrits de M. de Necker* published in 1805. See Vapereau, *op. cit.,* p. 1473–4.

[99] *Corinne ou l'Italie* (1807), Madame de Staël's second novel, was set in Italy.

turned me into whatever she wanted. Moreover, her Italy was proving effective as a correction to the depiction given to me by President Dupaty's *Lettres*.[100] I should also say that *Corinne* was not without influence in effecting my reconciliation with Rome, about which Fleury and many others had given me a more than limited concept. In this field, which I had only ever seen tilled by the most prosaic Gallicanism, I was finally encountering poetry. In my enthusiasm for Madame de Staël, I wanted to convert her to Catholicism, and I suffered greatly from the thought that she had died outside the Church. In a word, this was a year of very confusing reading for my young brain, but a revolution was brewing for the day when my mind would become permeated with distinct concepts and precise, ordered facts. It would take some time for this to come about, and the young fifth-year pupil, however ardent he was, still had to wait a few years in order to understand what would remain his ultimate conviction. The essential thing was that his faith, which thanks to God was vigorous and passionate, did not fail.

As for his moral conduct, it was secure as long as his mind was eagerly pursuing serious reading. I became noticeably more solemn, and this together with the seriousness with which I fulfilled my religious duties – although still without true devotion – led one of my colleagues to christen me with the name 'monk'. This sobriquet became very popular and it stuck until I left college. There was, however, no ill will towards me on the part of those who used it. The pupil who had given me this nickname was called Geffroi,[101] a frank Picard[102] whose personality was so given to mimicking people that we called him *Bobèche*.[103] In him, as in me, the traits

---

[100] Charles-Marguerite-Jean-Baptiste Mercier Dupaty (1746–1788), literary figure and jurisconsul who published both legal and literary works. His *Lettres sur l'Italie* appeared in 1785. See Vapereau, *op. cit.,* p. 677.

[101] This may be Jean-Marie-Michel Geoffrey (1813–1883), a famous actor in French theatre after 1844. See M. Prevost et R. d'Amat, *Dictionnaire de Biographie Française,* Paris, 1933–2004, v. 15, pp. 1139–40.

[102] That is, a native of the Picardie region in the north of France.

[103] The French word *bobèche* (candle ring) literally designates a small, moveable, flared metal attachment that is added to a candlestick in

uncovered at college proved to be true. I left Angers to enter seminary, and the goodness of God led me from a clerical vocation into the cloister. After leaving school, Geffroi joined the French theatre, where he distinguished himself and where he remains to this day. Our mutual colleagues often spoke about these two destinies, and on more than one occasion, even in my old age, they enjoyed reminding me of them.

I spent the holidays of 1821 in Le Mans. My father had been transferred to the college of this town as a teacher. The school in Sablé had collapsed following the foundation of the minor seminary of Précigné.[104] In its early days, due to its novelty value and the efforts of the clergy, this seminary took in the children from Sablé, with very few exceptions. My father could not hold out in the face of such competition. He therefore accepted the post that he was offered, and my elder brother who was a teacher in Évron[105] was also called to the college of Le Mans. During these first holidays spent in a town that was much bigger than Sablé, my thinking became more expansive. The cathedral[106] was far more imposing than the one in Angers, and it made an impression on me. The public library, the first significant source of literature that I had the chance to see, gave me real pleasure.[107] I made

---

order to catch dripping wax. At the beginning of the nineteenth century, however (during the First Empire and the Bourbon Restoration), it was also a stage name adopted by a famous popular actor who played mainly the role of a fool; the word then passed into popular usage in order to describe a fool or a buffoon. It is clear that the word is being used here in this latter sense. See E. Littré, *Dictionnaire de la langue française*, Paris, 1863, v. I, p. 361.

[104] A commune in the canton of Sablé, 52km from Le Mans. The minor seminary for the diocese of Le Mans was founded there in 1818. For further information, see Charles, *op. cit.*, pp. 187–90.

[105] A town situated 33km east of Laval. For further information, see Angot, *op. cit.*, v. II, pp. 133–49.

[106] The cathedral of Saint-Julian in Le Mans was begun in the eleventh century and was modified extensively over the centuries. For further information, see P. Joanne, *Dictionnaire Géographique et administratif de la France*, Paris, 1890, v. IV, p. 2444.

[107] This library was particularly well-stocked since the nucleus of its collection had been inherited after the Revolution from the former

the acquaintance of a former doctor of theology on the faculty at Angers, Canon Chevalier.[108] He was an old man full of sparkle, and was very welcoming towards young people. He had four or five thousand volumes, and he placed them at my disposal. I could hardly make the most of them during those brief holidays, but I was personally drawn to study contemporary ecclesiastical history in *L'Ami de la Religion,* which had been coming out for the past six or seven years.[109] I drew many erroneous ideas from this source, of which I would rid myself during the following years. Nevertheless, I also learnt a mass of facts about the Church and churchmen. This has been a great help to me as a basis for the knowledge of the Church that I have continued to seek ever since. Apart from Fr Chevalier, I did not see many people and, from then on, I thought seriously about entering the minor seminary to do my philosophy once I had finished my rhetoric at Angers.

I returned to school in October 1821. I found that my principal was Monsieur Grattet-Duplessis,[110] quite an insignificant man. The school had one major advantage for me: there was a teacher called Gavinet[111] who was able to nurture an attraction for literature in his pupils. He took an interest in me, and he is the only one of my schoolmasters for whom I retain fond memories. He read prose and verse perfectly, and he initiated us in the art of style by means of various literary models. This teaching was a great to help to me for learning techniques in the art of writing, which our education had until then completely failed to provide. Left to ourselves, although we

---

Benedictine abbey of Saint-Vincent (Congregation of Saint-Maur) in Le Mans. Most of its learned works from the sixteenth and seventeenth centuries came from this source, as did an impressive collection of ancient manuscripts. See Charles, *op. cit.,* pp. 68–9.

[108] Person currently unidentified.

[109] A bi-weekly ecclesiastical, political and literary journal founded in 1814. It was loyal to the restored Bourbon monarchy and to Rome, and was concerned with religion and its history (especially Catholicism) throughout the world.

[110] Pierre-Alexandre Grattet-Duplessis, appointed principal in 1821. See Port, *op. cit.,* v. 1, p. 81.

[111] Person currently unidentified.

read a lot we did not know anything about style. I felt new life within me and I wanted to compose French verse immediately. This came out quite well, but it was always serious in tone. In my passion for the *Martyrs*, I planned to translate its twenty-four books into French verse. I only carried out a tiny part of this project since I limited myself to translating an imitation of Chateaubriand's farewell to his muse, which he had placed at the beginning of book twenty-four.[112] I was occupied a little more seriously in a sort of epic on La Vendée. I even did quite a long episode featuring the abbey of Saint-Denis,[113] to which I made Henri de La Rochejacquelein[114] visit after the violation of the royal tombs.

As one would expect, this was all very adolescent, but since I was working quite assiduously on my verse I was deriving real benefit from it. In private, I showed these attempts to my close friend Charles Louvet[115] from Saumur. He later became not only mayor of his town, but also a *député* in the chamber, a representative in the republican assembly and a member of the legislative body. We shared a typical school friendship; we were regarded kindly in the house and Fr Pasquier gave us much preferential treatment. It was in this year that he gave me the *Soirées de Saint-Pétersbourg*[116] and the *Considérations sur la France* by

---

[112] See *Martyrs* 24, in Chateaubriand, *op. cit.,* v. 15, p. 265.

[113] The abbey of St-Denis-en-France in Paris, founded before 490, rebuilt by Dagobert (d. 638). Another basilica was completed under Charlemagne in 775, enlarged by Suger (d. 1152), and finally completed in 1281. In 1607 the abbey became the centre of the new Congregation, and in 1633 it was taken over by the Maurists. For further information, see Cottineau, *op. cit.*, v. 2, pp. 2650–57.

[114] Henri du Vergier, comte de La Rochejacquelein (1772–1794), Royalist general-in-chief and Vendéen.

[115] Charles Louvet (b. 1806), politician. He was elected mayor of Saumur in 1844, a *député* of the National Assembly in 1848, and a member of the legislative body in 1851 and 1857. For further information, see Firmin, Didot et Frères, *Nouvelle Biographie Générale depuis les temps les plus reculés jusqu'à nos jours,* Paris, 1855–66, v. 32, p. 54.

[116] *Les Soirées de Saint-Pétersbourg ou Entretiens sur le gouvernement temporel de la Providence* (1821). The central argument of this work states that everything happens by the will of God. The existence of evil

Joseph de Maistre to read. I was very drawn to these works, even though I was not yet in a position to understand them properly. It had been the same with the *Monarchie selon la Charte* by Chateaubriand; I read it with interest, but much later I realized that, essentially, I had understood nothing at all.

During this academic year, Louis XVIII called Bishop Frayssinous[117] to the ministry for public instruction. Since this minister had devised a plan to make the university Catholic, we watched with curiosity as all of our teachers carried out their Easter duties.[118] I will always remember Monsieur Damiron[119] and his manner of approaching the sacred table. He was devoted to philosophy and was not known for his great faith. At the end of the year, we were given the task of composing a compliment to the minister as the subject for our composition prize in Latin verse. The magnificent verse that opened my composition drew great admiration from the examiners: 'The priest, through whom Religion stands firm!'[120] These good men did not know that

---

on earth is a means for God to demonstrate his divine justice. No man is innocent, therefore everyone must be chastised. The earth is a vast altar upon which every living creature is immolated. See Vapereau, *op. cit.,* p. 1310.

[117] Denis-Antoine-Luc Frayssinous (1765–1841), ordained priest 1790; appointed bishop of Hermopolis, a peer of France, a member of the 'Académie française', grand master of the university, and principal chaplain to the king in 1821. He was appointed minister for church affairs and public instruction in 1824, and then private tutor to the duc de Bordeaux (1820–1888), son of the duchesse de Berry, from 1832. For further information, see L.-G. Michaud, *Biographie universelle* (also called *Biographie Michaud*), Paris, 1811–57 (85 vols with supplements), v. 15, pp. 48–55. Guéranger is mistaken in believing that Frayssinous became minister for public instruction as early as 1821.

[118] Traditionally, Catholics are bound to make their sacramental confession and receive Holy Communion at least once a year, normally at Easter or thereabouts. This practice is popularly called fulfilling one's Easter duties.

[119] Person currently unidentified.

[120] *Per quem Religio manet inconcussa Sacerdos!*

this verse was by Santeul[121] in a famous work presented to Bossuet.[122] I had read it two or three years previously in a book by Cardinal de Bausset.[123] Unfortunately, my own verses were not of the same standard; they were in fact very mediocre. I learned afterwards that the examiners had deliberated whether to give me the first prize as a reward for this unparalleled verse.

I am almost forgetting about the *Essai sur l'indifférence*[124] and the impression made on me by this work. I had very much liked the first volume and admired the second, whose ideas had been adopted by Fr Pasquier. While waiting to do my philosophy, I let myself be influenced by others since I was not in a position to judge for myself. Literature absorbed all of my intellectual powers, and a philosophical instinct was still slumbering deep within me. My understanding of positive controversy was more advanced, and hence I read with pleasure and profit the *Systema theologicum* by

---

121 Jean-Baptiste de Santeul (1630–1697), a canon-regular of Saint-Victor in Paris, who was ordained only to the sub-diaconate. He was a renowned modern Latin poet who distinguished himself as much in secular as in sacred compositions. He was in demand for inscriptions on monuments, published several secular poems, and composed Latin hymns for the liturgy of Paris. See Vapereau, *op. cit.*, p. 1821.

122 Jacques-Bénigne Bossuet (1627–1704), entered the college of Navarre, Paris in 1642; ordained priest and awarded a doctorate in theology in 1652; appointed bishop of Condom in 1669 (an appointment that he resigned since he was chosen by Louis XIV as the Dauphin's private tutor from 1670–79). He was chaplain to the Dauphin, before being appointed bishop of Meaux in 1682. He was a renowned preacher and an ardent Gallican. See Vapereau, *op. cit.*, pp. 301–6.

123 This book was undoubtedly Cardinal de Bausset's four-volume *Histoire de Bossuet*, Paris, 1814.

124 *Essai sur l'indifférence en matière de religion* (1817–1823) by Hughes-Félicité de La Mennais, later known as Lamennais, (1782–1854), writer and Catholic priest. This work, which was very influential in its day, pleaded for the importance of the Christian religion, both for individuals and for nations. It argued for the authority of the Church against individual 'private' religion, and attempted to prove the danger posed to society by the lack of organized religious belief. See Vapereau, *op cit.*, pp. 1174–7, esp. p. 1175.

Leibnitz[125] and the *Entretiens* by Starck[126] about the reunion of Christian communions.

---

[125] Gottfried-Wilhelm, baron de Liebniz (commonly spelt Leibnitz) (1646–1716), a famous German philosopher. His *Systema theologicum* was not published until 1819, but was subsequently translated into German (1820) and French (1848). See Vapereau, *op. cit.,* pp. 1218–20.

[126] Jean-Auguste, baron de Starck (1741–1816) *Entretiens philosophiques sur la réunion des diverses communions chrétiennes* (2nd ed.), Paris, 1821.

Seminary

My year of studying rhetoric, for which I retained such pleasant memories, came at last to a close. My ecclesiastical vocation had not wavered, and it was just a question of deciding whether I would go back to school to do my philosophy under Monsieur Damiron, or do it at seminary. Fr Pasquier and Dr Chevalier thought that I should go to seminary, and so this was the direction that I chose. At that time, philosophy students were reared outside of the major seminary in a place that had once been the Tessé mansion.[127] Later on, the bishop's palace was built there and philosophy was combined with theology at the major seminary. The rector of the house was Fr Fillion,[128] a respectable priest who had been reared at Saint-Sulpice[129] under the regime of the First Empire, but whose intelligence and learning were very ordinary. On Sundays and feasts, the pupils of the minor seminary (called the philosophy students) went to Mass and Vespers in the choir of the cathedral, and exercised the

---

[127] The former home of René de Froulai, comte de Tessé (1651–1725), a Marshal of France who had been born in the Maine region and who became its governor in 1680. For further information, see Larousse, *op. cit.,* v. 14, p. 1663.

[128] Louis-Jean Fillion (1788–1871), spiritual director of the college of Château-Gontier; appointed rector of the minor seminary in Le Mans in 1813, made an honorary canon in 1818. He was the brother of Claude Fillion (1817–1874), who was bishop of Le Mans from 1862. See *Le Chapitre du Mans depuis le Concordat par un de ses membres,* Le Mans, 1912, *passim,* (hereafter, *Le Chapitre*).

[129] A Parisian major seminary founded in 1642.

offices of cope-bearer, thurifer, chaplain to the bishop and so forth.

It was in November 1822, around the feast of St Martin,[130] that I joined the Tessé and donned the cassock. The class was made up of sixty-seven pupils, of whom barely forty reached holy orders. We had a retreat preached by the directors of the major seminary. This retreat did me much good, and during this year I received a distinct grace from God that opened my heart to the devotion of which I had, until then, been hardly aware. I did not understand completely, but it was no longer just an instinct that was guiding me towards an ecclesiastical vocation; I felt God's presence and was striving to let him reign supreme within me. Due to a complete lack of teaching about spirituality, however, I was ignorant (and would long remain so) of many truths that would have been a great help to my progress; I did not even suspect their existence. The method of prayer using petitions and responses, with all of their divisions and subdivisions, seemed completely impossible to follow, and this conviction has remained with me. I did not have anything with which to compare it, however, and the good Fr Fillion would have been incapable of giving it to us. The *Examens* by Tronson[131] were read to us each day but, due to a lack of explanation, I could not really see where all this was heading. I did notice one thing that has stayed with me: namely, that Tronson always brought his subject back to Our Lord at the beginning of each *Examen.* This was an illumination for me, however feeble it was.

The divine mystery of the Incarnation was indeed the object of my faith but, due to a lack of teaching, I barely perceived its consequences or applications. The role of the Blessed Virgin in God's plan was hidden from me, and during this year I was still talking superficially about the Immaculate

---

[130] 11 November.

[131] Louis Tronson (1622–1700), theologian who entered the Congrégation de Saint-Sulpice in 1656, of which he was elected superior in 1676. A two-volume collection of his complete works was published posthumously many years after his death (*Oeuvres complètes,* Paris, 1857). See Vapereau, *op. cit.,* p. 1995.

Conception. Nevertheless, I was happily praying to Mary as possessing superior powers of intercession, but that was all; I had no idea of her greatness. Her bodily Assumption seemed to me to be against sound reason. I had a profound contempt for all the acts of the saints that Mésenguy and Fleury did not accept as genuine, and I spoke about this as though I was a man who knew what he was talking about.

I was just as unenlightened with regard to religious aesthetics. It should be said in my defence, however, that if I had felt otherwise, I would have been the only person in France to do so. Be that as it may, I was proud of my cassock with its long train, and of my surplice with pleated wings, and of my pointed hat with its enormous, heavy crest. I was one of the smart set at seminary, and I was very careful to bring my large, silk sash with its wide fringe right up to just beneath my arms. As for fiddle-back chasubles, stiff copes and wide-ended stoles, I thought that they were perfect and had no desire for anything else. Nevertheless, I dare say that if I had suddenly seen the ancient forms, I would have found them better since the paintings and statues that I had managed to see at the museum in Angers[132] and elsewhere had prepared me for them. The fact is though that my aesthetic sensibility was not demanding them. The ogival architecture attracted me, but it was quite beyond me to analyze my impressions and still more to classify the different styles of the Middle Ages. All I knew was that I found this style more poetic than Greek monuments.

I began my philosophy, for which we were using the *Institutiones* of Lyons.[133] This work did not interest me very much; I had extreme difficulty in reproducing the method

---

[132] The museum in Angers opened in 1801 and included collections of sculptures, paintings, natural history, medals, liturgical vestments, enamels and archaeology. For further information, see Port, *op. cit.*, v. 1, pp. 86–8.

[133] *Institutiones Philosophicae auctoritate DD. Archiepiscopi Lugdenensis, ad usum scholarum suae dioceses editae*, Lugduni, 1782 (5 vols). This work was originally published for the use of seminarians belonging to the diocese of Lyons, and was already outdated during Guéranger's seminary years.

of argumentation and could not manage to express myself in Latin. All this meant that I was quite an insignificant pupil. The teacher, Fr Arcanger,[134] looked kindly upon me, and I was in any case quite interested in philosophy. At this time the Lamennaisian controversy concerning the foundations of certainty[135] was being conducted with too much intensity for my lively mind to become fired up either for or against. Ever since my rhetoric, I was already convinced and declared myself quite openly to be a Lamennaisian. Our teacher was of this persuasion, as was the tutor, Fr Nourry.[136] Although we spoke very highly of common sense, none of us had any. Our Cartesian friends, however, lacked it even more than we did. I did not understand these questions, and many others, until after I left seminary and could at last study as a man.

At the end of the academic year, on 10 August 1823, I received the tonsure. This step made a great impression on me since, thanks to God, I was well prepared for it. I began my holidays, and made the most of them to make the acquaintance of Fr Bouvier,[137] the rector of the major seminary, under whose regime I was going to enter. He showed me great kindness, and from then on I began a close

[134] Félix Arcanger (1797–1859), ordained priest 1820. He was professor of philosophy at the minor seminary in Le Mans; parish priest of Champgénéteux; dean of Milocorne; parish priest of Notre-Dame de Mayenne; made an honorary canon of Le Mans in 1844, and again from 1850–59; vicar general of the diocese of Le Mans. See *Le Chapitre, passim*.

[135] The theory of certainty called 'the philosophy of common sense' considered the rational philosophy of the eighteenth century to be in opposition to the authority of general reason, whose authority rests in the unanimous assent of the whole human race. The source of general reason goes back to the primitive revelation preserved by universal tradition.

[136] Auguste Nourry (1792–1836), an assistant priest at the Tessé. See F. Pichon, *Essai Historique sur les séminaires du Mans, 1802–1875*, Le Mans, 1879, p. 117.

[137] Jean-Baptiste Bouvier (1783–1854), ordained priest 1808. He was professor at Château-Gontier, then at the minor seminary in Le Mans from 1811; made an honorary canon of Le Mans in 1817; bishop of Le Mans (1834–1854). For further information, see A. L. Sebraux, *Vie de Mgr Jean-Baptiste Bouvier, évêque du Mans*, Angoulême, 1886.

friendship with him. This lasted until November 1837, when it collapsed due to a quarrel that continued, so to speak, until his death.[138]

He gave me access to the seminary library. I spent long hours there every day and it was then that I began to discover books. I experienced unparalleled happiness in finally studying the 'folio' editions. These editions of the Church Fathers delighted me. I had never handled them before, but the analyses of Fleury had given me a foretaste. Historians and hagiographers, especially the Bollandists,[139] all made a great impression on me. I felt that I was living a more intense life since, from then on, I truly knew what books were.

I began major seminary in November 1823. I discovered that my teacher was Fr Heurtebize,[140] a young, talented priest,

---

[138] Following the appointment of Guéranger as first abbot of Solesmes in September 1837, Bishop Bouvier refused to accept Guéranger's authority to confer minor orders on monks whom he wished to call to the priesthood. This was because the bishop was unhappy with the concept of monastic exemption from diocesan authority. In November 1837, he declared that he would not confer the sub-diaconate on monastic candidates who had received the minor orders from the abbot of Solesmes. He also insisted that the local bishop of a candidate's diocese of origin should present the dimissorial letters for a monastic ordination, and not the abbot of Solesmes on his own authority. Later on, he quarrelled with the abbot of Solesmes about his use of pontificalia and about the priory founded in Paris from Solesmes in 1842. For further information, see G.-M. Oury, *Dom Guéranger – moine au coeur de l'Église,* Solesmes, 2000, pp. 163–77.

[139] The French Jesuit Jean Bolland (1596–1665) is the original source for this name, which was given in 1641 by the Father General of the Jesuits to the group of scholars (of whom Bolland was one of the pioneers) working to publish detailed lives of the saints. For further information, see G. Jacquemet, (ed.), *Catholicisme – hier, aujourd'hui, demain,* Paris, 1948–2000, v. 5, p. 488.

[140] Benjamin Heurtebize (1796–1867), ordained priest 1819. He was professor of philosophy at the minor seminary in Le Mans, then professor of dogmatic theology at the major seminary. He was made an honorary canon of Le Mans in 1823, and went on to become rector of the major seminary and vicar general of the diocese of Le Mans. For further information, see A. Ceuneau, *Prêtre d'autrefois M. le chanoine Benjamin Heurtebize, Vicaire Général du Mans (1796–1867),* Laval, 1937.

although of shy disposition. He was a Lamennaisian and was responsible for the dogma course. I also had Fr Hamon,[141] a much older man, who was as foolish in his manner as he was rigorist in the ethics for whose teaching he was responsible. He was an anti-Mennaisian and a Gallican. Then there was Fr Lottin[142] who taught Sacred Scripture. He was learned, a Hebraist, not very sociable, but a good man who was a Lamennaisian and an Ultramontane like Fr Heurtebize. He did not know how to conduct his lessons, and we used to talk loudly throughout them to a greater or lesser extent. Three or four of us would sit near the podium in order to follow the lesson. Fr Bouvier was a moderate Gallican and was not very favourably disposed towards the philosophy of Fr de La Mennais. Shortly afterwards, he propounded his own philosophy that superseded what we had received in the minor seminary at Lyons, even though it was still substandard. In our theology, we were following the *Institutiones* of Poitiers[143] published in the eighteenth century, together with the treatises *De religione, De Ecclesia, De jure, injura et restitutione, et de contractibus* by Fr Bouvier, who was not yet sensible enough to publish a complete theology.[144] There were no courses in ecclesiastical

---

[141] Joseph-Amable Hamon (1785–1850), entered the seminary of Angers in 1808. While still a deacon, he was appointed to the seminary of Le Mans, where he was appointed professor of philosophy in 1810 and then professor of theology in 1812. He remained in this post until 1839. He became an honorary canon of Le Mans in 1818 and a titular canon in 1834. See Angot, *op. cit.*, v. II, p. 396.

[142] René-Jean-François Lottin (1793–1868), ordained priest in 1818. He was curate at Château-du-Loir; parish priest of Luceau; then professor of Sacred Scripture in the major seminary of Le Mans from 1819–1830. He became bishop's secretary in 1830, a canon of Le Mans in 1831, and then vicar general of the diocese until 1839. He was a Greek scholar, as well as the author of several works in the field of local history. For further information, see Angot, *op. cit.*, v. II, p. 721.

[143] *Compendiosae institutiones theologicae ad usum seminarii Pictaviensis,* Poitiers, 1708–9, (4 vols). This work was originally published for the use of seminarians in the diocese of Poitiers.

[144] These treatises were written between 1818 and 1833; they eventually formed the basis for his six-volume manual *Institutiones Theologicae,* which was published in 1834. See Johnson, *op. cit.*, p. 61.

history, liturgy, canon law, ascetic or mystical theology, and neither was there much devotion in the seminary.

Every day, Fr Bouvier used to give a spiritual conference in a calm, paternal manner, but there was no sustained teaching. Several of Rodriguez's[145] treatises were read to us in these conferences, and I found them very interesting. Then we had the *Méthode de direction*[146] from the diocese of Besançon, a work of exaggerated rigorism whose maxims were in accord with our moral theology course, whose teacher swore by no one but Collet.[147] St Alphonsus Liguori was soon rejected although, as his conferences demonstrated, Fr Bouvier was from then on usually more moderate in moral theology. Since I needed firm principles, and since we were not taught from any other perspective, the natural logic of my mind settled on tutorism[148] for a number of years; basically, until I was able to understand another theory.

As regards dogma, I will say enough about this by asserting that not a single pupil read St Thomas, and this was all the more so for Suarez or every other significant theologian. Fr Heurtebize made his course interesting, but since we were entirely lacking in sound, general concepts, we were necessarily the victims of the completely false system that was teaching us with such authority. It was for this reason that I was taken in by Fr Carrière's[149] theory expounded in a note-

---

[145] Alonso Rodriguez (1526–1616), Spanish priest and writer of ascetic works. His principal work in French translation at the time was *Pratique de la perfection chrétienne,* Paris, 1688, (3 vols). See Vapereau, *op. cit.,* p. 1747.

[146] This was one of the many diocesan manuals prepared for the direction of penitents in the sacrament of confession.

[147] Pierre Collet (1693–1770), theologian who became a brother of Saint-Lazare, exercising the roles of professor of theology and then college principal. His numerous works enjoyed great success in their day. Guéranger was no doubt taught from his six-volume *Institutiones theologiae moralis,* Paris, 1758. See Vapereau, *op. cit.,* p. 488.

[148] A system of moral theology in which, when faced with a conscience matter, one is recommended to choose the surest option whenever the more generous option is not certain.

[149] Joseph Carrière (1795–1864), entered Saint-Sulpice in 1812 and taught theology at the seminary of Issy; he was ordained priest in 1817 and

book from Saint-Sulpice, which upheld the power of princes over Christian marriage contracts.[150] As for Roman doctrines, Fr Heurtebize taught them, albeit cautiously and with great restraint, whereas Fr Hamon dealt with them very badly. Fr Bouvier let us say anything, and trod the *via media*. Personally, I did not make any noise and listened very attentively. In the eyes of the class, I was one of those pupils whom no one talks about. I used to talk informally after class about dogma or moral theology with Fr Heurtebize or Fr Hamon. Since I did not make any disturbance in class and also avoided being questioned except as briefly as possible, no one (or almost no one) was tempted to attribute to me any partiality whatsoever for theology. This applies to my three years of major seminary. In the first year, I reread Fleury with pleasure and, since Fr Heurtebize had made me read Marchetti's[151] criticism of this historian, I took one more step down the road towards full orthodoxy.

I had still not been given the *mens divinior*,[152] and the dismantling of my Jansenist and Gallican edifice came about only gradually. The eyes of the heart[153] spoken of by St Paul were not yet open, and by some strange phenomenon my nature, which was more poetic than rational, could think of no other way of being raised to a supernatural state than by religious duty. It was then that the most merciful and compassionate Mary, Mother of God, came to my aid in a way that was as triumphant as it was unexpected. On 8 December

taught theology in Paris. He eventually became vicar general of Paris and, in 1850, superior general of the Société de Saint-Sulpice. For further information, see L. Bertrand, *Bibliothèque Sulpicienne ou Histoire Littéraire de la Compagnie de Saint-Sulpice*, v. II, pp. 272–81.

150 These seminary notes were eventually published as a book in 1837: J. Carrière, *De Matrimonio*, Paris, 1837, (2 vols).

151 Guiseppe-Salvagnoli Marchetti (1799–1829), *Critique de l'Histoire ecclésiastique de Fleury*, Besançon, 1818. This is a French translation made from the Italian edition of Venice, 1794.

152 A more supernatural understanding.

153 'The eyes of your heart be enlightened, that you may know what is the hope of his calling, and what are the riches of the glory of his inheritance in the saints' (Eph 1:18) (Douai Bible).

1823 I was doing my morning meditation with the community, and had broached the subject (the mystery of the day) with my usual rationalistic ideas. It was then that I felt imperceptibly drawn to believe in Mary's Immaculate Conception. Speculation and feeling were joined effortlessly in this mystery, and I experienced sweet joy in my assent to it. There was no transport of delight, but rather gentle peace accompanied by sincere conviction. Mary had deigned to transform me with her blessed hands without any fuss or wild enthusiasm. It was a case of one nature giving way to another. I did not say anything about this to anyone, especially since I was still a long way from experiencing the full significance of what had been such a revolution for me. There is no doubt that I was moved by it, but I am all the more so today since I now understand the full extent of the favour that the Blessed Virgin granted me that day. May she now ensure that I give thanks for it in blessed eternity.[154]

It was in this year that my first inklings of a vocation to the order of St Benedict occurred, or maybe a little later in the following year. I felt a burning desire to study ecclesiastical topics from their very sources; the beautiful 'folio' editions published by the Fathers of the Congregation of Saint-Maur were making my mouth water. Moreover, Fr Heurtebize often talked to me about the Benedictines of the abbey of Évron,[155] which was his birthplace. He had been raised by Dom Barbier,[156] the last prior of this monastery. Dom

---

[154] For a discussion of Guéranger's mariology and its contrast with prevalent ideas about Mary emanating from the seventeenth-century 'École française', see Bowen, *op. cit.,* pp. 81–97.

[155] Benedictine abbey founded by Haduin, bishop of Le Mans, in about 630. It was destroyed by the Normans in the ninth century, rebuilt and restored in the tenth century, before joining the Congregation of Saint-Maur in 1640. It was destroyed at the Revolution. For further information, see Cottineau, *op. cit.,* v. 1, pp. 1089–90.

[156] Alexandre Barbier (1741–1819), professed at Bourgeuil in 1758, appointed cellarer of Évron in 1771, and elected prior from 1778. For further information, see A. Ceuneau, *La réforme de Saint-Maur à l'abbaye Notre-Dame d'Évron (1640–1790) et son dernier prieur claustral Dom Alexandre Barbier (1741–1819),* Laval, 1949.

Barbier was a venerable man and a true Benedictine; a friend of Dom Verneuil[157] who had counted on him for the re-establishment of the Congregation at Senlis in 1817. These conversations made a very strong impression on me. I was well aware that in the secular priesthood I would not have the means to devote myself to ecclesiastical studies. Hence, I felt the desire to become a Benedictine and confided this to Fr Heurtebize, who liked this idea and ended up admitting that he was rather inclined to follow me. We could see no other way to do this than to leave for Monte Cassino[158] since there were no longer any Benedictines in France. As for a foundation in our own country, we did not even think of it. This was often the topic of our conversations, but God alone knew what would become of it. Throughout the whole of my time in seminary, I was always coming back to this idea. It disappeared when I changed my mind, only to reappear more strongly than ever, and in different circumstances, when divine providence had prepared the way.

On 10 August 1824, at the end of my first year of major seminary, I received minor orders from the hands of Bishop de La Myre,[159] who had conferred the tonsure on me that very same day the previous year. I then began the long three-month holidays. These were disastrous for me since, in my enthusiasm for study, instead of devoting myself to the

---

[157] Charles-François Verneuil (1737–1819), professed at Jumièges in 1758, elected prior of Bec in 1775, visitor of Normandy in 1783, and prior of St-Denis in 1788. See *Matricula Monachorum Professorum Congregationis S. Mauri in Gallia Ordinis Sancti Patris Benedicti* (Text arranged and translated by Y. Chaussy), Paris, 1959, p. 159 (hereafter, *Matricula*).

[158] The site in Italy, near Naples, to which St Benedict moved after c. 525 in order to found a more cenobitic form of monastic life. For further information, see Cottineau, *op. cit.*, v. 2, pp. 1913–16.

[159] Claude-Madeleine de La Myre-Mory (1755–1829), vicar general of Carcassone, then Bourges; parish priest of Preuilly; became a member of the assembly of clergy in 1785. He was in exile in Piémont, Venice, Salzburg, and then Moravia. He returned to France in 1800 and became the vicar general of Paris in 1810; he was bishop of Le Mans (1820–1829). For further information, see *L'Épiscopat Français depuis le Concordat jusqu'à la Séparation (1802–1905)*, Paris, 1907, pp. 328–9, (hereafter, *L'Épiscopat*).

youthful relaxations that were appropriate for my age and
health, I gave way to impulse. For three whole months I read
approximately one book per day: philosophy, theology,
politics, history and literature. It was a rage, but a tranquil
rage. Although I did not notice anything during the holidays,
I had hardly spent a fortnight at seminary (where I had
returned in November 1824 for my second year of theology)
when I felt an attack of the most severe gastroenteritis that
could ever afflict a human being. I had to return to my
parents' house and put myself under the doctor. The whole
of my digestive system was afflicted; my stomach could no
longer digest anything and there were constant severe
stomach pains in my abdomen, which meant that I could not
get any rest either during the day or the night. Every mental
task aggravated the pain and I had to give up reading
completely, even of less serious books. A conversation
conducted in my presence was beyond my mental powers,
and weakened me however little I followed it. My nervous
system was aggravated to the extreme by the constant suffering and insomnia. I was becoming very thin, and this greatly
increased my suffering during the long periods that I was
forced to spend in my bed. This was because the skin on my
spinal column had rubbed raw. This situation affected my
character; I was becoming morose to the extent that people
were taking me for a hypochondriac.[160]

At that time the medical profession had deplorable
methods for treating gastric illness, and I was made to submit
to them. My regime consisted of a most rigorous diet,
complete abstinence from fatty food, as well as a liquid
medication[161] and leeches. In addition to the pain, I was
coming to the end of my feeble tether. In the end I decided
to treat myself, and I realized that white cheese beaten into
sweet milk could pass through my stomach and give me
some sort of nutrition. The experiment was successful and I

---

[160] These days we would be more inclined to say 'a depressive'.

[161] Guéranger's text specifies the name of this medicine: 'eau de gomme'.
This now obscure liquid medication was clearly based on gum and
resin and was formerly used to treat gastric complaints.

made it my evening meal. Nothing happened for six months, until one day I saw a leg of ham that had been served up on a table and asked for a firm, pink piece. Everyone thought I was joking, but I insisted. Despite my parents' objections, which I ignored, my stomach, which for the past six months had been unable to digest even a spoonful of stock, came out of this trial with flying colours. I also had an irresistible craving for salad, and pounced on a salad bowl full of dandelions. I swallowed this raw plant trustingly, and it made its way down without coming back on me. At the same time, I naturally felt the need to soothe the intestinal irritation that was consuming me. I was the despair of the doctors and I therefore devised my own breakfast each morning, which consisted of a cup of lime-blossom tea mixed with milk. A little toast gave this brew the necessary consistency. The trial worked for me; I continued this diet for four or five months, and when the fruit season arrived, I managed to quell my internal fire by eating figs by the dozen and piles of cherries and redcurrants, not to mention fresh lettuce. It was in this way that my stomach managed to recover. After a year, nothing remained of this terrible illness except a tendency to feel dull stomach pains in my abdomen. This misery is still with me, and I feel it during the various changes of the seasons and as a result of tiredness. Nevertheless, it took several years before my stomach was completely restored to the excellent condition it was in before the gastroenteritis; in the end, my stomach overcame all these trials.

My mental powers came back more slowly. Mental exertion became a trial for me. Around May 1825 I began to read again. At first half a page, then a page, then two, choosing readings that were not very abstract. Imperceptibly, I mastered it again. I was able to read for half an hour, which seemed a lot. I continued, and by varying the subjects, talking more informally for a while, and moving around in some way, I carved out for myself several afternoons of study. I would not, however, have been able to tackle any book at all after a meal. I needed at hour or two for digestion, during which time I was as passive as a boa. This difficulty gradually changed with time, although it lasted several long years. It has been no more than ten years since I have felt able to try to read after a meal, and I still find this difficult.

Around July, my intellectual powers felt better and I was thinking of getting down to reading the Fathers. I was not in a fit state to return to seminary and, in any case, the courses would be ending in a month's time. Ever since my childhood, reading Fleury had aroused in me a strong desire to make personal acquaintance with the landmarks of ecclesiastical antiquity. I spoke about this with Fr Bouvier, who praised my project and allowed me to take volumes of the Fathers from the seminary library. I set to work and read the Apostolic Fathers, St Justin, Athenagorus, Tatian, Theophilus of Antioch and the Shepherd of Hermas. I had even begun St Irenaeus when the new seminary year began in November 1825.

I had lost my entire second year of theology as a result of my illness. Moreover, my feeble health meant that I could hardly follow the life of the seminary for a third year. Fr Bouvier's kindness came to my aid. Every year, a third-year seminarian was sent to the minor seminary with the rank of principal. He was entrusted with the duties of master of cere-monies at the cathedral, providing an hour of daily Latin instruction for the children of 'La Psallette',[162] and with keeping an eye on the area of the minor seminary called 'Le bas-Tessé'. He had a place on the rector's council, and voted for the admission of philosophy students to the tonsure. For theology, he only had to go to the major seminary for the moral theology lecture, which took place in the afternoon. This very free position promised to be better for my health than that of a seminarian, and I received it as a providential blessing. I regained much strength during this year. At the end of my illness, a tumour had formed on my left thigh. Shortly before I started seminary, it had burst painlessly of its own accord, releasing an abundant quantity of clear, serous fluid. The wound healed around January, leaving me with no more than a deep scar that I shall always have. It seems that this serous fluid had been unleashed by the inflammation,

---

[162] That is, the choir school.

and that its elimination indicated the end of the crisis. I could now work, as long as I was careful.

I finished reading St Irenaeus and began Clement of Alexandria. It goes without saying that I was analyzing all these readings in a notebook.[163] In this year, however, I did not manage to get any further in my reading of the Fathers. My duties took up a certain amount of time, I had to follow the moral theology course and prepare for my sub-diaconate exam at the end of the academic year. On the other hand, I had made the decision to dedicate my entire life to the study of ecclesiastical antiquity.

There had been some significant changes at the major seminary. Fr Heurtebize had been removed from his chair and promoted to the post of vice-rector. To replace him, Fr Moreau,[164] a diocesan priest, had been withdrawn from Saint-Sulpice to take up the chair of dogma. This is the same man who has since founded the Congregation of the Holy Cross.[165] He was not up to much as a teacher, lacking knowledge of ecclesiastical antiquity and history. He was teaching the treatise on Grace; I went to several lessons but did not go back after these, in accordance with the freedom at my disposal. Fr Moreau was also planning to reform the seminary, but he did not achieve this. It should be said that he was not a strong character, and also that he had no ideas

---

[163] Guéranger's notebook based on his reading of the Fathers is preserved in the archives of the abbey of Saint-Pierre de Solesmes: *Lecture des Saints Pères*, v. 1, novembre 1825–janvier 1827, pp. 265. Although entitled 'volume 1', there is no surviving evidence of further volumes. For a discussion of these notes and the centrality of early Patristic thought in Guéranger's subsequent work, see Bowen, *op. cit.*, pp. 42–68.

[164] Blessed Basile-Antoine Moreau (1799–1873), ordained priest in 1821; founder of the 'Congrégation des Pères et des Soeurs de Sainte-Croix' in Le Mans. He was beatified in 2007. For further information, see E. Catta, *Le T.R.P. Basile-Antoine Moreau (1799–1873) et les origines de la Congrégation de Sainte-Croix*, Paris-Montréal, 1950–1.

[165] The 'Congrégation de Sainte-Croix' was founded in Le Mans in 1837. This Congregation comprises both brothers and clerics and is devoted to preaching and to Christian education in schools. Some years later, a Congregation of sisters was also founded. For further information, see reference given above.

other than those of the degenerate Saint-Sulpice of our day. My time passed peacefully during this happy year. I was studying a little, the ceremonies for which I was responsible interested me, the class I was giving was neither too long nor too difficult (I found that I had the future father of our organist, Monsieur Édouard Chévreux,[166] among my pupils), I was continuing to study moral theology under Fr Hamon and, as a special favour, Fr Bouvier allowed me to follow the diaconate course even though I was not yet in holy orders. It was in this way that, although I had to leave seminary a long time before the age for priesthood, I would not have to go back there any more except for the ordinations.

I was then very involved, as were all men of letters within the French clergy, in the serious discussions generated by the philosophical system of Fr de La Mennais.[167] Monsieurs Gerbet[168] and de Salinis[169] were giving this utopian idea a big

---

[166] The seventeen-year-old Édouard Chévreux was appointed organist of Solesmes on 15 May 1859 and remained in the post until 27 September 1861, when he left to become the organist at Saint-Lô. See *Diaire de Dom Guéranger – 1852–1874, Archives Dom Guéranger, V/3,* Solesmes, 2007, pp. 161, 211.

[167] Hughes-Félicité de La Mennais (see above note 124). His early writings were Theocratic, Ultramontane and Legitimist. Around 1828 he started to call for the separation of Church and State, and in 1830 he founded *L'Avenir,* a liberal Catholic journal. His ideas veered increasingly towards identifying the divine will with the will of the people, meaning that the people became the vehicle for truth and faith and that the Gospel was assimilated into the cause of social revolution. After the condemnation of his ideas by Gregory XVI in both 1832 and 1834 he refused to submit, and eventually abandoned the Catholic Church. For further information, see Voisin, *op. cit.,* pp. 598–9.

[168] Philippe-Olympe Gerbet (1798–1864), ordained priest 1822. He became one of the chaplains at the lycée Henri IV in Paris, before leaving this post to follow de La Mennais to La Chênaie. He reluctantly abandoned de La Mennais after the refusal of the latter to accept the condemnation issued by Gregory XVI in 1832. He then lived in the college at Juilly (1836–9), before spending ten years in Rome (1839–49). He became the vicar general of Amiens on his return to France, and was consecrated bishop of Perpignan in 1854. For further information, see *L'Épiscopat,* pp. 474–5.

[169] Louis-Antoine de Salinis (1798–1861), ordained priest in 1822. Along with Fr Gerbet, he became one of the chaplains at the lycée Henri IV

push in the *Mémorial catholique*,[170] books were being
published for and against, and a tremendous struggle was
going on. Fr Bouvier set himself among the anti-Mennaisians.
All the teachers except Fr Hamon were in the other camp,
even Fr Moreau. The pupils were equally divided. I was
holding out strongly for 'general reason', although still not
without my own doubts regarding the true principles for the
analysis of the Faith, and thus confusing the best elements of
the natural and supernatural orders. I had an excuse: in my
day we were not taught the treatise *De fide*[171] at seminary.
While waiting for my ideas about these important questions
to clarify, my powers of reasoning were becoming extremely
tired. Nature on the one hand, and Christian faith on the
other, protected me from Pyrrhonism,[172] to which such
badly phrased questions had easily led me.

There was then another more enduring and salutary crisis
taking place in the French Church. Gallicanism was taking a
real battering, and was collapsing after two centuries of domi-
nation. De La Mennais had overcome it by open attack, and
many of the studious young clergy were running after this
athlete. The book entitled *Du Pape* by Joseph de Maistre was
far beyond the level of the clergy of those days. We needed a
bold, eloquent and passionate priest to translate the Roman
ideal; such a priest had been found.[173] He was not alone, and

in Paris; he opened a college in Juilly with his friend Fr Bruno-Casimir
de Scorbiac (see footnote 556, p. 214) in 1828, and became its first
principal. He broke off his friendship with de La Mennais after the
latter's refusal to accept the condemnation of Gregory XVI in 1832. He
became vicar general of Bordeaux and professor of Sacred Scripture on
the theology faculty of this town in 1841. He was consecrated bishop
of Amiens in 1849, and transferred to become the archbishop of Auch
in 1856. For further information, see *L'Épiscopat*, pp. 44–5, 79–80.

[170] A monthly Catholic review founded by Frs Gerbet and de Salinis and
published from 1824–30.

[171] *De Fide, Spei et Caritate,* in F. Suarez, *Opera Omnia (editio nova),*
Paris, 1838, v. 10.

[172] A form of philosophical scepticism taught by the ancient Greek
philosopher Pyrrhon.

[173] That is, de La Mennais.

the *Mémorial* of 1826 was packed with learned, enlightening articles. We looked forward to them each month, and its convictions became stronger with each issue. For my part, I was making immense progress. Although I still did not understand the Church in the way that God would later allow me to, I was witnessing the collapse of my old ideas about the papacy, which had already been undermined for a long time, to be replaced by the true theory. With the exception of Fr Hamon, the seminary was entirely of the same opinion. As for Fr Bouvier, he had somewhat mixed, complicated feelings that worried me somewhat. Nevertheless, at least he was not seeking to hinder things.

In the spring of this year (1826), de La Mennais struck his decisive blow by the publication of the second part of his admirable book, *De la religion dans ses rapports avec l'ordre politique et civil.*[174] In this work, he not only made mincemeat of the last three articles of the *Déclaration* of 1682,[175] but also attacked the first one and overthrew it entirely. This boldness made a great sensation and led to two things: the *Déclaration* of the bishops[176] to the king in disobedience to the Roman doctrine, and the proceedings undertaken to condemn de La Mennais. Instead of stopping the movement, such acts advanced it, and a lasting dogmatic split occurred between the old French Church and the new

---

[174] Guéranger has made a slight error in transcribing the title of this work. The correct title is, *De la Religion considérée dans ses rapports avec l'ordre politique et civil,* Paris, 1826.

[175] The *Déclaration sur la puissance ecclésiastique* was a statement composed of four articles drawn up by Bossuet in 1682 and adopted by the assembly of clergy. They affirmed the absolute temporal independence of the king from ecclesiastical control, the superiority of ecumenical councils over the pope in spiritual matters, the need for papal decisions to respect the freedom and customs of the Gallican Church, and that the decisions of the pope were not irrevocable. For further information, see Larousse, *op. cit.,* v. 7, p. 247.

[176] In a letter to the king of France on 3 April 1826, fourteen French bishops declared their support for the full, absolute, temporal independence of the king in civil matters from the authority, either direct or indirect, of any ecclesiastical power. For the full text of this statement, see *L'Ami de la Religion,* 47 (1826): 274–6.

one, which originated from the Concordat of 1801.[177] Fr
Bouvier formally declared that he was opposed to the attacks
directed towards the first article. Was this simply due to his
inability to change his mind, or to the political direction that
he wished to follow? Perhaps both these factors were
involved. Whatever the case may be, he was not persecuting
us and limited himself to criticizing. This whole movement
was sweeping me along, my outlook was becoming clearer by
the hour and light was streaming in.

In June, Bishop de La Myre was struck by an apoplectic fit that
forced us to give him the last rites. As master of ceremonies, I
accompanied the Chapter when it brought him Holy Viaticum.
Before receiving the sacred host, the prelate said in the presence
of his assistants that he was dying in the faith of the Catholic
Church. He then added that he was also dying in perfect conformity to the doctrines of the old Sorbonne, that he was united
to the *Déclaration* which had just been made by the French
bishops, and that he was asking for this news to be communi-
cated to the minister Frayssinous. Listening to this strange declaration, which did not scandalize any of the old canons present, I
was far from thinking that I would later give this prelate the last
rites and suggest to him a very different declaration.

Bishop de La Myre did not succumb to this first attack, but
his right side remained paralyzed. The great ordination day
was approaching, and we had to get another bishop to come.
This was Bishop Duperrier-Dumourier,[178] bishop of Bayeux,

---

[177] This Concordat, between Pius VII and the Emperor Napoleon I, was signed
on 15 July 1801; it recognized the prerogatives of the Emperor and the State
over the Church in France after the collapse of the monarchy in the wake of
the French Revolution. The Catholic religion was no longer the official
State religion, but simply the religion of the majority of French citizens.

[178] Charles-François Duperrier-Dumourier (1746–1827), appointed canon
of Le Mans and then vicar general of the diocese in 1767 by Bishop de
Gonssans, and became archdeacon of Laval in 1782. After refusing to take
the constitutional oath at the Revolution, he went into exile in Germany
until 1797, when he secretly returned to France and administered the
diocese of Le Mans. In 1802 he was appointed vicar general of Le Mans
once again. He was then appointed bishop of Tulle in 1817, but never
took possession of his diocese. He was transferred to become the bishop
of Bayeux in 1823. For further information, see *L'Épiscopat*, pp. 102–3.

the former vicar general of Bishop de Gonssans,[179] who had administered the diocese of Le Mans throughout the Revolution, and who was greatly esteemed throughout the whole province. At this ordination, which took place in July, the day before the holidays, I had the honour of receiving the order of sub-deacon. I give thanks to God, who on that day deigned to admit me to the company of the ministers of his altar. I thus began to recite the breviary,[180] which I was proud and happy to do. I found everything about it to be wonderful, and was far from thinking that the day would come when I would cast this book aside as being radically incapable of fulfilling its aim. I must say, however, that some of the antiphons preserved from the Roman liturgy, for example those of the Circumcision, Corpus Christi and the Nativity of Our Lady, etc., made a particular impression on me. I used to experience another kind of sweetness with these antiphons that I certainly did not find disagreeable, and which even interested me. I had also noticed the passage from Bishop de Froullay's[181] letter at the beginning of the breviary, in which he revealed the motives that had led to the retention of these various pieces. These motives made a certain impression on me, but I was far from thinking that I would one day develop them in a work that was to cause a sensation.[182]

---

[179] François-Gaspard Jouffroy de Gonssans (1723–1799), parish priest of Lieu-Croissant (1766); consecrated bishop of Gap in 1774; transferred to Le Mans in 1777. For further information, see A. Jean, *Les Évêques et les Archevêques de France depuis 1682 jusqu'à 1801,* Paris, 1891, pp. 32, 430–1.

[180] The breviary for the diocese of Le Mans.

[181] Charles-Louis Froullay de Tessé (1687–1767), became the comte de Lyon in 1711, and bishop of Le Mans in 1723. See Jean, *op. cit.,* pp. 429–30. (See also p. 197, footnote 521.)

[182] The *Insitutions Liturgiques,* Paris, 1840–51 (3 vols).

Secretary to Bishop de La Myre

My seminary years had come to an end, and I was barely twenty-one. I had to wait until I was old enough for the diaconate and priesthood. According to the custom of the diocese, I was temporarily destined for the teaching profession. The second-form post at Château-Gontier was awaiting me after the holidays, which I was not very pleased about. There was no way of getting out of it, however, and I had to bid farewell to my beloved study of patristics and ecclesiastical studies. After leaving Château-Gontier, I was to find a curacy and set out on the path followed by all young priests at this time.

Divine providence came to my assistance when I was least counting on it. Bishop de La Myre was not to die from this first attack, but we could see that the end was near. His private secretary was a young priest from Le Mans called Fr Ligot.[183] He was much favoured by Fr Bouvier, the dean of the cathedral and a character from the now bygone *Ancien Régime,* who tended to achieve everything that he took on. The parish of Fresnay had just then become vacant, and Fr Bureau persuaded the bishop to appoint Fr Ligot there. Since Fr Ligot needed a successor in the prelate's service, Fr Bureau suggested that I take his place. I was a parishioner of the cathedral, and the good priest was kindly disposed towards me. As soon as he had sounded out the bishop, who

---

[183] René Ligot (1798–1835), ordained priest in 1824; curate in Mamers; made an honorary canon of Le Mans in 1825. See *Le Chapitre,* pp. 40, 56.

welcomed the idea favourably, he came to see me at my parents' home and made me the offer. It was not difficult for him to show me that I would have more free time for my studies at the bishop's palace, where my duties would be reduced to a minimum, than I would have in Château-Gontier, where my class would have made anything else impossible. In addition, I would have libraries in Le Mans, which were non-existent in Château-Gontier. I soon made my decision and was presented to the bishop immediately, who received me very well. Two weeks later, I moved into the episcopal palace.

Bishop de La Myre had suffered greatly from his apoplectic fit. The paralysis kept him in a state of great dependence, and his intellectual powers had been affected. His memory of the past had remained intact, but the doctors forbade him to deal with business matters and even to recite the breviary. As for Mass, the paralysis made it impossible for him to celebrate. Business matters were dealt with in his name. He appeared at the council meeting held in the bishop's palace every week, but he no longer governed. Fr Bouvier, who was the principal vicar general, had complete power within the administration and to all intents and purposes was really the bishop. The second vicar general was Fr Bourmault,[184] the former parish priest of Meslay;[185] he was a virtuous priest but was completely brain dead. He was not kindly disposed towards me due to my reputation as a Mennaisian. Another priest called Fr Dubois,[186] who exercised the function of pro-secretary at the bishop's palace and who played a role later on, was greatly loved by the bishop, whom he had served as private secretary before Fr Ligot. On the other hand, he

---

[184] René Bourmault (1776–1847), mayor of Évron (1800–1807), ordained priest in 1810, parish priest of Meslay (1821–1824), vicar general of Le Mans (1824–1842). For further information, see Angot, *op. cit.,* v. I, pp. 392–3.

[185] Situated in an arrondissement 21km south-east of Laval. For further information, see Angot, *op. cit.,* v. III, pp. 27–32.

[186] Pierre Dubois (1797–1875), ordained priest 1819; appointed honorary canon of Le Mans in 1823. For further information, see *Le Chapitre,* pp. 37, 123.

enjoyed the special antipathy of Mademoiselle de Cassini,[187] who had made him leave the bishop's palace and forced him to lodge in the town.

Mademoiselle de Cassini was the bishop's niece, and kept house for him. He had always had her with him since he returned from emigration, except when she had escaped: once to become a Carmelite in Poitiers,[188] and another time to become a Trappistine at La Val-Sainte[189] under the direction of Fr de Lestrange.[190] Her desire to become a religious had a second wind when she turned fifty. She wanted to become a Sacred Heart sister, and she planned to leave her uncle after she had got him to resign his bishopric. She was said to be a difficult character. I had the good sense not to intrude on her territory, and we lived together in total peace until she parted from her uncle. She left him, after he had handed in his resignation, in order to enter the Sacred Heart sisters, where she did not stay.

This new life was advantageous to me on several counts. Firstly, I had a lot more time to myself and books in abundance. Secondly, since I had until then only had dealings with books, it was time for me to experience something of human society. The bishop's palace had been maintained on

---

[187] Cécile de Cassini (1777–1867), entered the Sacred Heart sisters in Amiens in 1803 and left in 1806. Towards the end of her life she returned to the order, although in Orléans and without taking vows. For further details, see the archives of the French province of the Sacred Heart sisters.

[188] The Carmel de l'Incarnation in Poitiers has now relocated (since 1957) from its former city centre location to Migne-Auxances in the surrounding countryside. There is no record of Mlle de Cassini in their archives since she did not stay long enough to make profession.

[189] A monastery of Cistercian nuns in the diocese of Lausanne, Switzerland. Founded as a Charterhouse in 1294, it was suppressed in 1778 and became a house of Cistercian nuns from 1791–1825. It was restored as a Charterhouse in 1863. See Cottineau, *op. cit.*, v. 2, p. 3266.

[190] Louis-Henri-Augustin de Lestrange (1754–1827), Trappist monk who became abbot of Val-Sainte (note that this is not the same monastery as La Val-Sainte mentioned above) when the community of La Trappe sought refuge there after the Revolution. He spent much of his monastic life in refuge, and lived variously in France, Switzerland, Russia, America and Italy. See Larousse, *op. cit.*, v. 10, p. 412.

a grand scale; Bishop de La Myre kept up the traditions of the old hierarchy. Many people used to come to the bishop's palace; members of the prelate's extensive family were often there, and they would come either in succession or as a group. This contact was for me an extremely useful initiation into real life, which I had until then neglected. I found in the old bishop an extremely interesting storyteller, from whom I learnt many things for which I would have searched in vain in books. Bishop de La Myre was at once a man of the world and a priest of the *Ancien Régime*. He was born in 1755 in Picardie and had belonged to the royal court through his father,[191] who was the captain of the guards to the prince de Conti,[192] and by his mother, who was the princess' lady-in-waiting. In his childhood he had known Bishop de La Motte,[193] the famous bishop of Amiens. In his youth he had composed some verse and prose for the amusement of the princess de Conti. Having resolved to take up an ecclesiastical career even though he was the eldest child in the family, he had taken his degree at the college in Navarre. He had entered Saint-Sulpice during the happy period of Fr Bourachot,[194] a famous era of this house that then counted among its seminarians the prince de Talleyrand[195] and a whole host

---

[191]   François-Jean de La Myre (b. 1723).

[192]   Louis-François de Bourbon, prince de Conti (1717–1776). From 1744 he was the commander of the French army that fought at Piedmont. He distinguished himself in battle against Germany (1745) and Flanders (1746). For further information, see Larousse, *op. cit.*, v. 4, p. 1085.

[193]   Louis-François-Gabriel d'Orléans de La Motte (1683–1774), vicar general in the diocese of Arles; administrator of the diocese of Senez (1728–1733); consecrated bishop of Amiens in 1734. He was reputed to be a bishop of great holiness and ability. For further information, see Jean, *op. cit.*, p. 310.

[194]   Claude Bourachot (1697–1777), entered the 'Société de Saint-Sulpice' in 1720; taught philosophy at Lyons, before returning to Paris to complete his theological studies. He became professor of theology at the major seminary in Clermont in 1726, and then rector of the minor seminary in Paris in 1732. He became rector of the major seminary of Saint-Sulpice in 1770. For further information, see Bertrand, *op. cit.*, v. 1, pp. 354–8.

[195]   Charles-Maurice de Talleyrand-Périgord (1754–1838), diplomat and political figure. Ordained priest in 1779, seemingly against his will;

of other candidates, who also became bishops like him and who played a role in the Concordat of 1801. After priestly ordination, Fr de La Myre was chosen as vicar general by a bishop who was favoured at the royal court, in accordance with the custom of those who wanted to get on. This bishop was de Puységur of Carcassonne.[196] He was then transferred to the archbishopric of Bourges, where he was accompanied by Fr de La Myre. My bishop was present at the last assembly of the clergy, among the *députés* of the second order.[197] Like all the other assemblies, it was a means of advancement for many young priests of good background, making the acquaintance of well-placed prelates, the archbishop minister and influential ladies.

There was no lack of benefices for Bishop de Puységur's vicar general. Firstly, he had the abbey of Preuilly[198] in the

---

appointed bishop of Autun in 1789; promoted the cause of the Revolution and invited his priests to swear the oath to the civil constitution of the clergy; excommunicated by the pope and renounced his episcopal office. He undertook an ambassadorial role in England, and lived there as a political refugee (1792–94) before spending two years in America. He was laicized in 1802, became minister of foreign affairs, and held several other important positions in Napoleon's government. At the Bourbon Restoration he changed sides and won favour at the royal court, which earned him the position of minister of foreign affairs and the titles of the 'prince' de Talleyrand and honorary peer of France. He was ambassador to London (1830–1834), and was reconciled with the Church shortly before his death. For further information, see Voisin, *op. cit.,* pp. 1003–4.

[196] Jean-Auguste de Chastenet de Puységur (1740–1815), consecrated bishop of St-Omer in 1775; transferred to the see of Carcassonne in 1778; archbishop of Bourges (1788–1801). He was opposed to the civil constitution of the clergy and sought refuge in England and Germany during the Revolution. See M.-M. Michaud, *Biographie Universelle – Ancienne et Moderne* (2nd ed.), Paris, 1842–1865, v. 34, p. 569.

[197] Shortly before the Revolution, a meeting of the *États Généraux* was convened by the king on 5 May 1789 at the palace of Versailles. This event brought together the king and 1,200 *députés* for a consultative meeting. The first order *députés* were members of the nobility, the second order were members of the clergy, and the third order accounted for the rest. See *Les Dates,* p. 133.

[198] The Benedictine abbey of Saint-Sauveur and Saint-Pierre, founded at Preuilly-sur-Claise in 1001. It is situated in Loches, Indre-sur-Loire, in the diocese of Tours. See Cottineau, *op. cit.,* v. 2, pp. 2363–4.

diocese of Tours, whose rent was bringing him a private income of six thousand livres.[199] This abbey was not attached to any Congregation and the monks (there were seven or eight of them) eventually gave up conventual life and lived in houses in the village, from which they went to the church for the divine office. Apart from the abbey of Preuilly, Fr de La Myre still owned the priory of Oizé,[200] which was bringing in revenue of about 1,500 francs. The extraordinary thing was that this priory was in the diocese of Le Mans, near La Fontaine-Saint-Martin[201] in the canton of Foultourte.

When visiting the parish of La Fontaine-Saint-Martin after becoming the bishop of Le Mans, Bishop de La Myre came across a man whom he had baptized the previous century, when he had come to take possession of the priory of Oizé. By administering the baptism, he had wanted to fulfil the functions of a simple parish priest.

My bishop had seen Rome under Pius VI.[202] He could talk about the papal secretary, Cardinal de Bernis,[203] who had welcomed him kindly. On his advice, he had studied the Roman Congregations and had written a report on the work done by these dicasteries. He had seen Naples and Venice, and had taken part in the famous carnival in the latter town. I must say that his trip had been completely useless as far as art and architecture were concerned; he had only seen the social society of this country. He had returned to France for two or three years, when the Revolution toppled his hopes for advancement in the Church and cast him into foreign lands.

Like many émigrés, he was banking on only a squall of wind

---

[199] A 'livre' was formerly a unit of monetary currency in France.

[200] The Augustinian priory of Saint-Jean. See Cottineau, *op. cit.*, v. 2, p. 2124.

[201] A commune in the canton of Pontvallain, 28km from Le Mans. For further information, see Charles, *op. cit.*, pp. 286–7.

[202] Pius VI (1717–1799), pope from 1775. For further information, see Levillain, *op. cit.*, pp. 1330–4.

[203] François-Joachim de Pierre de Bernis (1715–1791), ordained priest 1759; appointed archbishop of Albi in 1764, with the title of cardinal; he held many different curial positions. For further information, see Prevost et d'Amat, *op. cit.*, v. 6, pp. 123–6.

and did not initially get past Piémont when he fled. He lost a sister in Turin, who was a Carmelite nun and who had withdrawn to a convent in this town.[204] To the very end of his life he had a tender veneration for this saintly religious, who seems to have loved him very much. Piémont was soon no longer a safe haven for émigrés, and my bishop thought of putting a safe distance between himself and the Revolution. He went to Brünn in Moravia,[205] where he withdrew to the house of baron de Schrattenbach, the bishop of this town.[206] I do not know how he had got to know him. He spent most of his time in exile in this town: that is, from about 1793 until 1800, when he returned to France. The bishop of Brünn had provided him with a benefice and gave him board and lodging at the bishop's palace. He was a German bishop in every sense of the term: a baron of the Empire, very much a man of the world and a keen fighter before the Lord. The dinners of his Chapter were also no exception to German customs. My bishop took all this in his stride, and when the exiles were recalled the mutual farewells were very cordial. Shortly afterwards, the imperial choice transferred baron de Schrattenbach from the see of Brünn to the prince-archbishopric of Salzburg.

On returning to Paris, Fr de La Myre became part of the new metropolitan Chapter under Cardinal Archbishop de Belloy.[207] He successfully devoted himself to preaching, and

---

[204] Alexandrine-Emilie de La Myre-Mory (1764–1795), discalced Carmelite nun. She entered the Carmel in Chambéry in Savoie, but died in exile in Turin. See Saint-Allais, *Nobiliaire Universel de France,* Paris, 1872, v. 2, p. 34.

[205] Present day Czechoslovakia. There was a high percentage of Germans (almost 30%) among the population of Moravia.

[206] This section is historically inaccurate. Vincenz-Joseph-Franz-Sales, prince von Schrattenbach (1744–1816) was the bishop of Brünn from 1800 until his death. Seigmund-Christoph-Graf, prince von Schrattenbach (1698–1771) was the prince archbishop of Salzburg, Austria from 1723 until his death. The bishop of Brünn during the period of Bishop de La Myre's exile was Johann-Baptist Lachenbauer, who governed the diocese from 1787 until 1799. See www.catholic-hierachy.org/bishop/bschras.

[207] Jean-Baptiste de Belloy (1709–1809), priest and canon of Beauvais; bishop of Glandève (1752); *député* in the assembly of clergy (1755); bishop of Marseilles (1755); archbishop of Paris (1802–1808); made cardinal in 1803. For further information, see Larousse, *op. cit.,* v. 2, p. 522.

celebrated the stations in the churches of the capital. I once heard him in the pulpit of his cathedral during the jubilee of 1826, where he repeated one of his old sermons. Its basic content was nothing out of the ordinary, but the delivery and animation were of rare distinction. Unfortunately for Fr de La Myre, Cardinal Maury[208] came to take up the see of Paris, supposedly in the name of the metropolitan Chapter, which had delegated him with a more than doubtful jurisdiction. During the disgrace of Fr d'Astros[209] (who used to function as the cardinal's vicar general), Maury managed to frighten Fr de La Myre by telling him that he was known to have been in touch with the pope in Savona for a marriage dispensation needed by someone in his family (Monsieur Henri de Cassini[210]). The cardinal added that the only way to avoid Vincennes[211] was to take the job of vicar general immediately, which the Chapter had just so cowardly and so irregularly taken from Fr d'Astros. Fr de La Myre weakened and made the mistake of accepting the offer. He tried to reassure his conscience by considering himself as not His Eminence's

---

[208] Jean-Siffrein Maury (1746–1817), prelate and orator. An ardent Royalist, he was preacher to the king and a member of the assembly of clergy. He fled France after the Revolution and was appointed cardinal archbishop of Nicée *in partibus,* and bishop of Montesfiascone and Corneto in 1794. He became archbishop of Paris in 1810 on the orders of Napoleon I and refused to resign when instructed to by Pius VII, who was in captivity at Fontainebleau. He eventually received a papal pardon after 1814. See Larousse, *op. cit.,* v. 10, pp. 1365–6.

[209] Paul-Thérèse d'Astros (1772–1851), ordained priest in 1797; vicar general of Paris from 1805, although he was removed from this office in 1811 after Napoleon imprisoned d'Astros at Vincennes as a punishment for circulating Pius VII's bull that excommunicated him. D'Astros was restored as vicar general in 1814. He became bishop of Bayonne (1820–1830), archbishop of Toulouse from 1830, and was made a cardinal in 1850. He had been designated to draw up the Imperial catechism in 1806. He was a Gallican, and became a leading figure among the French bishops opposed to Guéranger's liturgical work. For further information, see *L'Épiscopat,* pp. 111, 624–5.

[210] Alexandre-Henri-Gabriel, vicomte de Cassini (1781–1832), a magistrate and botanist. See http://fr.wikipedia.org/wiki/Alexandre.

[211] A château in the town of Vincennes that was made into a prison under Napoleon I.

vicar general but as an assistant to the Chapter. This caused no less scandal, and the unfortunate vicar general had the sorrow of witnessing his family distance itself from him, as well as a whole host of other honest people turn their back on him.

The Restoration put an end to this unfortunate situation. My bishop received the comte d'Artois,[212] and gave him a solemn speech in the cathedral of Notre-Dame before the Chapter. The prince, who did not know him, said that he must be Fr d'Astros. My bishop had to reply that he was only Fr de La Myre. There was, however, no hope of favour at the royal court when such a large number of vacant bishoprics were nevertheless raising the aspirations of noblemen who belonged to the old clergy. The hundred days' crisis worked to Fr de La Myre's advantage; he had the bright idea of following the king to Ghent and everything was forgotten. Cardinal de Périgord,[213] the king's principal chaplain, showed him great favour, and when the Bourbon throne was restored and the Concordat of 1817 concluded, Louis XVIII appointed Fr de La Myre to the see of Troyes. The governmental difficulties caused by the new Concordat prevented many clergymen chosen by royal appointment in 1817 from reaching the episcopate. Fr de La Myre, still urged on by the king's principal chaplain, was among those who found a place in the bishoprics of 1801, which were becoming vacant one after another. Bishop de Pidoll, the bishop of Le Mans, died in 1819 and the bishop-elect of Troyes was promoted to the see of St Julian. His consecration took place on 19 March

---

[212] Charles-Philippe de Bourbon, comte d'Artois (1757–1836), the future king Charles X.

[213] Alexandre-Angélique de Talleyrand-Périgord (1736–1821), chaplain to the king, then consecrated coadjutor bishop of Reims in 1766. He succeeded to the archbishopric of Reims in 1777. He emigrated at the Revolution and was one of thirty-six prelates who refused to resign their see at the Concordat. He became principal chaplain to the exiled Louis XVIII in 1808. At the Bourbon Restoration he became a peer of France and was entrusted with the ministry of ecclesiastical affairs. He resigned from the see of Reims in 1816. He became a cardinal in 1817 and was finally installed as archbishop of Paris in 1819. See Jean, *op. cit.*, pp. 451–3.

1820, and the new prelate did not delay in taking possession; he was more than sixty years old.

This was the character with whom I was henceforth going to live. I made the most of his memories, and drew out from them many ideas about the people and features of the world and Church of a previous age, for which I would have searched elsewhere in vain. I was often with the prelate; he went out in his carriage every day and I used to accompany him. I did not have many letters to write since everything concerning the administration was in the hands of Fr Bouvier. The other vicar general, Fr Bourmault, was a useless man who did very little.[214] There was a council meeting at the bishop's palace every Friday. The good bishop used to put in an appearance, but he did not stay until the end since the doctor had forbidden him to exert himself for fear that he would have a relapse. An excellent dinner, at which all the council members participated, followed the meeting.

The custom of the bishop's palace was that when the prelate came into choir, he was assisted at his throne by two honorary canons, one of whom was always his personal secretary. Not being a priest, I was not named an honorary canon, but the bishop still wanted me to don the outfit. He told me that during the *Ancien Régime,* this was called 'giving someone the cloth'. This innovation gave me the honours of a rochet,[215] an aumusse[216] and a mozetta,[217] and caused something of a sensation, especially among the young clergy who were already bereft of traditions. The old canons were not bothered by it.

---

[214] For a more positive assessment of Canon Bourmault's capabilities as vicar general, see Angot, *op. cit.,* v. I, pp. 392–3.

[215] A variant of the the surplice worn by ecclesiastical dignitaries such as canons, monsignori and bishops. It has narrow sleeves and is often made of lace.

[216] The fur cap with which canons sometimes covered their heads and which they usually carried over their arm. Bishop de La Myre's permission for the Chapter of Le Mans to wear the aumusse was given only on 7 December 1827, two days before Guéranger's installation as an honorary canon of Le Mans. See *Le Chapitre,* p. 44.

[217] The short cape worn over the rochet by ecclesiastical dignitaries such as canons, monsignori and bishops.

An incident that portrays rather well the canonical situation of the French Church at this time marked the first days of my stay at the bishop's palace. The papal nuncio, Macchi,[218] sent a letter to the bishop in which he expressed his concern about the powers exercised by the diocesan authorities in Le Mans with regard to marriage dispensations. He said that Rome was surprised that, in this diocese, uncles sometimes married their nieces and aunts their nephews, whereas there was no evidence of marriage between cousins. There were therefore grounds to think that dispensations from the second degree of kindred were granted in the diocese of Le Mans, which could not be legitimate. This was because Rome never granted such a privilege, and even in cases where it had existed previously it would have been repealed by the Bull of the 1801 Concordat. Consequently, the papal nuncio exhorted the bishop to examine this affair in the light of his conscience. In fact, dispensations from not only the fourth and third degrees of consanguinity, but even from the second were being issued from the secretariat of the bishop's palace every day, and with no hint of an apostolic indult. These latter dispensations were taxed at three hundred francs and were dispatched all the time, especially on Mondays. This was making considerable annual revenue for the secretariat, the diocese then joining together two *départements*.

The bishop disclosed the papal nuncio's letter to the council. The majority were of the opinion that it should be ignored, and the privileges of the diocese of Le Mans maintained. Fr Bouvier was of the opposite opinion, since his general inclination was to have closer links with Rome. If he was later considered as one of the representatives of

---

[218] Vincenzo Macchi (1770–1860), ordained priest in 1792. He was consecrated titular archbishop of Nisibis in 1818; appointed papal nuncio to Switzerland in 1818; papal nuncio to France from 1819–1826, when he became an official in the Roman curia. He was made a cardinal in 1826 and appointed prefect of the Congregation of the Council in 1834. In 1844 he became secretary of the Congregation for Universal Inquisition in 1844 and also appointed bishop of Porto e Santa Rufina in Italy. He became bishop of Ostia in 1847. See www.catholic-hierachy .org/bishop/bmacv.html.

Gallicanism, this is because he was overtaken by the Roman movement. Furthermore, he set himself limits that he had decided never to cross, especially when he became the bishop. In the present circumstances he held out resolutely for the rights of the Holy See, which was entailing the nullity of numerous marriages contracted with only episcopal dispensation. He instituted an examination of the grounds for dispensation. The defenders of the alleged right of the bishops of Le Mans extolled the authority of Bishop Duperrier, then the bishop of Bayeux, who had been the vicar general of Le Mans both before and after the Revolution, and to whom this practice dated back. The authentic grounds for nullity he had bequeathed were being discussed. Once the examination had been made, it was clear that these were limited to a list of acts of dispensation between cousins, the oldest of which went back no further than 1770. This was rather flimsy since, for validity, prescriptions against the rights of the Holy See must be at least a hundred years old. Fr Bouvier was triumphant, and on this occasion I remember a rather curious remark that well portrays the situation of the Church in France at this time. We were at table for dinner, and the subject of conversation was the dispensations. Suddenly, Fr Dubois began to speak and, addressing the bishop, he said: 'My Lord, it seems to me that this is a question of canon law, whose solution can be found easily since you have Durand de Maillane[219] in your library.' The future vicar general was suddenly aware, after a week of discussions, that here was a question of canon law and as far as he was concerned Durand de Maillane and canon law was one and the same thing.

To conclude the matter, the bishop bowed to the advice of Fr Bouvier and had a letter written to the papal nuncio stating that he was renouncing the use of his alleged right. Sometime later, he received a papal brief from Rome absolving his censures, in which a penance of reciting the seven

---

[219] Pierre-Toussaint Durand de Maillane (1729–1814), author of *Dictionnaire de droit canonique et de pratique bénéficiale*, Avignon, 1761, (2 vols); Lyons, 1770, (4 vols). See Vapereau, *op. cit.*, p. 682.

penitential psalms[220] and the litany of the saints was imposed upon him. Furthermore, he was given the power to dispense *in radice* all marriages in the diocese rendered null due to the lack of an apostolic dispensation. Broadcasting this news about would have caused serious problems, and Fr Bouvier was of the opinion that strict silence should be kept about this concession, leaving in good faith the large number of families that it concerned.

Bishop de La Myre had founded a house of Sacred Heart sisters in Le Mans, for which he had a great affection. I used to go there with him from time to time, and I was quite a close friend of the chaplain. On 21 November 1826, I preached for the first time, which happened in the chapel of this community. On that day, the feast of the Presentation of Our Lady, the sisters renewed their vows. This beginning was not a happy one for me since I had to get my notebook out of my pocket and finish my sermon as a reading. The same thing happened to me another four or five times, due to the extreme difficulty I had in memorizing sentences. I would have given up preaching were it not for an occasion that taught me that I was capable of improvising a sermon. The following year, I had been invited to preach for the establishment of a confraternity of the Blessed Sacrament in the rural parish of Ardenay,[221] twelve miles from Le Mans.[222] The congregation was not intimidating and I launched forth fearlessly. I made my listeners cry, and descended from the pulpit firmly resolved to no longer try to learn sermons by heart.

In the spring of 1827, my bishop left with Mademoiselle de Cassini to take the waters in Bourbonne, whose benefits against paralysis were recognized. I then returned to my parents' home and was able to devote myself to study

---

[220] In Christian Tradition, the seven penitential psalms are 6, 31, 37, 50, 101, 129 and 142.

[221] A commune in the canton of Montfort, 19km from Le Mans. See Charles, *op. cit.,* p. 301. Its name changed to Ardenay-sur-Mérize in 1933.

[222] At this point Guéranger's text speaks of a distance of 'four leagues', a unit of land measurement that is now archaic. A league was usually a distance of about 3 miles (5km).

without any distractions. My health was gradually improving and, prudently, I worked at my own pace. The Roman doctrines concerning the authority of the Holy See were the principal object of my labours, and I made extensive researches in the great landmarks of ecclesiastical antiquity. This enabled me to gain a fairly good mastery of these questions.

Diaconate and Priesthood

On 4 April I entered my twenty-second year and Fr Bouvier sent me the dimissorial letters for the diaconate, which I was to receive from the hands of Bishop Montault in Angers on Holy Saturday. Bishop Montault was the bishop of this town and welcomed me with great kindness, giving me lodgings at the bishop's palace. I was the only candidate at this ordination, which I received with great consolation since I had always had a high ideal of and a great love for the order of the diaconate. I returned to Le Mans on Easter Monday and resumed my usual daily life.

I am forgetting to relate how Fr Dubois had been made the vicar general.[223] As I have said, he was the pro-secretary of the bishop's palace and, since he was always needing the signature of one or other of the vicars general for the documents he was sending off, he thought that if he was the vicar general himself then he would no longer need to send the porter at the bishop's palace on endless errands to request the signatures he needed. Before the bishop left, he went to see him after lunch one day and explained his desire to him. The kind old man, who had never thought about this before, was taken aback and initially seemed to refuse. His affection for Fr Dubois, however, won the day, and he signed the document that Fr Dubois was holding out ready for him. The

---

[223] Fr Dubois was only an honorary vicar general of the diocese of Le Mans, retaining this post under Bishops Carron and Bouvier. See *Le Chapitre*, p. 123.

bishop's paralyzed hand wrote in barely legible characters, but there was something recognizable in the end. I entered the prelate's room a few moments later. He was embarrassed and said to me: 'Father, you have a compliment to offer Fr Dubois.'

'What compliment is that, My Lord?'

'I have just made him the vicar general,' he replied. The good bishop duly repeated the reasons that the candidate himself had put forward. He then added: 'But what is Mademoiselle going to say?' Suddenly the door opened and Mademoiselle de Cassini rushed over to her uncle in a rage, objecting to what he had just done. Fr Dubois had gone to see her straight after leaving the bishop so as to inform her of his promotion. This was to brave the storm, but he had preferred to anticipate it rather than be pursued by it. The poor bishop looked like someone under sentence. His niece was insisting that he withdraw from Fr Dubois the document that he had just signed, but the bishop did not have the courage for that. During the day, I saw Fr Bouvier, who did not hide his displeasure. The deed was done, however, and the consequent benefit for Fr Dubois is that he has been the vicar general almost continually ever since. On more than one occasion, he has stood a good chance of being appointed a bishop. He and I got on very well together at this time.

Before his departure the bishop had signed yet another document, but this one was for my benefit and was done willingly. I was to receive the priesthood during the prelate's absence, and he wanted me to be installed as an honorary canon without waiting for him. This distinction could be no surprise to anyone, being until then regarded as the private secretary's right.[224] The bishop had the letters sent off and, out of kindness to me, he did not want a vicar general to sign them in his name since he was keen to append his own signa-

[224] It is true that the post of private secretary to the bishop had long been associated with an honorary canonry, but Guéranger's claim that it was regarded as a right is probably an overstatement. For further information, see L. de Courville, *Le canonicat du Mans 1827–1837* (unpublished).

ture to them. The ensuing scribble certainly did not look human in form, but everyone could understand the prelate's intentions in my regard, realizing at the same time that only a paralytic was capable of drawing such shapeless signs. I therefore kept this title in my possession until the day when it would be useful to me, not suspecting what would happen to me.

The bishop's palace had obtained for me an age dispensation of eighteen months, which allowed me to be presented for priestly ordination from 4 October, subject to the *extra tempora* that had been granted in the same way. Both the bishop and Fr Bouvier intended me to make the most of this dispensation. It was therefore agreed with Fr Bouvier (who was directing me) that my ordination would take place on Sunday 7 October. I chose the archbishop of Tours to ordain me. The reason I gave preference to the metropolitan was that the good bishop of Angers, from whom I had received the diaconate, had been consecrated a bishop in the constitutional Church,[225] and I did not want to be de Talleyrand-Périgord's[226] grandson in my priesthood. We wrote to Archbishop de Montblanc,[227] who will feature in these

---

[225] The Church in France established after the proclamation of the civil constitution of the clergy in 1790, and which lasted until the Concordat of 1801. The model for this church was that of a democratic state, with dioceses comprising a single civil *département* and bishops elected to their sees. The constitutional church was condemned by Rome, with many French clergy loyal to the Holy See refusing to take the constitutional oath of loyalty to the state, the law and the king, and choosing instead to live in foreign exile. For further information, see Larousse, *op. cit.*, v. 7, pp. 247–8.

[226] Guéranger is mistaken in believing that Bishop Montault had been consecrated bishop in a line descended from de Talleyrand. In fact, Montault was consecrated bishop by Pacereau, the bishop of Gironde, who was himself consecrated by Saurine, the bishop of Landes, who owed his episcopate to de Gobel, the first schismatic archbishop of Paris. See des Mazis, *op. cit.*, 138.

[227] Augustin-Louis de Montblanc (1767–1841), ordained priest in Italy during the emigration, and did not return to France until 1814. He was appointed to the bishopric of Saint-Dié in 1817, consecrated coadjutor bishop of Tours in 1821, and became archbishop of Tours in 1824. For further information, see *L'Épiscopat*, pp. 632–3.

memoirs later on, and I reached him on Saturday 6 October. The Gallican customs of my day meant that I was ignorant until the following year of the remarkable grace that Our Lady worked for me by placing my priestly ordination on a day that had been dedicated to her in Rome and throughout the entire Catholic world. Neither the breviaries of Le Mans nor of Tours made any mention of the Holy Rosary on this day, so Mary did not receive any special homage from me then. This will always be something that I regret, all the more so since I have no doubt that this day for my priestly ordination had been chosen by her. In this year, 1827, the feast of the Holy Rosary fell right on 7 October, which is the anniversary of the victory of Lepanto.[228] This day contained yet another mystery, of which I did not become aware until much later: in the order of St Benedict it was the feast of St Justina of Padua.[229] It was under her auspices that the fifteenth-century Benedictine reform began which resulted in the Congregation of Monte Cassino. Our Congregation is affiliated to this one and, through the ministry of one of its abbots,[230] it received my monastic profession.[231] All this was

---

[228] A Christian naval victory by a combined fleet of papal, Spanish and Venetian ships over the Turkish fleet on 7 October 1571, in memory of which Pius V (1504–1572) instituted the feast of the Holy Rosary.

[229] St Justina of Padua (c.300), virgin and martyr. A church in Padua was dedicated to her in the sixth century, and the monastery attached to this church was reformed in the eleventh century according to the Rule of St Benedict. From 1408 onwards, the monastery was reformed again by Lodovico Barbo. This monastery became the centre for the reformed Cassinese Congregation. See Farmer, *op. cit.*, p. 296.

[230] Vincent Bini (d. 1843), professed in 1791 in the abbey of St Peter, Perugia; prior of Rome (1817); abbot of St Salvatore de Scandriglia (1820); abbot of Perugia and visitor of the Cassinese Congregation (1821); abbot 'fontisvivi' and procurator general of the Cassinese Congregation (1825); abbot of Farfa and procurator general of the Cassinese Congregation (1827); abbot of Saint Paul-outside-the-walls and procurator general of the Cassinese Congregation (1831–1838); abbot president of the Cassinese Congregation (1838–1841). See the archives of the abbey of Saint Paul-outside-the-walls.

[231] Following the approval by Rome of Solesmes as a monastic Congregation on 9 July 1837, Guéranger made monastic profession on 26 July 1837 in the Roman basilica of St Paul-outside-the-walls. See Oury, *op. cit.*, p. 158.

hidden from my eyes even though, barring my frailty and great imperfections, I had done as much preparation for my ordination as I could.

I was ordained in the chapel at the archbishop's palace during the prelate's Low Mass. He was assisted by the vicar general, Fr Dufêtre[232] (who has since become the bishop of Nevers), and by Fr David,[233] a member of the Picpus Congregation and the seminary rector, each of whom was holding a pontificale. Once the ordination had started, I followed all of its rites, which were very familiar to me, with recollection. After the litanies, I noticed that neither the bishop nor the priests present were laying hands on me, but had passed on immediately to the words: *Oremus, fratres carissimi, Deum Patrem omnipotentem.*[234] I also noticed that neither the bishop nor the priests were holding their right hand on me. I was worried sick about this omission, which was going to make my ordination doubtful, and felt that I should complain: 'My Lord,' I said to the archbishop, 'you are forgetting the laying on of hands.' Surprised by this interjection from an ordinand, the prelate replied: 'We have thought of everything, Father; you take care of yourself.' He then continued to read through the rite as though nothing had happened, still without the imposition of hands. I insisted once again, and finally the two priests read the rubrics before the allocution more attentively and alerted the archbishop, who then said to me naïvely: 'You are right, please forgive me.' Immediately, he came over to me and laid his hands on me, and the priests did

---

[232] Dominique-Augustin Dufêtre (1796–1860), ordained priest in 1819; he became vicar general of Tours (1824–1842), and then bishop of Nevers (1842–1860). For further information, see *L'Épiscopat,* pp. 406–7.

[233] Isidore David (1771–1847), the first disciple of Pierre-Marie-Joseph Coudrin (1767–1834), who founded the Picpus Congregation in 1800. David was professed in 1801 and became superior of the Picpus community in Poitiers in 1802. He then became rector of the major seminary of Tours in 1819, and of the major seminary of Rouen from 1829–41, when he moved to Paris. See the archives of the French province of the Picpus Congregation.

[234] 'Let us pray, beloved brethren, to God the Father Almighty...' These are the opening words of the prayer that was said immediately after the imposition of hands during the rite of priestly ordination.

the same after him. God granted me the grace of not being disturbed by this incident, which could have been a cause for concern for the rest of my life. The ordination continued, and ended with great recollection on my part. I was conscious of God throughout, who from that moment was engraving me with the august character of the eternal Priest.

At lunch with the archbishop, there was no reference to the incident that could have had such major consequences. We had all received a lesson on the need to pay the greatest attention to the rubrics when administering the sacraments. We went our separate ways after the meal; several people went to the Chapter Mass but I had a pilgrimage to make that was dear to my heart, and I was keen to make it while still moist with the holy oil that had consecrated me. I was sufficiently familiar with the cult of St Martin to have banked on making the most of my trip to Tours by paying him my respects on the ruins of his sanctuary. I therefore made my way alone to Marmoutier.[235] After crossing the Loire, I took a right turn alongside the river and finally reached a vast portal that had survived the walls which surrounded it in former times. I walked through it and soon found myself on the site where Marmoutier had once stood. There was nothing but rubble everywhere, but it was still possible to make out the location of a large cloister, whose walls had been razed almost to the ground. The precinct of the regular places was also recognizable from the fragments of wall that had not been torn down entirely. There were vines and tended gardens within this enclosure. The location of the great abbatial church was likewise desolate. I remember quite a large outbuilding that had remained standing. The sight of these ruins made a great impression on me and I was very moved as I crossed this desolate enclosure, stepping over the remains of the walls and

---

[235] The monastery founded by St Martin of Tours in 372. It was occupied by canons around 850, before its destruction by the Normans in 853. It was then re-established by canons of St Martin of Tours and given to monks around 982. After passing through various monastic congregations, it became affiliated to the Congregation of Saint-Maur in 1637, under whose helm it founded more than 124 dependent priories. For further information, see Cottineau, *op. cit.,* v. 2, pp. 1762–6.

inspecting everything with an attitude of religious awe. I was alone, and I approached the grottoes carved in the rock that had once been within the enclosure of the abbey. A little later, I learnt that St Martin's presence had sanctified one of them, and that St Brice[236] had lived in the other one.

I then caught a glimpse of a large, solid, half-broken down tower and ended up on a terrace, on which stood a modern chapel. The platform was reached by a gentle slope that had been planted out as an English garden. Fortunately, the door of the chapel was open and, since I really needed to pour out my heart in prayer, I went in immediately. Above the altar, there was rather a mediocre reproduction of *La Messe de Saint-Martin* by Le Sueur.[237] Nevertheless, this painting moved me, and while I was kneeling before the altar I implored the great bishop to take under his protection the poor newly-ordained priest whose devotion to St Martin had drawn him to these ruins. I then recalled thoughts that I had entertained on more than one occasion in the past: the idea that monastic life could one day be mine. I was moved to the depths of my soul by the sight of the ghastly devastation before my eyes, and I started to recite the stanzas of the *Rorate*.[238] I found expression to what I was feeling in these words from Isaiah: *Ecce civitas Sancti facta est deserta ... Jerusalem desolata est, domus sanctificationis nostrae et gloriae tuae, ubi laudaverunt te patres nostri.*[239] The rest of

---

[236] St Brice (d. 444), educated at St Martin's monastery of Marmoutier, he eventually became his successor as bishop of Tours in 397. For further information, see Farmer, *op. cit.*, p. 77.

[237] Eustache Le Sueur (1617–1655), painter and founding member of the 'Académie de Peinture' in 1648. *La Messe de Saint-Martin, évêque de Tours* was painted in 1654 and belongs to a series of large-scale religious paintings that Le Sueur carried out towards the end of his life. For further information, see Larousse, *op. cit.*, v. 10, pp. 412–413.

[238] An Advent chant composed mainly of verses drawn from the prophet Isaiah. The first line runs as follows: *Rorate, caeli, desuper, et nubes pluant iustum* ('Drop down dew, O heavens, and let the clouds rain on the just' (Is 45:8).

[239] 'The city of your sanctuary has become a desert ... Jerusalem is desolate. The house of our holiness and of our glory, where our fathers praised you' (Is 64:10–11).

the canticle, where sin is shown to be the cause of such dismal abandonment, moved me no less. The inhabitants of Marmoutier dispersed like a leaf blown by the wind, the Lord who turned away his face and allowed wickedness to follow its course; these lines were strikingly true. At the third stanza I prayed ardently, uttering these words: *Mitte quem missurus est*.[240] I asked God to raise up zealous men to revive these ruins, so as to release Holy Church from the yoke of captivity that had weighed her down ever since she had been deprived of the sacred institutions that were her freedom and glory. Having reached the fourth stanza, *Consolamini, consolamini, popule meus, cito veniet salus tua*,[241] I remained silent. None of my predictions pointed to the return of monastic life and the restoration of these ruins. I was still faced with the desolation, and nothing consoled me.

On coming out of the chapel, I found an old woman at the door. Her countenance of respectability led me to tell her how moved I was by the sorry sight before my eyes. She understood, and started to tell me with great emotion about the dreadful scenes of the profanation and destruction of Marmoutier. Among other things, she told me that the wreckers had demolished the stained-glass windows of the great church with huge hammer blows; they could not be bothered to dismantle them. 'We could hear,' she said, 'this horrible noise from the other side of the Loire, and the hammer blows pierced us to the heart.' I left this place with a sorrowful soul and set out for the town. I was conscious of my priesthood throughout the entire journey of one and a half miles,[242] and I was praying to St Martin to come to my aid. The two towers, the only fragments of his former basilica, guided me to the second pilgrimage that I wanted to make. Having returned to the town, I walked through various streets and finally found the remains of the august temple before me, where the patron saint of France had received the homage of so many nations during so

---

[240] 'Send whom you will send' (Ex 4:13).
[241] 'Be comforted, be comforted, my people, your salvation will come quickly' (*cf.* Is 40:1).
[242] Guéranger's text reads 'half a league'.

many centuries. A few streets and a vile market now filled this most hallowed place. I could not kneel down in public so, standing, I prayed to the great St Martin, that he might have mercy on France, which was so unfaithful to his memory. I finally set out for the city, but with a sorrowful heart.

I attended Vespers and sermon, and returned to the archbishop's palace for dinner. The archbishop was very gracious when I bid him farewell. This prelate was a very ordinary man and was in poor health, but he had a good episcopal bearing. He will feature again in these memoirs. The archbishop's secretary, Fr Boullay,[243] was still a canon in Tours at this time and was a dilettante of the first order.[244] I had seen the portrait of Paganini[245] and other virtuosi in his bedroom. I agreed to go for a walk with him in the streets of Tours by the light of the night sky. He started talking to me about the Roman question, which was such a burning issue at this time; he did not seem pleased to discover that I was an Ultramontane.

The next day, I left early in the morning for Le Mans by stagecoach in the illustrious company of Dom Antoine Saulnier de Beauregard,[246] the abbot of Melleray.[247] I had seen him at the

---

[243] Jean-Alexandre Boullay (1797–1873), ordained priest in 1820. He was a curate at Ambroise and then at the cathedral (1822); appointed an honorary canon of Tours in 1825, and became the bishop's secretary in the same year. He became a titular canon in 1828 and honorary vicar general in 1836. See the archives of the archdiocese of Tours.

[244] In contemporary parlance, dilettantes are people who pursue an activity without passion or real competence. They are nothing to do with those of the nineteenth century, who were devotees of music and Italian melodies.

[245] The Italian virtuosi were well known in the provinces at this time. Nicolo Paganini (1784–1840), was the most brilliant violinist of his generation. See Larousse, *op. cit.,* v. 12, pp. 19–20.

[246] Antoine Saulnier de Beauregard (1764–1839), doctor of theology and counsellor in the parliament of Paris; ordained priest in 1789; canon at Sens; refused to take the constitutional oath and emigrated to Belgium and then London. He was professed as a Trappist at Lulworth, England in 1796, elected superior in 1810 and blessed as first abbot in 1814. When the English government suppressed Lulworth, he led his community to France and took over the former abbey of Notre-Dame de Melleray in 1817. See des Mazis, *op. cit.,* 137.

[247] A Cistercian monastery in the diocese of Nantes originally founded in 1145. See Cottineau, *op. cit.,* v. 2, p. 1813.

archbishop's palace and he had attended my ordination. He did not lay hands on me, however, since he was in secular clothes, according to his custom when outside the monastery. I already knew this great monk via a visit that he had made to the bishop's palace in Le Mans on his way to Paris. He came again the following year. I have never experienced anything more enjoyable and scintillating than Dom Antoine's conversation. His speech was always perfectly fitting, demonstrating a sparkling wit and an aura of the *Ancien Régime*. You could tell he was a nobleman a mile off, and he had what was then called the manner of the former royal court down to a tee. The *Life*[248] that has been published about him does not by any means give an adequate portrait of him. My bishop, very much a man of the world, paled in comparison with him and yet it was always obvious that Dom Antoine was a monk. He was much favoured at court and in the homes of the *faubourg* Saint-Germain,[249] and every year a trip to Paris was *de rigueur*. He took a friendly liking to me, and confided to the bishop that he was coveting me for Melleray. The bishop told me to be on my guard, but there was not much to worry about. I felt no attraction for La Trappe, where I would have had to give up my studies. I had a very pleasant journey with this wonderful old man, and reached Le Mans in the evening of 8 October.

The following day was the day of my first Mass, the feast of St Denis.[250] At this time, I was still burdened by my

[248] *La vie du R. P. Antoine Saulnier de Beauregard, abbé de la Trappe de Melleray, redigée par deux de ses amis, sur les notes fournies par les religieux de Melleray,* Paris, 1840.

[249] A relatively central part of Paris (south of the river Seine) comprising many large and expensive town houses. During the time to which Guéranger refers, it was one of the wealthiest parts of the city.

[250] St Denis (d. c.250), bishop and martyr, was the first bishop of Paris. From the middle of the fourth century he has been wrongly identified with Pseudo-Denis the Areopagite, a mistake that Guéranger makes here. Furthermore, it was wrongly thought that Pseudo-Denis the Areopagite was the disciple called Dionysius who was converted to Christianity by the preaching of St Paul in Athens about the 'Unknown God' (Acts 17:16–34). Since the end of the nineteenth century, Pseudo-Denis the Areopagite has been identified as a Christian mystical theologian dating from the end of the fifth/early sixth century. For further information, see Farmer, *op. cit.*, p. 143.

seventeenth-century prejudices concerning the value and authority of the writings of the divine areopagite. This meant that I was completely unaware of God's grace in ordaining that I should offer the mystical sacrifice for the first time under the auspices of this great initiator into the sacred mysteries. I regarded St Denis as only a martyr and the apostle of Gaul and, such was my complete entanglement in the web of modern errors, I would have willingly fought to defend the fact that he went back no further than the middle of the third century. God wanted me to tread the paths from which I would later strive to turn others away.

The grace of my ordination truly permeated my being. I was physically aware of it, so to speak, through a sense of recollection and the feeling of transformation that the priesthood had produced within me. I blessed God for this grace, which helped me to offer the divine sacrifice with a respect and an ease that strengthened me in Jesus Christ, the great High Priest. I have never been so richly alive, yet without transports of delight and artificial excitement. During my retreat in preparation for ordination, I had given a lot of attention to Fr Olier's treatise entitled, *Sur les Saints Ordres,*[251] and to the rites of the pontificale. I celebrated my first Mass in the cathedral, at the altar dedicated to Our Lady behind the main altar. I was assisted by Canon Bureau, the cathedral dean, who had got me in at the bishop's palace.

I have said that my bishop made me an honorary canon from the very day of my priesthood. The day after my first Mass, Fr Dubois offered to introduce me during the visits that I was to make to all the titular and honorary canons. We made these visits during the course of the next few days, and on Sunday (the octave day of my ordination) I was presented to the Chapter before the Chapter Mass, in the room where the canons had already assembled. I lay down my letters of institution, and everything seemed to be going straightforwardly

---

[251] Jean-Jacques Olier (1608–1657), ecclesiastical writer and founder of the 'Société de Saint-Sulpice', who was ordained priest in 1633. The work to which Guéranger refers is actually entitled: *Traité des Saints Ordres*, Paris, 1676.

when an old canon from the former Chapter, a very stiff man called Fr de Saint-Chéreau,[252] claimed that he had not been convened. The other canons tried to uphold the convocation on the basis of my visits during the previous week, arguing that things were never done any differently. Fr de Saint-Chéreau then fell back on the signing of my letters of institution, whose signature, as I have said, was a shapeless scribble. In vain, the cathedral dean pleaded in my favour, saying that everyone knew the bishop's intentions towards me, and that the characters, such as they were, were obviously in his hand. Fr de Saint-Chéreau pressed his point, and the other canons were so taken aback that I decided it was no longer appropriate to prolong this scene. I took back my letters and, after announcing to the Chapter that I was going to appeal to the bishop who would return the following month, I withdrew from the room. I went to recount the incident to Fr Bouvier, who did not seem too surprised. At this time, I did not yet realize what became obvious to me shortly afterwards: since I was already wearing a canon's outfit, the public did not notice what had happened to me.

I had very friendly dealings with the community of the Sacred Heart sisters, and they invited me to let them benefit from my Mass until the bishop's return. This incident, of no importance in itself, was to have an immense significance for my future work and on the whole direction of my life. This community was using the Roman missal and, so as not to depart from its customs, I fell into line with the chaplain, who celebrated the community Mass – the same Mass that I was often asked to celebrate – from the Roman missal. Despite my lack of enthusiasm for the Roman liturgy, which I had not in any case studied very seriously, I was soon permeated by the greatness and majesty of the style employed in its missal. The use of Sacred Scripture, which was of such solemnity and authority, the sense of antiquity emanating from this book with its black and red lettering, all

---

[252] René-Louis Pillon de Saint-Chéreau (1758–1845), became a canon of Le Mans cathedral in 1781. At his death, he was the last surviving canon from before the Revolution. See *Le Chapitre*, pp. 8, 73.

made me realize that I had just discovered in this missal a living work from the ecclesiastical antiquity for which I felt so passionate. From then on, the tone of modern missals seemed devoid of authority and divine unction, appearing as the work of a single country during a single period, as well as something entirely personal. I had been converted, and the mercy of Jesus the great High Priest had willed that my conversion would take place at the altar, during the very celebration of the divine mysteries. I certainly did not feel these impressions as clearly from the beginning as I am describing them here. Nevertheless, I felt their presence strongly enough at first for me to soon start thinking about adopting the Roman breviary, which I felt would complement the missal. Soon I did not want to celebrate Mass anywhere other than at the Sacré-Coeur convent since there was nowhere else where I could find this beloved missal that spoke just like the Holy Fathers, whereas the other missal spoke like just anyone.

I was thinking like this when my bishop returned with his niece during November. The bishop's palace immediately became my home once again. The bishop had not regained his health in Bourbonne, but the doctors had declared that a second trip was necessary the following year, and that this might have a beneficial effect. Mademoiselle de Cassini immediately declared that it would be me who would accompany her uncle during this second trip. As for her, the time had come to enter religious life, which she could not delay any longer due to her advancing age. She had been admitted to the Sacré-Coeur novitiate, and by keeping her distance from her uncle during his trip to the waters, she was preparing him for a definitive separation. She also told me about her plan, which was to get the old man to resign his see, whose duties he could no longer fulfil adequately due to his infirmity.

Meanwhile, the good bishop thought it urgent to make amends for the unfair treatment that the Chapter had bestowed on me regarding my installation as an honorary canon. Fr Bouvier had a ready-prepared plan, however, which consisted of getting the bishop to nominate three new canons, after whom I would come fourth. The trick worked, and Fr Bellenfant,[253] the rector of the minor seminary of Précigné, Fr Clocheau,[254] the director of the major seminary, and a third whose name I forget,[255] were installed ahead of me, even though they were appointed eight months after me. This quadruple installation took place on a Sunday towards the end of November.[256]

From its outset, the year 1828 found me earnestly preoccupied with the idea of adopting the Roman breviary for my personal use. Poussielgue in Paris was publishing an edition of this breviary. I had it sent to me with an *Ordo,* but before I could use it I needed to find out my bishop's opinion. On 26 January, the vigil of St Julian, I had the following conversation with him: 'My Lord,' I said to him, 'I am thinking of asking you for permission to recite the Roman breviary.'

'Permission,' he replied, 'but it is us who would rather need permission *not* to say it.'

'Since you have agreed, My Lord,' I added, 'I intend to begin from today.'

'Very good, Father. But I am warning you, it is longer than ours. I know this from having recited it during exile.'

'My Lord, the breviary brings with it the missal. Since I have the privilege of saying Mass for you every day, will you agree to my celebrating it from the Roman missal?'

'Why not, Father? Surely the Roman missal is just as good as ours?'

After a discussion that was perfectly balanced on both sides, the only thing left for me to do was to thank God and make it my duty to fulfil the desire he had inspired within me. I therefore began to use the Roman breviary at first

---

[253] Claude Bellenfant (1792–1845), ordained priest in 1815. See *Le Chapitre,* pp. 44, 74.

[254] Julien Clocheau (1799–1883), ordained priest in 1824. *Ibid.,* pp. 45, 139.

[255] Basile Horeau (1737–1830), acquired and founded the minor seminary of Précigné in 1816. He was a professor and then rector at the college at Château-Gontier. *Ibid.,* pp. 44, 49.

[256] Guéranger is mistaken here since the installation took place on 9 December 1827. *Ibid.,* p. 44.

Vespers of St Julian. This was a solemn moment in my life.
The daily recitation of the Roman breviary, together with the
daily celebration of Mass from the Roman missal, took me
ever deeper into the innermost understanding of the
Church. As I continued to use it, I came to understand
numerous things that had remained hidden from me, and
about which I would certainly have always been ignorant if
God had not been pleased to open this avenue for me. I
obtained a Roman missal, which Poussielgue had also just
printed, and from then on this missal always formed part of
my luggage on all the journeys that I made with the bishop.
I carried it around with me into all the churches where I was
to celebrate Mass and, in all honesty, this precaution must
have seemed somewhat strange in more than one sacristy in
1828.

Journey to Bourbonne

I spent the winter dealing with the relatively few tasks of my office, and with my beloved studies, for which I had enough free time. After Easter, the trip to Bourbonne had to be planned. We (the bishop, Mademoiselle de Cassini and I) left towards the end of April. On the way, I saw Chartres cathedral, whose magnificence and mysterious harmony struck me very deeply. I was still a long way from understanding the architecture of the Middle Ages, but Notre-Dame de Chartres was the first complete cathedral I had seen at that time. I do not mention Saint-Gatien[257] in Tours, which was a complete church but whose proportions were far inferior to those of the choir of Saint-Julian in Le Mans, and which could not elicit any admiration from me. In Chartres, on the other hand, it was impossible not to feel strong emotions in the face of such a marvel, however vague my feelings were. In France at this time, ideas about the architecture of the Middle Ages had been reduced to the feeble chapter in the *Génie du christianisme* that Chateaubriand had entitled, *Des Églises Gothiques.*[258] It has to be admitted that if this chapter was admiring and respectful, it was not enthusiastic. The word 'gothic' was thought to express everything that could be said. Even if it did not shed any light on the style,

---

[257] The cathedral of Saint-Gatien in Tours was begun in 1170 on the site of a previous cathedral that was destroyed by fire in 1166. For further information, see Joanne, *op. cit.*, v. VII, pp. 4926–7.

[258] *Génie du Christianisme*, in Chateaubriand, *op. cit.*, v. 12, pp. 124–8.

however, I must say that there was at least no lack of poetic feeling. These coloured stained-glass windows, the sacred half-light that they produced in the whole building, the elevation of the arches, the five naves and the perimeter of the choir with its numerous statues, all delighted me. Yet I also felt wonder and an almost pitiful tenderness when I looked at the appalling, monstrous *Assomption* by Bridan[259] on the main altar. I prayed with faith and devotion before the *Madonna* displayed on the pillar, but was still profoundly ignorant of the Chartres' tradition concerning the *Virgo paritura*.[260] I celebrated Holy Mass joyfully in this sanctuary and then went back to my elderly bishop at the hotel, although not before admiring the façade, the aerial spires and the two superb porticoes to the north and in the middle.

Paris soon drew my attention, but without eliciting any enthusiasm.[261] There were too many vulgar houses and ugly streets. The Tuileries and the Louvre were on too small a scale; in a word, everything was beneath my expectations. I said Holy Mass at Sainte-Geneviève on the vigil of Pentecost since we had arrived the previous day. I went to

---

[259] Charles-Antoine Bridan (1730–1805), sculptor. The *Assomption de la Vierge* was placed behind the main altar of Chartres cathedral in 1776. See Larousse, *op. cit.*, v. 2, p. 1261.

[260] 'The Virgin who is to give birth'. According to E. Male, *Notre-Dame de Chartres*, Paris, 1963, p. 8: 'The origin of the *Virgo paritura* remains shrouded in mystery. There is no documentary allusion to the statue of the "Virgin who is to give birth" before the end of the fourteenth century. It was in 1389, in the *Vieille chronique*, that it was mentioned for the first time.'

[261] Guéranger wrote to his brother Édouard in a letter of 25 May 1828: 'The domes of Les Invalides, Sainte-Geneviève and Val de Grâce seemed to me a terrible jumble of houses: this was Paris. We were weighed at the toll-gate and soon found ourselves on an embankment, on the banks of the river Seine. The entrance to Paris from Le Mans is magnificent. There is nothing on earth more beautiful than the rue de Rivoli. The Tuileries, the Seine, the Bourbon Palace, the Place Louis XV and a thousand other things all caught my eye; they inspired me with wonder and admiration that far exceeded my expectations. This is because, I will admit, Paris surprised me. I used to think I knew it without having been there; I was wrong.' Reproduced in *Lettres de Dom Guéranger à sa famille (Archives Dom Guéranger, XIII)*, Solesmes, 2004, pp. 11–16, esp. p. 13.

Notre-Dame for the day Mass of Pentecost, where Arch-bishop de Quélen[262] was officiating. He gave the appearance of great dignity, except for a slight display of affectation. The whole function was conducted with wonderful precision, with everyone knowing what to do. This was the first time that I heard the pontifical blessings after the *Pater*.[263] Notre-Dame seemed a beautiful and noble vessel to me, but far inferior to Chartres cathedral in terms of its mysterious, moving effect. The Sainte-Chapelle was still used as a magistrate's office, but one could just about catch a passing glimpse of it. I had studied the monuments of Paris in Monsieur de Saint-Victor,[264] and found everything beneath my expectations: edifices, arcs de triumph and the rest. I had become very pro-Bourbon and wanted to see the monument of Louis XVI[265] in the cemetery of La Madeleine. I felt such strong emotions there, and admired everything with complete happiness. The diorama[266] was then showing the inside of St Peter's in Rome when the pope was praying. I ran over to it, and felt great joy. Later on, when I was actually in this place, I was able to judge the exquisite faithfulness of the artist, who had worked from real-life proportions.

My bishop could not even think of an audience with the king,

[262] Hyacinthe-Louis, comte de Quélen (1778–1839), ordained priest 1807; became coadjutor bishop of Paris in 1819 and succeeded to this see in 1821. He became a member of the Chamber of Peers in 1822, and a member of the 'Académie Française' in 1824. For further information, see R. Limouzin-Lamothe, *Monseigneur de Quélen, archevêque de Paris,* Paris, 1955–56.

[263] During Pontifical Mass, after the *Pater noster* and the fraction of the host but before the *Agnus Dei,* some missals included a solemn blessing by the bishop. Although found in certain ancient Roman sacramentaries, the custom was most common in the Gallican liturgy. This blessing was maintained as late as the new missal for the diocese of Paris published in 1841. See J.-B.-E. Pascal, *Origines et Raison de la Liturgie Catholique en forme de Dictionnaire,* Paris, 1844, pp. 156–61.

[264] J.-B. Bins de Saint-Victor, *Tableau historique et pittoresque de Paris,* Paris, 1822.

[265] Louis XVI (1754–1793), king of France (1774–1792). For further information, see Voisin, *op. cit.,* pp. 649–51.

[266] A large-scale painted canvas highlighted by a frame and a light, so as to give the impression of a real scene.

his semi-paralyzed state making it totally unsuitable for him to be presented at court. He resigned himself to this, and fell back on visits to the higher echelons of the clergy. I accompanied him on a visit to Archbishop de Quélen, whose rare distinction I could appreciate even though it concealed a man who was in fact very ordinary. We met up in the archbishop's drawing room with Cardinal d'Isoard,[267] who had obtained a red hat via his membership in the Roman Rota, and who held the metropolitan see of Auch at the time. His Eminence's simplicity greatly endeared him to me. He was a very short, gentle man, and was wearing Roman-style secular clothes. I had not yet seen a cardinal until that day. My bishop then paid a visit to the bishop of Hermopolis[268] in the Tuileries, where he was living as the king's principal chaplain. The bishop of Beauvais had already succeeded him as the minister of public instruction, and everyone was expecting some sort of outburst against the Jesuits. I liked Bishop Frayssinous on account of his affability, his gracious simplicity and his easy manner. During the course of the visit, Bishop Tharin,[269] bishop of Strasbourg and private tutor to the duc de Bordeaux,[270] came by. I was less fond of this

---

[267] Joachim-Jean-Xavier d'Isoard (1766–1839), entered seminary as a young man but progressed no further than receiving the tonsure. He then became auditor of the Roman Rota in 1804. By 1824 he had become the senior member of the Rota. He was finally ordained priest in 1825 and made a cardinal in 1827. He was appointed bishop of Auch in 1828 and later bishop of Lyons in 1839, but died before he could take possession of his diocese. See Prevost et d'Amat, *op. cit.,* v. 18, pp. 222–3.

[268] That is, Bishop Frayssinous. See footnote 117, p. 25.

[269] Claude-Marie-Paul Tharin (1787–1843), ordained priest in 1811. He became a professor and then the rector of Saint-Sulpice, and later rector of the seminary in Bayeux, a post from which he subsequently resigned. He was appointed bishop of Strasbourg in 1823, but resigned in 1826 when he became private tutor to the duc de Bordeaux, the son of the duc and duchesse de Berry. For further information, see Larousse, *op. cit.,* v. 15, p. 45.

[270] Henri-Charles-Ferdinand-Marie-Dieudonné d'Artois, duc de Bordeaux, comte de Chambord (1820–1883), the posthumous son of the duc de Berry and the last representative of the elder line of the Bourbons. Proclaimed king of France (as Henri V) by his grandfather Charles X (who abdicated in his favour immediately after the 1830 July

prelate, who was still young, of slender build and with a hatchet face, although he did have a kindly manner. He seemed rather curt to me, and somewhat narrow-minded. This first impression of his character proved to be correct, although he was also an exemplary and devout prelate. At the hotel *Bon Lafontaine*, where we were staying, my bishop received a visit from Bishop Fallot de Beaumont,[271] one of his friends from seminary. He had been the bishop of Vaison[272] under Pius VI, but was moved at the Concordat to another see (I do not know which one[273]), until finally appointed by the emperor to the see of Piacenza during the disagreement with Pius VII. He had governed the Church of Piacenza until the Restoration with the faculties of the Chapter, and had then returned to France, where the Bourbons left him without a bishopric. I have often seen him since then as he came frequently to see my bishop when the bishop lived in Paris. His language revealed a sincerely devout man who was very preoccupied with God's judgements. I do not know if he blamed himself for his administration at Piacenza, and it was not my place to ask him to give an account of it, particularly in the presence of my bishop, who had been Cardinal Maury's vicar general.

After staying in Paris for about ten days, we left for Marolles,[274] a village near Grosbois in the region of Seine-et-

---

Revolution), he was never recognized as such by France and followed his family into exile. He made several unsuccessful bids during his lifetime to be recognized as king of France. For further information, see *La Grande Encyclopédie*, v. 10, pp. 315–318.

[271] Étienne-André-François-de-Paule Fallot de Beaumont (1750–1835), ordained priest in 1773. He became vicar general of Blois (1780); coadjutor bishop of Vaison (1782), and succeeded to this diocese in 1786. His see was suppressed in 1791 and he sought refuge in Rome. After the Concordat he resigned his see in 1801, was appointed bishop of Ghent in 1802, then transferred to the see of Piacenza in 1807. He was appointed archbishop of Bourges in 1811. This appointment never obtained Roman approval. Hence, he governed his new diocese as vicar capitular and retained the see of Piacenza. He resigned this see in 1817 and died in exile in Paris. For further information, see Prevost et d'Amat, *op. cit.,* v. 13, pp. 542–4.

[272] Vaison-la-Romaine (Vaucluse).

[273] The see of Ghent (see note 271 above).

[274] A commune 13km from the canton of Betz. See Joanne, *op. cit.,* v. IV, p. 2503. Its name changed to Marolles-lès-Saint-Calais in 1894.

Oise.[275] One of the bishop's nieces[276] was living there in quite a nice château, and was married to Monsieur de Broin, a Burgundian minor noble. This family, consisting of father, mother and their four children, gave an example of a very respectable Christian household. We stayed there for more than a month. Mademoiselle de Cassini had her own plans, and did not accompany us; she retired to the Sacré-Coeur convent in Paris until her uncle's return.

People in the Marolles region were living in a state of complete ignorance with regard to their religious duties. In terms of the parish, the village was dependent on another slightly more populated village called Santeny.[277] Their parish priest was a Flemish former canon regular of Prémontré called Van Ekolt.[278] He was a respectable man, to whom I went for confession. I was getting him to recount as much information as possible about his order and about Fr L'Écuy,[279] the last abbot general, who died a canon of Notre-Dame de Paris and who wrote a large number of mediocre Gallican articles in Michaud's *Biographie universelle*.[280]

---

[275] Guéranger is mistaken here since Marolles is in the region of Seine-et-Maine.

[276] Ernestine-Marie-Louise de La Myre-Mory (b. 1787) was married to Edné-Seguin de Broin, on 30 August 1809. See Saint-Allais, *op. cit.*, v. 2, p. 35.

[277] A commune 6km from the canton of Bouissy-St-Léger. See Joanne, *op. cit.*, v. VI, p. 4404.

[278] Person currently unidentified.

[279] Jean-Baptiste L'Écuy (1740–1834), professed in 1761; ordained priest in 1764; taught theology at Prémontré and in Paris, before becoming secretary to the abbot general in 1771. He was appointed prior of the college in Paris in 1775, while also remaining secretary to the abbot general. He was elected abbot of Prémontré and abbot general of the order in 1780. The events of the French Revolution forced him to renounce his abbacy in 1790, and he withdrew to live in the country. In 1801 he moved to Paris, where he became an honorary canon in 1803 and chaplain to the comtesse de Survilliers in 1806. In 1824 he became a titular canon and vicar general of Paris. He left a vast corpus of literary work in Latin, French and English. For further information, see B. Ardura, *Prémontrés – Histoire et Spiritualité*, Saint-Étienne, (CERCOR Travaux et Recherches VII), 1995, pp. 317–26.

[280] Louis-Gabriel Michaud (1772–1858), bookseller and literary figure. His *Biographie universelle* (also called *Biographie Michaud*) was inspired by his ardent Royalist sympathies and his extreme animosity for the

Among other licentious behaviour in the village of
Marolles, there was the pest of civil marriages. There were
easily a dozen of them out of the two hundred inhabitants
who lived there. I undertook to regularize them; I went to
meet the couples, and almost everywhere I encountered
goodwill. I then wrote to the bishop of Versailles[281] to ask for
faculties. Very graciously, he was willing to grant them to me
through the intermediary of Fr Blanquart de Bailleul,[282] his
vicar general, who has since become the bishop of Versailles
himself and then later the archbishop of Rouen. At the time,
I was looking after the extremely poor church of Marolles,
where the parish priest of Santeny came on horseback every
Sunday to celebrate a first Mass. With the help of Madame de
Broin and her daughters, the church was cleaned and the
poor sacristy put in order. I sang the High Mass every Sunday
and, since it was Corpus Christi, I decided to have the
procession of the Blessed Sacrament. To the great astonish-
ment of the people, most of whom had never seen this spec-
tacle in Marolles, I got through it. The simple and tasteful
altar of repose prepared at the château was a great success.

At the same time, I was continuing the business of regu-
larizing the marriages. Nine of them were blessed, and all of
the spouses went to confession beforehand. They were all
the more amenable since I celebrated their marriages
without asking for stipends. This is because the excuse that
they all gave for remaining in this detestable cohabitation
was that they were loath to spend their money on a church
wedding celebration; such was the depressing state of these
people. Couples with children brought them along with
them and, after giving the nuptial blessing, I regularized

---

people and events of the eighteenth century, especially the French
Revolution. The work was reprinted from 1842–1865. See Vapereau,
op. cit., p. 94.

[281] Jean-François-Étienne Borderies (1764–1832), bishop of Versailles
(1827–1832). For further information, see *L'Épiscopat,* pp. 682–3.

[282] Louis-Marie-Edmond Blanquart de Bailleul (1795–1868), ordained
priest in 1819; bishop of Versailles (1833–1844); transferred to become
archbishop of Rouen (1844–1858); after his resignation he retired to
Versailles. For further information, see *L'Épiscopat,* pp. 542–3, 683–4.

these children in the name of the Church by means of the rite contained in the diocesan rituale.

At last, around the middle of June, it was time to leave for the waters. We left our kind hosts and made our way to Troyes. It was in this town that the bishop received the edition of the *Moniteur*[283] that contained the royal dictates of 16 June.[284] We finally reached Bourbonne-les-Bains around 20 June, where we stayed until 10 August. The bishop experienced some relief, as in the previous year, but there was no hope of a cure. Any stay in Bourbonne is very tedious since these waters are hardly used except by the paralytics and lame people who abound there. I found a useful way to occupy myself by studying, and I read a lot of modern literature as a distraction. The parish priest, Fr Mathey,[285] was a refined and energetic priest; a devout man and a true pastor. He saw the bishop frequently, and I made the most of his company. The doctor at the waters, Dr Ballard,[286] was also one of our regular visitors. He was rather a plump, spiritual man who had accompanied the armies of the Empire.

The church in Bourbonne is very ugly. Beneath one of its drain pipes in the cemetery lay the body of Cardinal Roverella,[287] who extorted the brief of Savona from Pius VII. On his return to Rome, he was struck with paralysis and the

---

[283] *Gazette Nationale – Moniteur Universel* (often referred to by its sub-title, which from 1811 became its only title) was a paper founded in 1789. It reported the debates of the National Assembly, internal and foreign political events, and contained complete transcriptions of public acts, treatises and other official documents. See Vapereau, *op. cit.,* p. 1424.

[284] Acts issued by the government of Charles X on 16 June 1828, which concerned the reform of secondary education. These dictates expelled the Jesuits from working in secondary education in France. See *Les Dates,* p. 156.

[285] Edné-Honoré Mathey (1768–1844), ordained priest in 1791 and became a curate in Vroncourt. He was parish priest of Chalvraines (1804–1813) and then Bourbonne-les-Bains (1813–1844). He was made an honorary canon of the diocese of Langres, and became honorary vicar general in 1821. See the archives of the diocese of Langres.

[286] Person currently unidentified.

[287] Aurelius Roverella (1748–1812). For further information, see *Dictionnaire des Cardinaux,* Paris, 1857, pp. 1481–2.

doctors sent him to Bourbonne, where he died. The parish priest told me that he had written to the family to get them to reclaim the body and had not received a reply.

The bathing season had come to an end and we made our way to Besançon, where the bishop wanted to spend the solemnity of the Assumption. He was going to this town to visit another of his nieces, who was married to the comte de Laurencin.[288] We spent a week with this family, who made a great fuss of the prelate. I took the opportunity to make the acquaintance of the Besançon clergy. Roman doctrines were flourishing there, but all scholarly effort was turning to the philosophical ideas of Fr de La Mennais. I would have preferred these men to be somewhat more theological. Among other people, I saw Fr Doney,[289] a canon who is currently the bishop of Montauban and also a well-known extreme Mennaisian. I also saw Fr Gousset,[290] who is today the cardinal archbishop of Reims. He was a seminary professor, and spoke passionately to me about the success enjoyed in the seminary by the doctrine of common sense.[291] As a present, he gave me a copy of a book he had published about loans at interest, in which he defended the extreme position.[292] Everyone knows how much that position has

[288] Aimé-François, comte de Laurencin (1760–1833), general and *député* under the Bourbon Restoration. For further information, see Firmin et al., *op. cit.,* v. 29, p. 926.

[289] Jean-Marie Doney (1794–1871), taught philosophy in the minor seminary of Ornans then in the Collège Royale in Besançon; became honorary vicar general of Besançon in 1829 and vicar capitular in 1833; he was consecrated bishop of Montauban in 1844. See Jean, *op. cit.,* pp. 366–7.

[290] Thomas-Marie-Joseph Gousset (1792–1866), ordained priest in 1817. He was professor of dogma, then of moral theology in the major seminary of Besançon; vicar general of Périgueux, before becoming bishop of the same diocese (1836–1840); archbishop of Reims (1840–1866); made cardinal in 1850. See *L'Épiscopat,* pp. 469, 500–3.

[291] The philosophy was taught from a manual by Fr Doney, which was based on the Mennaisian theories of common sense and general reason: J.-M. Doney, *Institutionem philosophicarum ad usam juventutis praesertimque seminariorum,* Besançon, 1828.

[292] M. Gousset, *Exposition de la Doctrine de l'Église sur le Prêt à Intérêt,* (3rd ed.), Paris: Gauthier, 1827. In this work, the author defends the idea that loans at interest are contrary to the natural, divine law.

changed since then, and how the matter is now viewed. All
his other works on moral theology come after this period,
and the old principles were still holding sway in the school of
Besançon. As I have just said, Roman doctrines were flourishing in this diocese, although scholarly effort had not
yielded great results in these subjects. The strength of this
Church in Besançon, which had stood up to Bishop Le
Coz[293] for fourteen years, was such that when Archbishop de
Villefrancon,[294] one of the signatories of the 1826 *Déclaration*, returned to the fold of this excellent body of clergy, it
was not long before he disowned this participation in the
resurrection of Gallicanism with words of bitterest regret. He
had died shortly before our arrival in Besançon, and people
were already talking about Fr de Rohan[295] as his successor.

I was very interested in the town of Besançon as a fortress,
which was the first one that I had seen. Its Spanish appearance impressed me, but its churches did not move me. The
cathedral has two apses and so can only be entered through
the side doors. To my great disappointment, I could no
longer see the Holy Shroud. It disappeared during the Revolution, leaving no trace other than the layout of the cathedral, one of whose apses was dedicated to it. After staying a
week, we left for Paris, having received, as far as I was
concerned, much for which to praise the kindness of the de
Laurencin family and the very friendly welcome of the clergy,
especially those who were called Mennaisians. Among the

[293] Claude Le Coz (1740–1815), elected constitutional bishop of Ille-et-
Vilaine in 1791; appointed bishop of Besançon in 1802. He was a loyal
promoter of the Emperor Napoleon I, and tried to erase memories and
practices that predated the Concordat. See *L'Épiscopat*, pp. 130–1.

[294] Paul-Ambroise, comte de Frère de Villefrancon (1754–1828), became
archbishop of Adana *in partibus* and coadjutor bishop of Besançon in
1821; succeeded to the see of Besançon in 1823. For further information, see *L'Épiscopat*, pp. 132–3.

[295] Louis-François-Auguste de Rohan-Chabot, duc de Rohan (1788–1833),
married in 1808; widowed in 1815; ordained priest in 1822; consecrated bishop of Besançon in 1828; made cardinal in 1830; fled to
Belgium and then Rome after the 1830 July Revolution, where he
remained until 1832. He returned to his diocese and died prematurely
the following year. See *L'Épiscopat*, pp. 133–4.

seminary professors I had seen there was Fr Mabile,[296] who later became the bishop of Saint-Claude and then Versailles. We headed for Paris via Dijon, where we arrived at night, having travelled a good stretch by stagecoach. When the bishop was properly settled into a hotel, I wanted to go and pray for a while in a church. I looked for the cathedral but it was closed. Having noticed that another church in the same square seemed to be open, I went in and knelt down to say my prayers. Some time afterwards, I heard the noise of horseshoes on the cobblestones and realized that there was rather a strong smell of hay. I was in the church of Saint-Philibert, which had been converted into a military stable. I hurried to get out of this desecrated place and returned to my bishop, who teased me about my disappointment.

The next day we set off on the road once more and, after spending two days near Provins in the château of the marquise de Clermont-Mont-Saint-Jean,[297] one of the bishop's old acquaintances, we went once again to Marolles and the de Broin family, where we spent the rest of August and September. At the beginning of October, we left for the château of Le Gué-à-Trême, six miles[298] beyond Meaux. This land, which had belonged to the prelate's brother before the Revolution, had not left the family. The comte de La Myre,[299] who was the bishop's nephew and a staff officer attached to the minister of war, was living there. He was married to Mademoiselle de Lur-Saluces[300] from Bordeaux, who was

[296] Jean-Pierre Mabile (1800–1877), ordained priest in 1820; became vicar general of Montauban in 1844; bishop of Saint-Claude (1851–1858); bishop of Versailles (1858–1877). For further information, see *L'Épiscopat*, pp. 555, 685.

[297] Louise-Adélaide Clermont-Mont-Saint-Jean (née de Mascrany) married Jacques, marquis de Clermont-Mont-Saint-Jean (1752–1827) on 1 October 1780. See A. Robert and G. Cougny, *Dictionnaire des Parlimentaires Français*, Paris, 1889–91, v. 2, pp. 135–6.

[298] Guéranger's text mentions a distance of 'two leagues'.

[299] Auguste-Jacques-Anne de La Myre-Mory (b. 1794). See Saint-Allais, *op. cit.*, v. 2, pp. 35–6.

[300] Louise-Alexandrine-Jeanne de Lur-Saluces (1801–1852). She was married to bishop de La Myre-Mory's nephew Auguste on 12 May 1824. See www.jean.gallian.free.fr/saluces/images.

accomplished in every respect. We stayed in this house until after All Saints' day. Priests were very scarce in the diocese of Meaux; I therefore took on a neighbouring parish, where I used to say a second Sunday Mass after saying a first one at the château.

Finding myself in the neighbourhood of Germigny, I went to visit this country house that had belonged to Bossuet. I was moved as I visited the interior of the château and the avenues in the park. I visited several neighbouring houses in order to see items of furniture that had belonged to the famous prelate. In the parish church, I saw the old, worm-eaten pulpit in which he sometimes used to preach to the villagers. I also saw a pew at the entrance to the choir where he used to sit, so I was told, whenever he gave catechism classes to the children from time to time. I pushed on as far as Meaux, whose cathedral I visited. There I saw the pulpit in which Bossuet had preached so many times, and into which I impertinently wanted to climb. Behind the altar, I found the prelate's marble tombstone. I knew that this inscription had been moved, and that Bossuet's body was resting in front of the altar. This is where it was in fact discovered several years ago.

After a very pleasant stay, we left Le Gué-à-Trême in the first few days of November and were soon making our way back to Le Mans, where I was glad to return. Mademoiselle de Cassini returned with us, so as to force the moves that would result in her uncle's resignation. She enlisted Fr Bouvier in the plan, and this resignation that was so longed for by his niece, and which was in any case very much motivated by the prelate's infirmities, was finally given. Henceforth, Mademoiselle de Cassini was free; she stayed at the bishop's palace for a few months during the winter, and left for Paris with her uncle in the spring.

I found myself without a position and was daydreaming about the decision I still had to make when, shortly after my return, I received a letter from the comte de La Myre that settled my uncertainties. He was proposing that I should accompany the old bishop to Paris and stay with him, assuring me of suitable financial provision. The advantage of this arrangement was that I would be well-placed to pursue my studies in Paris. I was not yet twenty-four years old, and could therefore make the most of my youth.

In Paris

Few people in Le Mans were sorry about Bishop de La Myre's departure. His episcopate had in reality been short, and his infirmity had gradually isolated him from everyone. The resignation was only sent to Rome in the spring and, after the prelate's departure, Fr Bouvier continued to govern the diocese as before. We left for Paris in January, and for the time being the prelate moved into the hotel *Bon Lafontaine*. As for Mademoiselle de Cassini, she went off to the Sacré-Coeur convent, where she soon took the veil. Later on she made her vows, and later still she was dismissed.[301] She then entered the Vintras sect,[302] until she finally came back to her faith and common sense and ended her adventurous life as a Christian.

My bishop planned to take lodgings at the 'Missions Étrangères'[303] but an obstacle threatened to block this

---

[301] Guéranger is mistaken in believing that Cécile de Cassini entered the Sacred Heart sisters in 1829 (see footnote 187, p. 49). It is possible that he has accidentally inverted the order in which she first tried her vocation with the Carmelites in Poitiers, and the year that she first joined the Sacred Heart sisters in 1803.

[302] A pseudo-mystical sect founded by Pierre-Eugène-Michel Vintras (1807–1875) under the name of *Oeuvre de la Miséricorde* (Work of Mercy), which spread throughout France, Italy and Spain, and which included several priests in its midst. Rome condemned this sect on several occasions. It veered towards Occultism after 1875. For further information, see Jacquemet, *op. cit.*, v. 15, pp. 1174–6.

[303] The seminary of the 'Missions Étrangères' was founded in Paris by Jean Duval in 1663. It was suppressed and sold during the Revolution, but reopened by Imperial decree under the Concordat. For further information, see G. Chatenet, *Missions Étrangères: La paroisse S. François-Xavier à Paris,* Paris, 1971.

otherwise very suitable arrangement. The prelate was counting on frequent visits from his nieces and great-nieces, and the seminary rules were an obstacle to the ready admittance of women into the house. The prelate thought of making his needs known to Fr des Genettes,[304] the parish priest of the 'Missions Étrangères',[305] who was not lacking in influence over the seminary superiors. We paid him a visit, and asked him to take up the cause of an old, infirm bishop who could not be deprived of his family's attention during his last days. Fr des Genettes, then in the prime of life and full of charm and kindness, graciously undertook to sort out the matter. Shortly afterwards, he came to see the prelate at the hotel. Fr des Genettes informed him that the superiors had decided that, since the lodgings where he was to live were on the ground floor, women could be allowed access to them provided that they refrained from climbing the staircase.

As soon as we had moved in, I began looking for a spiritual director and soon made my choice. My bishop went to a Jesuit priest for confession, who was informed when he was needed and came to see the prelate. He was called Fr Varin,[306] one of stalwarts of the Society of the Fathers of the Faith, who entered the Society of Jesus in 1814. It was he who founded the Sacred Heart sisters in Amiens in around 1802; his life has been published by Fr Guidée.[307] I liked this

---

[304] Charles-Éléonor Dufriche des Genettes (1778–1860), ordained priest 1805, became parish priest of Monsort; he was curate (1819) and then parish priest of the 'Missions Étrangères' (1820–1830); emigrated to Switerland (1830); returned and became parish priest of Notre-Dame-des-Victoires (1832–1860); founded the 'Archconfraternity of the Blessed and Immaculate Heart of Mary' in 1836. He was always an ardent supporter of Guéranger's work. See des Mazis, *op. cit.*, 146.

[305] The seminary chapel of the 'Missions Étrangères' also served as a parish church.

[306] Joseph-Désiré Varin d'Ainvelle (1769–1850), army officer; ordained priest in 1796 and became a member of the 'Fathers of the Faith' suppressed by Napoleon; entered the Society of Jesus in 1814, which had been re-established in France at the beginning of the Bourbon Restoration. He was the superior of the house in Paris from 1825 until 1833. See des Mazis, *op. cit.*, 147.

[307] Achille Guidée (1792–1866), Jesuit; ordained priest in 1817; made

religious, and I trusted him. He grew fond of me, and did me much good. This was the first time I had spoken to a religious, and my dealings with him helped to form many of the ideas and attitudes that I would never have had under the direction of Fr Bouvier, whom I saw until I left for Paris. In this kind old man, I encountered common sense, love for God and sweetness of manner, together with an authority that I had never come across anywhere else. In a word, without having a very clear perception of it, I started to have some sense of what it meant to be a religious.

My dealings with Fr Varin opened up the Jesuit library to me, which was already very extensive. The proximity of their house at 35, rue de Sèvres was very convenient for me, and I went to work there several times a week. There were a vast number of foreign ecclesiastical works from Italy, Germany etc., which surprised me.[308] I realized that my concepts of bibliography formed in the libraries of Le Mans, which hardly contained anything but the works of French authors, were very incomplete. This delighted me and gave me renewed enthusiasm. One single aim inspired all of my work: the defence of Roman doctrines. There was still something of the seminarian in my manner, but I was gradually ridding myself of this every day.

It seemed to me that a large-scale historical/dogmatic work about the rights of the Holy See was needed at this time. My work in Le Mans had paved the way in the field of ecclesiastical antiquity, and I decided to devote myself to writing this book. It seemed urgently needed in the all too incomplete polemic that Roman supporters were waging against the Gallican school, which was still vigorous since it was defended by the old episcopate and the government. The

---

socius to the provincial of France in 1833; provincial of the province of Paris in 1836, the French Jesuits being by then divided into two provinces: Lyons and Paris. For further information, see Prevost et d'Amat, *op. cit.*, v. 17, p. 74.

[308] For further information on this library, see P. Delattré, *Les établissements des Jésuites en France depuis quatre siècles. Répertoire topo-bibliographique*, Paris, 1939.

year 1830 had not yet arrived in order to overcome the
divide.

At that time, Fr de La Mennais was revelling in all his glory,
not because of his philosophical system, which was unsus-
tainable, but by his zeal and eloquence in defending Roman
doctrines. He was the uncontested and venerated head of
the school that was then called Ultramontane. During the
first weeks of my stay in Paris, I thought that it would not be
indiscreet to write him a long letter, in which I explained the
plan for my work and asked him to enlighten me with his
advice.[309] I was not made to wait for the reply, and on 27
February I received the following letter:

La Chênaie, near Dinan, Côtes du Nord
22 February 1829

Dear Sir,

There is no doubt that work you have spoken to me about
will be very useful. So as to be read easily, it should not be too
long, especially if it is simply aiming to establish the divine
prerogatives of the Holy See by means of tradition. A history
of the popes would perhaps be more interesting, and would
be of greater use than a simple dogmatic treatise; I think that
it would also make more of an impression, especially on lay
readers. When you have decided on the above, I shall try to
point out to you several works that seem to me to be well
worth consulting. Returning trust for the trust that you have
shown me, I should tell you that several people are currently
engaged in work that is similar to what you have planned. It
would be highly desirable to coordinate these various works,
so as to somehow make one common effort from all of these
partial and differing attempts. This could only be achieved
successfully by forming a body especially devoted to studies.
This body already exists, or at least its first members have
gathered together. If your time is at your own disposal, as
what you have said leads me to believe, and if zeal for God

---

[309] For a discussion of the relationship between de La Mennais and
Guéranger, and for details of their correspondence, see Johnson, *op.
cit.*, pp. 80–95.

and his Church inspires you to consider joining those who are united in the same zeal, I suggest that you come in with us. You will have a lot of help from books here, and you will find among us freedom and hearts ready to love you. In any event, I ask you to keep this letter confidential. If providence were to call you elsewhere, I would remain no less united to you.

With my affectionate regards,
Félicité de La Mennais

I received this kind letter with great pleasure. I recognized in it the tone of a man of conviction, whose principal concern was for the Church. There was no hint of the terrible storms of pride that would arise in this soul, and of the distressing shipwreck in which it would perish.[310] As far as the suggestion contained in this letter was concerned, I was not even tempted to accept. I venerated the man who had written it as someone providential for our French Church. Nevertheless, I did not want to launch out into the unknown by giving myself to him, and neither did I want to abandon the pleasant freedom with which God had provided me.

I wrote a second letter about the same subject, and received the following reply:

La Chênaie, 15 March 1829

Dear Sir,

Here is a very brief account of my thoughts about the work that you are planning. I think that it could be very useful, and

---

[310] Following the condemnation of his later ideas by Gregory XVI in 1832, de La Mennais gradually became estranged from the Church and was forbidden to function as a priest. This decline was hastened by his publication of a pamphlet entitled *Paroles d'un croyant* (1834), which was condemned by Gregory XVI in the same year. De La Mennais published an account of his break with the Church in *Les affaires de Rome* (1836), in which he attacked even the institution of the papacy. See Vapereau, *op. cit.*, pp. 1174–7, esp. p. 1176.

I strongly urge you to continue with it. For two reasons, my only wish is that it should to be less wide-ranging than a complete ecclesiastical history. Firstly, a hard-working person of genuine learning and real talent has been busy with this latter work for quite some time already. Secondly, the important aim that you particularly have in mind will be more surely attained if there is nothing else to distract the reader's attention. Moreover, long books are not read very much these days. I feel that if you limit yourself to demonstrating the use and development of papal power, your book could be no longer than four volumes without omitting anything essential or really useful. This will put it within the reach of many more people.

Apart from this, you are quite capable of judging for yourself how best to proceed. In order to do this well, you must limit yourself to what has been clearly and properly thought out. I understand that your position at this time is fixed by providence. When this same providence changes it, and if it suits you to combine your efforts with ours, then I would be delighted. One of the advantages of the state we have chosen is that each man, whether he is devoting himself to study or to some other work, is completely free from all cares, worries and temporal contingencies.

With my affectionate regards,
Félicité de La Mennais

A third letter about the same subject, also in reply to me, was couched in these terms:

La Chênaie, 28 April 1829

Dear Sir,
    I have been ill, which has prevented me from replying to you sooner. I am making the most of an odd moment when, although still weak and suffering, I nevertheless feel a little more able to encourage you once again to carry out the useful project that you have formed. Apart from the Fathers, the Councils, the letters of the popes and the decretals, it seems indispensable to me to consult several other great

anthologies: Dom Bouquet,[311] Muratori (*Rerum Italiae scriptores*),[312] the capitularies of Baluze,[313] the old German chronicles, of which a collection similar to Muratori's has been established; Orsi's, *De Irreformabili R. Pontif. In definiendis fidei controversies judicio,* 3 vol. in-4°, etc.[314]

This is what strikes me as being most important. There are also many books concerning particular points of history or discipline, but for the most part they will be referred to by means of your own research. The history of Gregory VII and his period by Voigt must be read.[315] This work is in German, and I do not think it has been translated. One of the most important things is for you to form correct ideas about the social system of the Middle Ages, and about society in general. Your work would lose much of its interest and usefulness if you were to limit yourself to purely theological considerations.

You better than anyone will see what ought to go into it when you finally decide on the plan.

With affectionate regards from your humble and obedient servant,

Félicité de La Mennais

---

311 Martin Bouquet (1685–1754), Benedictine monk of the Congregation of Saint-Maur, and librarian of the abbey of Saint-Germain-des-Prés in Paris. He produced the first eight volumes of the great collection entitled: *Rerum gallicarum et francicarum scriptores,* Paris, 1738–52, which was continued by his colleagues. See Vapereau, *op. cit.,* p. 313.

312 Louis-Antoine Muratori (1672–1750), Italian historian and compiler, who specialized in gathering and organizing historical sources for the study of Italian history. The work to which de La Mennais refers is the collection entitled: *Rerum italicarum scriptores praecipui ab anno 500 ad annum 1400,* Milan, 1723–51, (29 vols). *Ibid.,* p. 1457.

313 Étienne Baluze (1630–1718), librarian then professor of canon law at the collège Royal. The work to which de La Mennais refers is his two-volume, *regum Francorum capitularia,* Paris, 1677–1780. *Ibid.,* pp. 189–90.

314 Giuseppe-Agnostino Orsi (1692–1761), Dominican ecclesiastical writer. His work, *De Irreformabili R. Pontif. In definiendis fidei controversies judicio* was published in 1740. *Ibid.,* p. 1515.

315 Jean Voigt (1786–1863), German historian. The work to which de La Mennais refers is: *Hildebrand als Papst Greg. VII und sein Zeitalter,* Weimar, 1816. A French translation of this work first appeared in 1837. See Vapereau, *op. cit.,* p. 2046.

My subsequent dealings with Fr de La Mennais, which I shall recount, were focused exclusively on serving the Church, the defence of which he had embraced with such zeal and talent, especially since 1826. In these dealings, we never discussed his famous philosophical system with one another. I was focusing on one thing only: the true nature of the Church, which needed to be defended and vindicated against the misrepresentations it had suffered from Gallican teachings. It seemed to me that any Catholic who realized the truth about this important matter ought to join in with Fr de La Mennais, whose mission was so self-evident.

It was a delight to devote myself to ecclesiastical studies with a focused goal. This particular purpose, however, had the drawback of delaying my aspirations towards forming a synthesis. I became aware of many things, my mystical understanding was awakened and my narrow tendency towards false criticism had disappeared, but my intellect was waiting for a sign in order to blossom and make more fruitful the attraction that was driving me towards erudition. It was the liturgy that gave me this sign, and very much in spite of myself. The school of Fr de La Mennais looked for general ideas in all things. I understood the dogma of the Incarnation as the centre to which I should bring everything back; I also saw that the dogma of the Church was contained within that of the Incarnation. The sacraments, the sacramentals and the poetry of the prayers and gestures of the liturgy all seemed ever more radiant to me. I felt that the future of my intellectual work lay in these areas. Fr Gerbet published his *Dogme générateur de la piété catholique* on the Eucharist;[316] I was delighted with it, but did not sense the voice of tradition in this book. There was nothing that recalled the Fathers, or the tone of antiquity; everything seemed to date from yesterday. This was not yet what I was looking for. It is also true that I was just an adolescent, being twenty-three, and that I needed more time, reading and reflection for my ideas to eventually achieve some sort of order. Our seminary education had

---

[316] P. Gerbet, *Considérations sur le dogme générateur de la Piété Catholique*, Paris, 1829.

been so intellectually impoverished that I had not yet opened St Thomas Aquinas' *Summa* even once. History for me was no more than a succession of facts, with which I was fascinated to a greater or lesser extent, and in which I sought out the Church as more of a polemicist than a theologian. Literature was a pleasure for me, but nothing more, and I was completely ignorant of style. There was some sort of latent fermentation in my mind, but it would not be until I was well past thirty that I would finally reach the understanding that God has been pleased to bestow upon me.

In Paris I had social dealings only with my bishop's family, and I did not wish for any others. I enjoyed their kindness, and I pursued my education in this distinguished, delightful environment. The ideas there were very much of their time: there was not much awareness of what was lacking in society at the time, yet there were solid Christian virtues combined with great dignity, simplicity, a strong family spirit and the patriarchal customs found in the heart of Paris. All this was found, with its own nuances, in the de Broin family just as much as in the de La Myre family. I sometimes met people who interested me (because I had heard of them) in the drawing room. For example, I remember the comte de Marcellus,[317] whose political speeches and poetry I had noticed. He was an eighteenth-century Catholic.

Among the clergy, I only had dealings with Fr de Valette,[318] a young priest who held a post in the parish of the 'Missions', whom I liked very much due to his easy manner and straightforward devotion. He was a former pupil of the *École Polytechnique*,[319] and had entered the ranks of

---

[317] Louis-Marie-Auguste Demartin de Tyrac, comte de Marcellus, (1776–1841), political figure and poet. He became a *député* after the Restoration and a peer of France in 1823. His published works of poetry include: *Odes sacrées, idylles et poésies*, Paris, 1825; *Odes sacrées tirées des psaumes*, Paris, 1827; and *Cantates sacrées*, Paris, 1829. For further information, see Larousse, *op. cit.*, v. 10, p. 1137.

[318] Person currently unidentified.

[319] A school founded by the State in 1795 to train personnel for the artillery and other branches of the military services. The students received a very high level of scientific training, and the school soon achieved a reputation for excellence. For further information, see Larousse, *op. cit.*, v. 7, pp. 120–1.

the clergy fairly recently. On being assigned to the parish of the 'Missions', he had succeeded Fr Sibour.[320] This latter had started to preach extensively during Lent and Advent, and later became bishop of Digne and then archbishop of Paris. I often had the opportunity to see him since he always enjoyed returning to the 'Missions'. We got on very well with one another.

In the spring, my bishop went to spend a month at Marolles in order to take the country air. I brought some books with me, and made the most of this stay. It was then that the prelate told me that he thought there was no point getting the parish priest of Senteny to come each week, and that henceforth he was asking me to hear his weekly confession while he was not in Paris and within reach of Fr Varin.

We returned to Paris at the end of April. Until then (and even since) I was accustomed to saying Mass every day at the Sacré-Coeur convent in rue de Varennes. This had established kind relations between these sisters and me. I often encountered Fr d'Héricourt[321] in the sacristy, whom Martignac's ministry[322] called to the see of Autun in this year

---

[320] Marie-Dominique-Auguste Sibour (1792–1857), ordained priest in 1818; administrator of the parish of Saint-Sulpice (1819), and then the 'Missions Étrangères' (1820); chaplain of the collège Saint-Louis (1821); vicar capitular of Nîmes (1837); appointed bishop of Digne in 1839; transferred to become archbishop of Paris in 1848. For further information, see *L'Épiscopat,* pp. 215–16, 460–1.

[321] Bénigne-Urbain-Jean-Marie du Trousset d'Héricourt (1797–1851), ordained priest in 1825; vicar general of Évreux and then briefly of Besançon; consecrated bishop of Autun in 1829; he refused the archbishopric of Avignon in 1835. For further information, see *L'Épiscopat,* pp. 86–7.

[322] Jean-Baptiste-Silvère Gaye-Martignac (1776–1832), politician, magistrate and publicist. He was an ardent Royalist and achieved rapid promotion under the Bourbon Restoration. He became attorney general of the royal court at Bordeaux (1815); procurator general of Limoges; *député* of Marmande (1821); state counsellor (1822); minister of state (1823); and minister of the interior (1828). He assumed a lower profile after 1829, when his liberalizing policies caused him to be sidelined by Charles X. For further information, see Larousse, *op. cit.,* v. 10, p. 1272.

(1829). He will feature again in this account later by way of Dom Pitra, his diocesan.[323]

Bishop de Bovet,[324] the former bishop of Toulouse, was also there; a venerable and extremely learned old man who has written against sceptics in the fields of chronology and the Egyptian dynasties. The religious sister who served as sacristan was Madame de Marbeuf,[325] the niece of the last archbishop of Lyons[326] before the great Revolution. My bishop had known her in the world, where she was an important figure and influential over her uncle, who was minister in charge of distributing ecclesiastical benefices. Apart from the saintly Mother Barat, mother general of the

---

[323] Jean-Baptiste-François Pitra (1812–1889), ordained priest in 1836, professed as monk of Solesmes in 1843, prior of Paris (1843–1845). Endowed with brilliant intellectual gifts, he was sent to Moscow by Pius IX for seven months (1859–1860) in order to study the liturgy and canon law of the Russian Orthodox Church. He was called to Rome to help prepare a new edition of the Greek liturgical books of the Byzantine rite. He was made cardinal in 1863, and in 1869 became the Vatican librarian. For a useful bibliographical summary, see C. Johnson, 'Guéranger and Study, Pitra and Migne' in *Ephemerides Liturgicae,* 121 (2007): 7–24, esp. 16–17.

[324] François de Bovet (1745–1838), ordained bishop of Sisteron in 1789, but was forced to resign after he refused to take the constitutional oath. After a period of exile in Switzerland, Germany and England, he returned to France in 1814. He was then appointed archbishop of Toulouse in 1816, although he did not take possession of his diocese until 1819. He resigned on health grounds in 1820, when he moved to Paris. His publications included: *Des dynasties égyptiennes* (1829); *Les dynasties égyptiennes suivant Manéthon* (1835); *L'histoire des derniers pharaons et des premiers rois de Perse selon Hérodote, tirée des livres prophétiques et du livre d'Esther* (1835). See Prevost et d'Amat, *op. cit.,* v. 7, pp. 86–7.

[325] Catherine-Salinguera-Antoinette Marbeuf (née de Gayardon de Fenoyl) (1765–1839), married the comte de Marbeuf on 20 September 1786. She was widowed soon afterwards and eventually made profession as a Sacred Heart sister in 1820. She spent most of her religious life as sacristan of the house in Paris. For further information, see the archives of the French province of the Sacred Heart sisters.

[326] Yves-Alexandre de Marbeuf (1734–1799), became vicar general of Rouen in 1761; consecrated bishop of Autun in 1767; appointed minister of ecclesiastical benefices (1772–1789); transferred to become archbishop of Lyons in 1788, but went into exile during the Revolution and died abroad. Guéranger is mistaken in believing that Madame de Marbeuf was the archbishop's niece. She was in fact his sister-in-law. See Jean, *op. cit.,* pp. 215, 222.

Congregation,[327] I also saw her famous assistant, Madame
Eugénie de Gramont,[328] who used to reign supreme among
the polite society of the *faubourg* Saint-Germain.

In the afternoon of 3 May, the feast of the Finding of the
Holy Cross, which fell on a Sunday that year, I received a
courier from these sisters, who informed me that the
Dauphine[329] had just told them that she wanted to come to
Vespers in their chapel that day. They were therefore asking
me to come and receive Her Royal Highness and celebrate
Vespers in her presence. I hurried to this invitation, much to
the satisfaction of my bishop. I was delighted to welcome the
orphan of the temple at the chapel door. I gave her holy
water, presented the cross for her to kiss and incensed her,
according to custom. After this I escorted her into the sanctuary and to the seat that had been prepared for her. At the
Magnificat, after incensing the altar I incensed the princess
three times, according to court ceremonial. She prayed with
great recollection during the office, but throughout her time
at the Sacré-Coeur convent her customary severe and almost
harsh expression did not desert her for a minute.

The acceptance of my bishop's resignation by the Holy
Father was still not forthcoming. The government felt that it
could appoint his successor while it was waiting. He was Fr
Gallard,[330] the parish priest of La Madeleine, who was the

---

[327] St Madeleine-Sophie Barat (1779–1865), foundress of the Society of
the Sacred Heart, which was devoted to the education of poor children. For further information, see Farmer, *op. cit.,* pp. 40–1.

[328] Eugénie de Gramont (1788–1846), professed in 1807; taught in boarding schools of the order in Amiens and Paris, and became the superior
of the house in Paris in 1833. For further information, see the archives
of the French province of the Sacred Heart sisters.

[329] Marie-Thérèse-Charlotte, duchesse d' Angoulême (1778–1851), wife of
Louis XVIII and daughter of Louis XVI. For further information, see
Larousse, *op. cit.,* v. 1, p. 380.

[330] Roman-Frédéric Gallard (1785–1839), ordained priest 1812, curate at
Saint-Aignan d'Orléans; held various roles in the *Grande Aumônerie*
(1814–1822); honorary canon of Paris (1820); honorary vicar general of
Notre-Dame de Paris (1822); titular canon of Paris (1824); parish priest
of La Madeleine (1825); consecrated bishop of Meaux in 1831; transferred to become archbishop of Reims (1839), but died shortly after his
installation. For further information, see *L'Épiscopat,* pp. 348–9.

king's choice. After visiting my bishop, he came to see me and asked to speak to me in confidence. I agreed to have lunch with him the following day and, on arriving at the appointed time, I discovered that the bishop-elect of Le Mans was very keen to become acquainted with everything that concerned the diocese. I satisfied all of his questions, but he concluded very strongly that he would not accept a Church like Le Mans, which seemed too imposing for him, a man of mediocre talent and learning. I realized that, to a large extent, the superiority he imputed to Fr Bouvier was responsible for most of his fear. He lost no time in presenting both his thanks and his excuses to the king, and Fr Carron,[331] the parish priest of Saint-Germain de Rennes, was appointed in his place. Later on, Fr Gallard accepted the see of Meaux, and died the archbishop of Reims.

Fr Carron also came to pay his respects to Bishop de La Myre. I saw him on this occasion, and it seemed to me that he would not scorn the bishopric of Le Mans. His nomination was motivated by the fact that he was related to the respected Fr Carron,[332] whose virtues and services had been appreciated in England by the Bourbons.

In June I went through the sadness of losing my mother. She had been suffering for a long time, and the letter from one of my brothers telling me that she was in her final moments reached me just a day before the one informing me of her death. I was denied the painful consolation of closing her eyes.

---

[331] Philippe-Marie-Thérèse-Gui Carron (1788–1833), ordained priest in 1809. Appointed curate of Saint-Germain in Rennes in 1812, and became parish priest there in 1817. He became vicar general of Nevers in 1823. He was consecrated bishop of Le Mans in 1829, a position that he held until his sudden death in 1833. See *L'Épiscopat,* p. 329.

[332] Gui-Toussaint-Julien Carron (1760–1821), ordained priest in 1782. He was appointed curate at Saint-Germain in Rennes, but refused to take the civil oath of the clergy at the Revolution. He went into exile first in Jersey and then in London (1796–1814). He devoted himself to many charitable works for the poor, both in exile and on his return to France at the Bourbon Restoration. For further information, see Prevost et d'Amat, *op. cit.,* v. 7, pp. 1263–4.

Death of Bishop de La Myre

In August my bishop set off with me for the château of Le Gué-à-Trême. It was there that we learnt of the change of government that was calling the prince de Polignac[333] to become president of the council. We were worried, and with good reason. Our host, the comte de La Myre, was kept on as commanding officer of the new minister of war. He was in Paris for his service on 30 August, and after a very peaceful evening everyone went to bed without anxiety. Towards 3.00 a.m., the bishop's valet came to inform me that his master was in the grip of the most violent apoplectic fit. Madame de La Myre was also informed, and arrived at the patient's bed at the same time as I did. A servant left on horseback to fetch a doctor and I heard the confession of the prelate, who was still fully conscious. The doctor prescribed some treatment, but warned us that the attack was very serious and that another one after this, even if less severe, would claim the patient's life.

The Blessed Sacrament was not reserved in the tabernacle of the chapel in the château. I celebrated Holy Mass in the bedroom of the prelate, to whom I had first administered the sacrament of Extreme Unction, and then gave him Holy Communion. I felt that I should first get him to confess the doctrine of the Holy See regarding the universality of the rights of the Sovereign Pontiff, in reparation for the unfortunate Gallican terminology to which he had clung when the sacraments were administered to him in 1826. With great effusion, he repeated after me that he was declaring his complete submission to the Roman Pontiff, and that he had no other faith and no other doctrine than that of the Roman Pontiff. Lastly, to abjure the principles he had received previously in the school of Paris, I also got him to declare that in his submission he was not separating the person of the Pontiff from the chair that he occupies.

I finished the Mass, during which the prelate had been given all the divine assistance he needed. During the day he was a little better. Madame de La Myre had dispatched an urgent message to her husband, who soon arrived. Over the following days, the prelate experienced some relief. On 7 September he came down to the drawing room after dinner and, when he retired at about 9.00 p.m., he asked me if he could receive Holy Communion the following day, the feast of the Nativity of the Blessed Virgin Mary. I told him that I could see no objection to this, and that I would celebrate Holy Mass in his bedroom since I did not want him to come down to the chapel in the château. Although we were far from being completely reassured, we got through the evening without anxiety. The next morning, around 4.00 a.m., we were all woken up in great haste; a new apoplectic fit had just begun. I ran to the prelate, who was unconscious. I hurried to give him absolution. The death rattle began, and the doctor arrived just as the patient was drawing his last breath. Bishop de La Myre died on a feast of the Blessed Virgin Mary, to whom he had always had an extraordinary and very fervent devotion. He died the bishop of Le Mans since the brief in which Pope Leo XII[334] released him from the bonds tying him to this Church arrived only after his death.

---

[334] Leo XII (1760–1829), pope from 1823. For further information, see Levillain, *op. cit.,* pp. 1031–5.

On that day I was due to stand in for the parish priest of Vareddes,[335] who was away, and celebrate a second Mass in the church of this parish, where many people would be gathered. This was because in this region, which in other respects was very irreligious, the suppressed feasts were still marked with solemnity. During the Mass that I celebrated at the château shortly after the bishop died, I had inadvertently swallowed the first ablution, so that I was no longer keeping a fast[336] and could no longer say a second Mass. Nevertheless, I made my way to Vareddes, where the people were expecting me in the church. I ascended the pulpit and, after telling them of the bishop's death, I informed them of the mishap that had happened to me. We sang Terce and Sext and, after solemn exposition, I gave Benediction of the Blessed Sacrament. The people seemed satisfied, and I hurried to return to Le Gué-à-Trême.

The comte de La Myre was of the opinion that his uncle's funeral should be carried out as simply as possible. Pressing economic constraints made this necessary since the prelate had left his affairs in quite an unfortunate state, which would later cost his family dearly. It was therefore agreed that we would not write to the bishop of Meaux, who was then Bishop de Cosnac,[337] and I was entrusted with assembling the clergy for the following day. I left on horseback and trotted back and forth for the entire afternoon. I managed to find eight parish priests, covering between fifteen to eighteen miles[338] and the same distance to get back. In itself this did not amount to much, but it was a lot for this region that was littered with vacant parishes. I had arranged the burial

---

[335] There is no mention of this place-name in P. Joanne, *Dictionnaire Géographique et administratif de la France*, Paris, 1890. It is therefore likely that Guéranger has recorded the name incorrectly.

[336] At this time, the discipline of the Eucharistic fast was very strict. It was not permitted to ingest anything at all before Mass, even water. Guéranger had done no more than accidentally swallow the water used to purify the sacred vessels during his first Mass of the day.

[337] Jean-Joseph-Marie-Victoire de Cosnac (1764–1843), appointed bishop of Meaux in 1819, where he remained until he was transferred to become archbishop of Sens in 1830. See Prevost et d'Amat, *op. cit.*, v. 9, pp. 750–1.

[338] Guéranger mentions a distance of 'five or six leagues'.

for the afternoon of the following day, 9 September.

I officiated at this sorrowful function. We performed the five prayers for the dead[339] according to the custom of the diocese, whose rituale then governed the entire liturgy, and we buried the body in the parish cemetery. In the evening, I wrote up my account of the prelate's last moments and death, which was to be sent to the Chapter of Le Mans. I was careful not to omit the profession of faith concerning the rights of the Roman Pontiff, which the bishop had made before receiving Holy Viaticum. The following day, I sang the solemn Requiem Mass, assisted by several parish priests who had come the day before for the burial. After the Gospel, I gave the prelate's funeral eulogy. The following day, I took leave of my hosts and returned to Paris.

I had only just returned to the 'Missions' when Fr de Valette came to see me and immediately began talking about what should be done in my situation. The diocesan adminis-tration of Le Mans did not look very kindly on me. On the other hand, I was already settled in Paris and a scholarly career was opening out for me there. Surely it was natural to stay where I was doing so well and apply for a job, which would give me a means of subsistence as well as leaving me with enough free time to devote myself to ecclesiastical studies? Fr de Valette agreed to put my case to Fr des Genettes, the parish priest of the 'Missions', and suggest me as his replacement. Fr de Valette himself had just been appointed chaplain to the page-boys at Versailles, and so his position was to be given to someone else. Fr des Genettes, who was favourably disposed towards me, agreed willingly and, although I did not belong to the diocese of Paris, Arch-bishop de Quélen appointed me an assistant priest of the parish of the 'Missions Étrangères'. Seven of us worked in this capacity, each entrusted with administering the sacra-ments and carrying out other functions for one day per week,

---

[339] At the end of the funeral rite, during the final commendation, the coffin is blessed with holy water and incensed. In the liturgical rite used here by Guéranger, this ceremonial was repeated five times for such dignitaries as bishops.

which was counted from midnight to midnight. Moreover, there was a curate, Fr Ausoure,[340] who became our guest at the abbey.

Fr des Genettes was very fond of me right from the beginning, even though his residual Gallicanism (which soon disappeared) meant that he found me rather too Ultramontane. He promised to give me light duties so as to leave me enough free time, and he kept his word. I took my turn to preach and to do my day of keeping an eye on the place, but I did not have to take catechism classes. My young age did not inspire many people with the desire to come to me for confession. Fr des Genettes entrusted me with instructing and preparing for first Holy Communion the son of the marquis de Moustier,[341] who was our parishioner. I gave this very gifted child a great deal of attention, and today he is the French ambassador to Vienna. I also had to instruct two young English boys, whose mother (called Mrs Wikerey[342]) had recently converted. Her husband had remained a Protestant, but he always received me very well. In November, I had to travel to Le Mans to bless the marriage of my brother Édouard,[343] but I only stayed for a short time. I saw

---

[340] Jean-Baptiste-Hippolyte Ausoure (1793–1875), ordained priest in 1818; curate at Saint-Denis-en-France; parish priest of Pierrefitte, Seine (1820); principal curate of Saint-Philippe du Roule (1825); parish priest of Saint-Séverin (1837); appointed vicar general of Paris in 1840 and promoter of the diocese in 1841; parish priest of Saint-Philippe du Roule (1842–1856). Following an incident that resulted in his disgrace in 1857, he retired to live at Solesmes as a permanent guest from 1861 until his death. Guéranger appears to be mistaken in thinking that he was a curate at the 'Missions Étrangères'. See the archives of the archdiocese of Paris.

[341] Léonel-Desle-Marie-François-René Moustier (1817–1869), diplomat and statesman. After his election to the legislative assembly in 1849, he became plenipotentiary to Prussia in 1853. He was appointed French ambassador first to Vienna and then, in 1861, to Constantinople. He was minister of foreign affairs (1866–1868), before becoming a senator. For further information, see Larousse, *op. cit.,* v. 11, p. 647.

[342] Person currently unidentified.

[343] Édouard Guéranger and Euphémie Gallois were married in November 1829.

Fr Bouvier, who was very kind to me, and hurried back to Paris.

Everything there was ablaze, and the Revolution was imminent. No one thought that the Polignac ministry would be successful. Fr de La Mennais had just published his book, *Les progrès de la révolution et de la guerre contre l'Église.*[344] Archbishop de Quélen had responded to this with a Gallican pastoral letter, to which Fr de La Mennais himself replied in strong terms. He had slipped into his book a sentence about the Jesuits that hurt them deeply since it considered them to be incapable of serving the cause of the Church and society effectively, despite their virtues and devotion to duty.[345] This important sentence unleashed displeasure against the school of de La Mennais from the old Fathers of the Faith, who still formed the majority of the Society at this time, and it led to certain consequences that would later affect Solesmes. The newly re-established Society was already none too keen on the philosophical ideas of the loner from La Chênaie. Nevertheless, there was no breakdown of relations, and many of the new Jesuits were even favourably disposed to this new doctrine. After the famous sentence, however, the spilt was sealed.

In private, I continued my good relationship with rue de Sèvres, and worked hard to prepare my *magnum opus* about the rights of the Holy See. From time to time I wrote to Fr de

---

[344] *Les progrès de la révolution et de la guerre contre l'Eglise,* Paris, 1829.

[345] Referring to what he considered to be the unjust action of the government in expelling the Jesuits from working in eight French minor seminaries in June 1828, de La Mennais stated that there was 'nothing more absurd, nothing more iniquitous and nothing more revolting than most of the accusations to which the Society of Jesus had been subjected.' He then went on to praise the zeal and virtue of its members. Nevertheless, de La Mennais immediately qualified his remarks by saying that he did not think that the Society was 'sufficiently adapted to present modes of thinking and to the current needs of the world.' Oddly, he concluded his reference to the Jesuits by remarking that he would be 'very distressed if he had let slip a single word that might grieve these venerable men.' See de La Mennais, *op. cit.,* pp. 169–70.

La Mennais, who encouraged me. Here is one of his replies, which had no small influence on my literary career:

La Chênaie, 31 December 1829

Dear Sir,

The plan you are proposing to follow in the work with which you are occupied seems very good to me. This will be a sort of dogmatic history about pontifical power, whose rights will be established by drawing on the major sources of tradition, and whose salutary influence throughout different generations will be highlighted in the facts that you are to relate. Four or five volumes will not be excessive to deal with such a subject properly. You may be helped by some of the German authors, both good and bad. There are some very beautiful insights into the Middle Ages in Frédéric Schlegel (philosophy of history).[346] The history of the constitution of the Church by Planck,[347] written from an opposing point of view, does nevertheless contain some remarkable conclusions and could supply valuable information about specific points. In general, historical research is much more advanced on the other side of the Rhine than in our own land.

I encourage you to give yourself an occasional break from your great work by preparing a few articles for the *Mémorial*. People need to be helped by writings of this sort.

Fr Gerbet has been away from La Chênaie for a fortnight, but he will soon be back. When he returns, I shall give him the message you have asked me to convey. He has spoken to

---

[346] Charles-Guillaume-Frédéric Schlegel (1772–1829), German writer and Orientalist. Although de La Mennais labels his work 'philosophy of history', his interests were far more wide-ranging. He published a novel, poems, a study of Greek and Roman history, a study of the language and philosophy of India, a history of ancient and modern literature, and a translation of *Corinne* by Madame de Staël. His *Philosophie der Geschichte* (1829), to which de La Mennais refers, portrays the Middle Ages as a period of enlightenment providing the sole explanation for the progress of mankind. See Vapereau, *op. cit.*, pp. 1843–44.

[347] Gottlieb-Jacob Planck (1751–1833), German theologian. The work to which de La Mennais refers is his five-volume *Gesch. der Entstehung und Ausbildung Christl. Kirchl. Gesellschaftverfassung*, Hanover, 1803–5. See Vapereau, *op. cit.*, p. 1609.

me about your plans, and I was delighted to learn that in all respects they accord with your views and preferences.

With affectionate regards and good wishes for a happy New Year,
Félicité de La Mennais

Fr de La Mennais was advising me to write for the *Mémorial catholique*. I took this advice seriously and was so enthusiastic that, even though I had not yet completed my twenty-fifth year, I soon presented Waille,[348] the editor of this review, with an article entitled, *Une thèse de théologie en Sorbonne*.[349] It was quite childish, but the editorial team was encouraging in its acceptance. From then on, I decided to give public voice to my thoughts about the liturgy by means of a series of articles in this publication.

The new position I had taken in joining Fr des Genettes guaranteed me some independence for my studies, but it seemed too precarious to my friends. The family of Auguste de La Myre was closely linked to Monsieur de Montbel,[350] one of Monsieur de Polignac's colleagues at the ministry. Moreover, Madame de La Myre, whose father Monsieur de Lur-Saluces was the close friend of Monsieur de Montbel, and who had the highest regard for her, thought that I should benefit from such great esteem. Initially, this was focused on nothing less than making me general secretary at the ministry.

The position had been taken immediately, however, and

---

[348] Person currently unidentified.

[349] *Une thèse de théologie en Sorbonne* (signed Y) in *Mémorial catholique* 1 (31 janvier 1830): 17–25. This article is Guéranger's first published work. It gives an account of the *viva voce* examination for the doctoral thesis of a certain Fr Kirwan, which was entitled: *Quodam est scutum fidei*. This examination was held on 18 January 1830 at the Sorbonne, Paris.

[350] Guillaume-Isidore Baron, comte de Montbel (1787–1861), 'chevalier de la Foi', mayor of Toulouse, an extreme right *député* in 1827. He became minister of ecclesiastical affairs and public instruction in 1829, and subsequently became minister of the interior and minister of finance. See des Mazis, *op. cit.,* 157.

given to Fr Vayssière,[351] who was later the editor of *L'Ami de la Religion*. At that time he was as young and unknown as I was. Attention then turned towards the king's chapel. The post of chaplain to the nobility or to one of the royal chateaus seemed suitable, and could be obtained easily at short notice. It was not long, however, before the July Revolution overturned all of these plans, with which I was in any case only ever half-taken, and launched me along the path where God was calling me. In the meantime, Monsieur de Montbel had the doors of the king's private library at the Tuileries opened to me, with permission to borrow books. The ecclesiastical studies section was very rich, and I made extensive use of it. Things were much easier for me than in the Jesuit library, where one was never allowed to borrow books.

At that time, Fr Caillau[352] from the 'Société des Missions de France' published his *Collectio selecta*[353] of the Church Fathers. He asked me to cooperate, and I got involved in a few volumes. Things did not get very far, again due to the July Revolution. I also had dealings with the bookseller Parent-Desbarres, who wanted me to continue the *Bibliothèque des dames chrétiennes*, a collection that had been started and since abandoned by Fr de La Mennais. We even had an agreement, but everything was broken off when I ended my stay in Paris.

---

[351] Person currently unidentified.

[352] Armand-Benjamin Caillau (1794–1850), priest of the 'Société des Missions de France'; rector of the basilica of Sainte-Geneviève (1826–1830); chaplain of the Marie-Thérèse Infirmary (1832); rector of Saint-Euverte in Orléans (1840). For further information, see *Bibliographie Catholique*, v. X, 1850, pp. 49, 97.

[353] *Collectio selecta SS. Patrum, complectens exquisitissima opera tum dogmatica et moralia, tum apologetica et oratoria*, Paris, 1829–42, (133 vols).

First Publications

In the spring of 1830 I began to make my mark in the *Mémorial catholique* with my first article on the liturgy, which was followed by another four.[354] I tried to present the respect and affection that I felt for the Roman liturgy, and established the need for the liturgy to be ancient, universal, authorized and holy. These principles directly contradicted the French liturgies.[355] I did not attack the abuse from the perspective of law since it seemed all too clear to me that Rome had given way in this area. I laid siege to the position by bringing it to a standstill, jeopardizing the Gallicanism in this disastrous liturgical expression by a simple confrontation with the very foundations of Catholicism. I felt that I had got off to a good start, and my vocation as a Catholic writer was settled.

My vocation as a polemicist did not take long to emerge. Picot,[356] the editor of the pathetic review *L'Ami de la Religion,* had been upset ever since the first articles, and lost no

---

[354] 'Considérations sur la liturgie catholique', in *Mémorial catholique* (28 février 1830): 49–57; (31 mars 1830): 79–90; (31 mai 1830): 181–9; (31 juillet 1830): 241–56. Reproduced in *Mélanges*, pp. 5–110.

[355] For a discussion of this issue, see C. Johnson, *Prosper Guéranger (1805–1875): A Liturgical Theologian – An introduction to his liturgical writings and work* (Studia Anselmiana 89, Analecta Liturgica 9), Rome, 1984, pp. 306–39.

[356] Michel-Joseph-Pierre Picot (1770–1841), literary figure and editor of *L'Ami de la Religion* from 1814–1840. For further information, see Larousse, *op. cit.,* v. 12, pp. 947–8.

time attacking them using notes supplied by Fr Tresvaux du Fraval,[357] a canon of Notre-Dame who belonged to another age and in whose eyes nothing could equal the beauty of the Parisian liturgy. The author of the article and his assistant had heaped up so many absurdities and untruths that it was easy for me to demolish them and overturn their arguments. They had been foolish and somewhat economical with the truth, although perhaps unwittingly since the prejudices of this time were so deep-rooted and its ideas so distorted. My victory displayed an outrageous insolence. Perhaps something should be attributed to the ardent enthusiasm of being twenty-five, and to my inexperienced style. Be that as it may, Fr Bouvier later got me to admit that I had gone a bit too far in the defence, and he boasted about this to Picot in an encounter that I shall describe later. As far as I can remember both sides replied, and the whole discussion that I had participated in was published partly in the *Mémorial*[358] and partly in the *Revue catholique.*[359] I remember that Picot called me a 'tough jouster' in *L'Ami de la Religion.*[360] I was somewhat milder in an article about the translation of the relics of St Vincent de Paul, which was celebrated in Paris on one of the Sundays of Paschaltide.[361] I signed my articles with all manner of initials, having taken a long time to overcome my repugnance for appending my name to my writings.

---

[357] François-Marie Tresvaux du Fraval (1782–1862), ordained priest in 1809 in the diocese of Saint-Brieux; curate at Triguier Derrier (1820); parish priest of La Roche Derrier (1820). He became an honorary canon of Notre-Dame de Paris in 1820, the same year in which he also became secretary to the archbishop of Paris (1820–1833). He was made a titular canon in 1825, and became vicar general of Paris in 1833. See the archives of the archdiocese of Paris.

[358] *Mémorial catholique* (31 juillet 1830): 241–56.

[359] *Revue catholique* (15 juin 1830): 151–73; (15 juillet 1830): 208–13.

[360] *L'Ami de la Religion* 1650 (2 juin 1830); 1652 (9 juin 1830); 1659 (3 juillet 1830).

[361] 'Translation des reliques du Saint-Vincent-de-Paul', in *Revue catholique*, 1 (15 mai 1830): 111–21.

In May, during the octave of the Finding of the Holy Cross, the parish of the 'Missions' went on a pilgrimage to Mont-Valérien,[362] and I was entrusted with preaching the stations on the mountain. I thus had the opportunity to see the royal family at close hand. The Dauphine came to a Low Mass that I celebrated, and I had to perform a custom of the French Court, which consisted of bringing the folded corporal to the princess and giving it to her to kiss before putting it back into the burse at the end of Mass. We then had a Solemn Mass attended by Charles X. I saw him singing the *Domine, salvum fac regem,*[363] with a naivety that was reminiscent of king Robert.[364] Bishop de Forbin-Janson,[365] bishop of Nancy and founder of the Missionary Institute of Mont-Valérien, did the honours for His Majesty, and Cardinal de Croy,[366] the archbishop of Rouen, assisted as principal chaplain. The

[362] A hill in the Seine region about 8km west of Paris, between Suresnes and Nanterre. Since at least the sixth century it has been a place of pilgrimage in honour of the Cross and Passion of Our Lord. Pilgrimages were especially popular during the former octaves of the feasts of the Cross on 3 May and 14 September. During the time to which Guéranger refers, Bishop de Forbin-Janson, the local bishop of Nantes, was a great devotee of this site. He had the church rebuilt and installed an exact replica of the tomb of Christ found in Jerusalem. For further information, see J. Migne, *Encyclopédie Théologique,* Paris, 1851, v. 44, pp. 1019–22.

[363] 'Lord, save the King', a liturgical acclamation drawn from Psalm 19:10.

[364] Robert II (971–1031), king of France (996–1031). Known as 'the wise' on account of his sound political judgement and 'the devout' on account of his religious fervour, he enjoyed singing and composed several hymns. For further information, see Michaud, *op. cit.,* v. 36, pp. 106–7.

[365] Charles-Auguste-Marie-Joseph de Forbin-Janson (1785–1844), ordained priest in 1811; became vicar general of Gap, then rector of the major seminary. He was consecrated bishop of Nancy in 1824. From 1830 he found himself in administrative difficulties that necessitated his absence from the diocese. During these years he spent much of his time preaching and evangelizing both in Paris and abroad. For further information, see *L'Épiscopat,* pp. 386–7.

[366] Gustave-Maximilian-Juste, prince de Croy-Solvé (1773–1844), bishop of Strasbourg (1817); archbishop of Rouen (1823); made cardinal in 1825. He was an ardent Legitimist and was close to the Royal family. He became principal chaplain of France in 1821. See Prevost et d'Amat, *op. cit.,* v. 9, pp. 1305–6.

princes performed the Stations of the Cross presided over by Bishop de Janson, who spoke very appropriately at each station. The Dauphine was singing some verses from the canticle *Au sang qu'un Dieu va répandre*[367] along with the congregation. The duchesse de Berry[368] was more distracted and less recollected. The clergy of the 'Missions' ministered to the king and princesses during their stations and, together with the cardinal and the bishop of Nancy, we escorted them to the farthest limit of the enclosure. I heard the king telling Bishop de Forbin that he had received news that morning from the Dauphin, who had led the expeditionary army to Toulon; the fleet was about to set out to sea and was heading for Algiers.[369] In the afternoon, large numbers of the faithful from Paris joined those who had left with us in the morning. When everything was ready, I preached the stations in the open air, according to custom.

At that time, Roman doctrines were fermenting more and more among the clergy, despite Gallican opposition. Fr des Genettes had finally given in and, with the feast of St Peter drawing near, he suggested that I should give an extended sermon about the rights of the Holy See at Vespers that day. The day passed as follows: at the first Mass, where there was hardly anyone except the poor, I extolled the prerogatives of St Peter. At the High Mass, Fr des Genettes braved the archbishop and the state council, giving a very colourful account of the history and composition of the 1682 assembly, and denouncing the *Déclaration*. Lastly, at Vespers, I spoke for

---

[367] 'To the blood that a God is going to shed'. The first line of the French translation of an eight-stanza canticle by Giovanni Battista Pergolesi (1710–1736), an Italian composer. The canticle is a meditation on the Passion of Christ. See http://www.musicologie.org/Biographies/p/pergolesi.html.

[368] Marie-Caroline de Bourbon-Sicile, the duchesse de Berry (1798–1870), the daughter of François I, the king of Deux-Siciles. In 1816 she married the duc de Berry, the nephew of Louis XVIII and second son of the comte d'Artois (the future Charles X). She was forced into exile in England, Scotland and Italy after the 1830 July Revolution, and secretly married the comte Lucchesi-Palli. For further information, see Larousse, *op. cit.*, v. 2, p. 611.

[369] Algiers was taken by the French on 5 July 1830. See *Les Dates*, p. 156.

more than an hour about the role of the Roman Pontiff in the Church. It goes without saying that the parish clergy seemed more surprised than the faithful at how this day had been used. It will be readily understood that there was no second church in Paris where such demonstrations would have been possible. This took place on the Sunday following the feast of St Peter, according to the custom in France. The next day I left for Le Mans, having received permission from my parish priest to take a month's holiday.

The 1830 Revolution

Before the end of July,[370] the terrible revolution broke out that carried away in a storm the senior Bourbon line, and the deplorable Restoration government that had been able to restore freedom to the Church and yet had not wanted to do so. The repercussions were quite violent in Le Mans, and on Sunday 30 July there were cries of death threats against the clergy in a huge gathering held in the Place des Halles. There was great uncertainty as to what the future held for the country, and the various efforts of the interim government were not achieving rapid success. Surely a reaction was about to break out in our western regions? In the end, peace held out everywhere. I saw Fr Bouvier every day, and was struck by the resolute way in which he viewed such events. At the height of the storm, he said to me: 'Rest assured that there will be no Royalist reaction, for those days are gone. Nor will there be a long period of anarchy. The party that caused this revolution will call the duc d'Orléans[371] to the throne. Foreign powers will not be happy about it, but they will not take up the cause of the fallen line. There will certainly be preferential treatment in the order of succession, but the

---

[370] The popular uprising known as 'Les Trois Glorieuses' (27–29 July 1830) forced the abdication of Charles X on 31 July. Before abdicating, he confirmed the appointment by parliament of the duc d'Orléans, Louis-Philippe, as lieutenant-general of the kingdom. Louis-Philippe became king of France on 9 August. See *Les Dates*, p. 156.

[371] The new king was Louis-Philippe I (1773–1850), king of France from 1830–1848. For further information, see Voisin, *op. cit.,* pp. 653–4.

same dynasty will stay on the throne. Mark my words, Europe will not stir and it will recognize the new king.'

I was struck by these words, which display Fr Bouvier's remarkable common sense at this period of his life (something that people have noticed about him on more than one occasion since), but they did not throw much light on things for me. A few days later, they were completely vindicated. Be that as it may, a serious question still remained for me that soon raised its head: should I return to Paris or stay in Le Mans? News from the capital revealed that the situation of the clergy there had become intolerable. Clerical dress could not be seen in the streets without exposing the imprudent priest wearing it to the final acts of violence from a misguided population. My family was alarmed at the prospect of my return and yet, on the other hand, Fr des Genettes was recalling me. I decided to return, but first I got myself kitted-out from head to toe in Le Mans in as secular a fashion as possible, giving myself the appearance of a young student from a good family. Towards the end of September I got into the stage coach dressed in my new outfit, and set out in the coupé with two travellers from Le Mans. These men were very worked up by events, and greatly lamented that the gradual quelling of the political commotion had not, in the end, led to the extermination of priests. One of them, well-known in Le Mans, said: 'Even if just one of them remains, he will still continue the fight for religion.' These good men had no idea that they had travelled with a priest, covering one hundred and fifty miles with him. I found a way to say my office, partly in Chartres, partly in Rambouillet[372] and the rest by heart.

After finally reaching Paris, I ran to see Fr des Genettes, who opened the door to me himself. My disguise was so complete that he did not recognize me, and it was a long time before he picked out my distinctive features. He then told me that he was about to resign, realizing that it was no longer safe for him to live in a town where the clergy were so

---

[372] A commune in the Seine-et-Oise region. See Joanne, *op. cit.,* v. VI, pp. 3780–1.

vulnerable. Paris would in any case soon be destroyed, and the prophecies of Orval[373] and others were being fulfilled. He told me that he had chosen to withdraw to the town of Fribourg in Switzerland. This unexpected announcement stunned me somewhat, although it did not surprise me too much since I knew the weak side of this good parish priest, who had believed Thomas Martin.[374] I was starting to regret returning to Paris since it was very unsafe, and I was about to lose my only support. Fr des Genettes strongly urged me to come with him to Fribourg, where several people whom I knew had already gone in the same panic; one of them was Monsieur O'Mahonny, one of my partners in crime at the *Mémorial catholique*. Fr des Genettes was planning a journal, a review called *L'Invariable*,[375] and he would have offered me a good position had I wanted to participate in it along with O'Mahonny. The review was published, and vegetated at Fribourg for several years. Fr des Genettes wrote to me many times urging me to come and join him.

In my disappointment, I informed my family of the situation and of the offers that I had been made. My father and brothers were of the opinion that I should leave Paris and return to the family in Le Mans. I soon made up my mind and, since I had no commitments to the archdiocese, Fr des

---

[373] Predictions of a millenarianist and apocalyptic style that proclaimed the return of the Bourbons to France after the 1830 July Revolution. One variation of their putative origins links them to a sixteenth-century manuscript belonging to the Cistercian abbey of Orval in Belgium. For further details, see *Le Grand Avénément précédé par d'un Grand Prodige*, Paris, 1873.

[374] A ploughman from Gallardon (Eure-et-Loir), who was a visionary and 'prophet' during the Bourbon Restoration. Thomas Martin proclaimed the survival of Louis XVII, whom he believed to be hidden somewhere in Europe, and campaigned against the so-called illegitimacy of Louis XVIII and Charles X. For further information, see G. Lenôtre, *Martin le Visionnaire (1816–1834)*, Paris, 1925.

[375] *L'Invariable* was founded in Switzerland in 1830 as the new *Mémorial catholique*. It fought against the teachings of *L'Avenir*, speaking out against *laicité*, political and moral individualism, scientific materialism, as well as romanticism in art and literature. It ceased publication in 1838. For further information, see Jacquemet, *op. cit.*, v. 1, pp. 351–7.

Genettes needed only to inform the administration of my decision to return to my diocese when he left the parish of the 'Missions', that is, at the end of October.

As soon as I arrived, I resumed my sacred ministry in the parish and continued this until the parish priest left. There was no sadder sight than this disguised clergy, with the tricolour ribbon in their buttonholes. We crossed the church in our lay clothes, which elicited strong reactions from the faithful. We recovered our cassocks in the sacristy and, after the service was over, we merged in with the crowd, leaving church in our secular clothes. No one today can have any idea of the ungodly character that the July Revolution had assumed; one priest had been shot point-blank at the altar in one of the churches in Paris. In particular, we felt very anxious whenever we had to bring the sacraments to the dying. In Paris, the same house was occupied by all sorts of people, which could lead to dangerous encounters. Among other things, I remember bringing Holy Viaticum to a house in rue de Sèvres, to the mother of one of the heroes of the July Revolution who had been very ill-disposed towards the clergy. He was not in, but he could have returned at any time. We carried the Blessed Sacrament in a small silver box containing the host. A sacristan or an altar boy followed at a distance, carrying a parcel containing a cassock, a surplice, a stole and some other items. We would dress at the sick person's home, and put on our lay clothes again after administering the sacraments. We then went on our way, but not without first looking all around and behind us. It was under such auspices that the reign of the Orléans branch was inaugurated. This pressure only ceased in 1832 during the cholera epidemic,[376] when it was possible for the archbishop of Paris to reappear in public.

---

[376] During the Parisian cholera epidemic of 1832, which caused over 10,000 deaths, Archbishop de Quélen placed his château at Conflans at the disposal of the authorities as a refuge for the sick. He also founded a charitable institute to help children orphaned during the epidemic. These actions salvaged his popular reputation to some extent. For further information, see Larousse, *op. cit.*, v. 13, p. 513.

Before leaving Paris, I had to make inquiries about the great crisis looming for French Catholics as a result of moves just made by Fr de La Mennais; he had suddenly declared himself to be a political figure, and announced that he intended to create a Catholic Liberal party in France. During my stay in Le Mans I had received the programme for the forthcoming journal, *L'Avenir*.[377] My ideas were completely overturned by the declaration of a utopia that seemed to transform the 1789 Revolution and its principles into benefits for the Church and real social progress. Things were much worse after I had contacted Fr de La Mennais and the editorial staff directly; it was then that I realized that this consisted of forming an alliance with the Revolution throughout Europe, and of using all possible means to help it. I remember, on seeing my disconcerted appearance, Fr Gerbet said to me: 'What do you expect? We must pass through a democracy at any price in order to return to a theocracy.' Fr de La Mennais did not back these words, which contained a final protest for Christian law. I could fully understand the right of Catholic citizens to take advantage of the freedoms inscribed in the *Charte* of 1830, which was more extensive than that of 1815,[378] for the benefit of their faith. I agreed to a temporary suspension of Christian law after the Christian majority had defected, but I could not accept considering this as either progress or as something permanent.

During this stay in Paris, thanks to my contacts with the staff of *L'Avenir*, I was present at the official opening of the

---

[377] A review founded by Frs de La Mennais and Gerbet, and published from 1830 until 1831 in succession to the *Mémorial catholique*. The review attacked *L'Univers* and *L'Ami de la Religion*, demanding complete separation of Church and State, and a renewed Christian society based on freedom of the press from censorship, freedom of education, freedom of religious and political association, universal suffrage and increased powers of local government. For a discussion of the relationship between Guéranger and *L'Avenir*, see Johnson, *op. cit.*, pp. 95–9.

[378] The *Charte* of 1830 went further than that of 1815 with regard to the toleration of religion in France. For further information, see J. L. Olsen-French, 'French Calvinists and the State, 1830–1852', in *French Historical Studies*, 15 (1967): 225–38.

free school that these gentlemen had decided to begin, in accordance with the article of the new *Charte* that promised freedom of education. In order to gain the immediate benefit of this freedom they had decided to act quickly, gathering together five or six children, with Fr Lacordaire,[379] Monsieur de Montalembert[380] and Monsieur de Coux[381] standing in as school teachers. Along with the three teachers, about a dozen of us witnessed this opening on the fourth floor. There were two nasty old tables made of blackened wood, and the kids wore overalls. We were all standing, and Fr Lacordaire began to speak. I can still see him, with his small black long-coat. He aimed his lively allocution at the children, who could not understand any of it and looked impassive. The orator spoke as though he was addressing a senate, proclaiming the era of freedom of education that had begun in this attic. He ended by telling the kids that they would be 'better than their fathers and worse than their children.' They had thus taken possession of education, but they had

[379] Jean-Baptiste-Henri Lacordaire (1802–1861), ordained priest 1827; joined de La Mennais at La Chênaie just before the July Revolution in 1830, but separated from him after his condemnation in 1832. He undertook to restore the Dominican order to France in 1838, and was professed in Rome in 1840. He returned to France and began a preaching tour of the principal cities, founding Dominican houses in areas where he was particularly successful. He was provincial prior of the order in France on two occasions (1850–1854 and 1858–1861). He founded a third order of teaching friars in 1852. For further information, see Prevost et d'Amat, *op. cit.*, v. 19, pp. 15–17.

[380] Charles de Montalembert (1810–1870), writer and politician. He became one of three editors of the journal *L'Avenir*, having special responsibility for covering foreign affairs. After the collapse of this journal and the condemnation of de La Mennais by Rome, Montalembert moved into politics, where he fought for freedom of education. He was elected to the 'Académie Française' in 1852. His liberal views on freedom of conscience were condemned by Pius IX in 1864. See Voisin, *op. cit.*, p. 746.

[381] Charles, comte de Coux (1787–1864), economist. He distanced himself from de La Mennais' ideas after the papal condemnation of 1832. From 1834 he taught political economics, geography and statistics at the University of Louvain. He became editor-in-chief of *L'Univers* in 1845, but left in 1848 to found the short-lived paper *L'Ère nouvelle* with two companions. For further information, see Jacquemet, *op. cit.*, v. 3, pp. 265–6.

no hold on the university, which the July regime had firmly resolved to maintain as one of its strongholds. A lawsuit followed, and Fr de Montalembert brought the case[382] before the Court of Peers,[383] where it lost to great aplomb. It was a fine attempt but, in a nation like ours that is so little used to freedom, it could not succeed. People laughed raucously about it around the country, and it took another ten years for French Catholics to become interested in the issue of public education. I left Paris feeling worried and troubled. The suppression of the *Mémorial catholique* ordered by Fr de La Mennais upset me; it was as though I realized that the theological aspect of the issues had ceased to interest him. Moreover, this measure meant that I was losing the public forum that had opened up for me, and I was far from insensitive to this. Fr de La Mennais and Fr Gerbet urged me to write in *L'Avenir*, but I was not at ease in this environment. My sole collaboration was limited to the two articles that I sent from Le Mans during the following months. Their subject was 'Prayer for the King'.[384] I established the meaning of this prayer, which was a custom as old as the Church, and with the help of St Paul and some liturgical formulas I demonstrated that the only aim of this prayer in a non-Christian society was to obtain peace and calm for the Church. I had undertaken these successful articles in order to combat the repugnance of the Gallican clergy, who continued to regard this prayer as the recognition of a political right in the so-called Legitimist sense.

---

[382] That is, the right to a free university as opposed to a public one.

[383] The Court of Peers was a tribunal composed of members of the Chamber of Peers, the upper legislative assembly of the French government, and existed from 1814 until 1848. The Court of Peers heard cases relating to protecting the safety of the State, high treason and various other accusations. For further information, see Larousse, *op. cit.*, v. 12, pp. 37–8.

[384] 'De la prière pour le roi', in *L'Avenir* 1 (24 octobre 1830); (28 octobre 1830). Reproduced in *Mélanges*, pp. 113–32.

Return to Le Mans

After returning definitively to Le Mans, I immediately saw Fr Bouvier, who was very concerned about the newspaper *L'Avenir*. He told me that he would wait to give his verdict on the paper until its beliefs and sympathies were expressed openly. I could not help being surprised when he added that the administration of *L'Avenir* had let it be known that it would grant shares at the rate of three thousand francs, and that he was minded to send this sum and become a shareholder in the newspaper. He asked me to write about it to Fr de La Mennais, who replied that he would accept the sum gratefully. Fr Bouvier sent his three thousand francs, which were lost down to the last centime when *L'Avenir* crashed in November 1831. The good superior never bragged about this escapade, and I kept his secret. Since then, I have realized that this move was a step towards politics on his part. The Revolution of 1830 had been an inspiration for him, but it was the July government rather than the school of *L'Avenir* that brought about his advancement. I should add that, from the very beginning, he disapproved of *L'Avenir's* tendency to insult the former government in several of its articles. This caused great scandal in the West and Fr Bouvier let his unhappiness be known several times, although without letting on that he was a shareholder in the newspaper.

I moved into my father's home in rue Saint-Vincent with the intention of devoting myself to ecclesiastical studies and the defence of Catholic truth, giving no thought to my future; God was guiding everything. I was still busy with my historical work about the rights of the Holy See, and was working through the principal sources at my own pace. Nevertheless, the current situation of the Church was preoccupying me more than anything else. I was worried about the appointment of bishops by the new government and, since the *Charte* of 1830 had removed the state religion that was still preserved by the *Charte* of 1815, the time seemed right to bring to the attention of Catholics the final article of the 1801 Concordat. This article expressed the necessity for the head of state to profess the Catholic religion in order to exercise the right of appointing to episcopal sees. The state religion no longer existed, and there was nothing to protect France from witnessing a heterodox prince on the throne. Surely there was good reason to demand a revision of the Concordat? It was a serious question but it was soon settled by the Holy See, which agreed to the appointments made by Louis-Philippe. A little later, the nomination of Fr Guillon[385] was an exception to this, for reasons that were personal to this cleric.

Unaware of this outcome, which took some time to arrive, I wrote my book, whose express aim was to get the French bishops to make a serious examination of such an important question. I sent a copy of the work to Archbishop de Quélen of Paris, who sent a very kind reply. *L'Avenir* carried two articles by Fr Lacordaire, who praised some things, naively confusing the freedom of the Church with Liberalism, and reprimanded others, notably, with regard to the Concordat of 1516.[386] This was because, without naming him, I had refuted his scandalous assertions about the Concordats in his defence speech during the trial of *L'Avenir*. Naturally, *L'Ami*

---

[385] Marie-Nicolas-Sylvestre Guillon (1760–1847), was an ardent defender of the Gallican church and defied the archbishop of Paris by administering the sacrament of Extreme Unction to the Jansenist Bishop Grégoire in 1831. For these reasons his nomination by Louis-Philippe to both the see of Cambrai and then the see of Beauvais was refused by Rome. In 1833 he was given as a compromise the title of bishop of Morocco *in partibus*. See Prevost et d'Amat, *op. cit.,* v. 8, p. 1629.

[386] This granted the sovereign the right to make episcopal appointments, which were then canonically instituted by the pope.

de la Religion attacked me, accusing me of Liberalism, even though I had carefully distinguished between the thesis and the hypothesis in the sense that has since been formulated by the Italian Jesuits of the *Civiltà cattolica.*[387] The book was entitled, *De l'élection et de la nomination des évêques.*[388] Six hundred copies were printed, which sold quite quickly, albeit without the author's name. These days it exists only in second-hand. The publication took place in spring 1831.

The publication took me to Paris to attend to the corrections of this book. I saw Fr de La Mennais and Fr Gerbet again and briefly saw Montalembert, but I avoided Lacordaire more than ever. I made the acquaintance of Sainte-Beuve,[389] with whom Fr de La Mennais had connections and who was a friend of Lacordaire. We were hoping to make a Catholic of him, but he was having none of it. Perhaps Fr de La Mennais' downfall contributed to his decline into the scepticism in which he has languished ever since.

At that moment, Bishop Grégoire died.[390] A huge crowd went to his town house in rue du Cherche-Midi on the morning of his funeral in order to see his body, which was clothed in *pontificalia* and laid out in his bedroom. Since I

---

[387] A Roman review edited and published by the Jesuits. It was founded in 1850 and was intended to fight against irreligion by means of wide-ranging and scientific articles. For further information, see Jacquemet, *op. cit.,* v. 2, pp. 1153–4.

[388] P. Guéranger, *De l'élection et de la nomination des évêques,* Paris, 1831. This was Guéranger's first book, and deals with the role of the government in episcopal appointments. It is an Ultramontane work, arguing that the appointment of bishops belongs to the successor of Peter and not to the State. Reproduced in *Mélanges,* pp. 139–345.

[389] Charles-Augustin Sainte-Beuve (1804–1869), poet and literary critic. For further information, see Larousse, *op. cit.,* v. 14, pp. 59–61.

[390] Henri-Baptiste Grégoire (1750–1831), ordained priest in 1775; professor at the college of Pont-à-Mousson; curate at Marimont-la-Basse (1776–1782); parish priest of Emberménil. He helped to draw up the civil constitution of the clergy and was the first person to take the oath in December 1791.When elected constitutional bishop in the *départements* of Loir-et-Cher and La Sarthe in 1791, he chose the diocese of Blois. He participated in a motion to abolish the royalty in 1792, and was opposed to both Napoleon and the Bourbon Restoration. See Prevost et d'Amat, *op. cit.,* v. 16, pp. 1139–42.

was dressed as a layman, I slipped into the crowd and approached the bed. I saw the emaciated Jansenist face of the old priest faithful to the constitutional oath, who had just died in dogged schism. A group of his political friends were in the bedroom, chatting to one another quite animatedly; they were all nasty, white and grey-haired characters. There was an unfortunate priest called Fr Parabère,[391] who was to perform the burial. He was wearing an alb and a stole, but did not dare to mingle with the friends of the deceased and seemed very ill at ease. The government had requisitioned the parish church of L'Abbaye-aux-Bois[392] so that the prelate's schismatic funeral could be celebrated there. Later on, I cast my eye over this sorry scene. Fr Parabère was singing the Mass, and he had a deacon and a sub-deacon of the same mould as him. An old Jansenist priest, whom I am told is called Fr Paquot,[393] was celebrating a Mass in black vestments at a side altar. I made a quick exit from this heretical and schismatic atmosphere, cursing the government whose cowardice had dared to soil with this shameless act a church consecrated to the religion professed by the majority of French people. I saw the Belgian republican Monsieur de Potter,[394] who was also an enemy of the Catholic Church, at the church door. He was protesting vigorously against the violation of religious liberty and stood outside during the entire ceremony, waiting for the procession to leave for the cemetery.

On returning to Le Mans, I resumed my usual work once

---

[391] Person currently unidentified.

[392] A monastery of Cistercian nuns founded in 1202 in the diocese of Noyen. It was transferred to Paris in 1654 and was suppressed during the Revolution. The church was demolished in 1906. See Cottineau, *op. cit.,* v. 2, p. 2194.

[393] Person currently unidentified.

[394] Louis-Joseph-Antoine de Potter (1786–1859), Belgium publicist and historian of strong Republican sympathies. He was twice tried and sentenced in Belgium for his protests against the political regime, and his second sentence in 1830 banished him from the country for eight years. It was then that he came to France and witnessed the July Revolution. For further information, see Firmin et al., *op. cit.,* v. 40, pp. 906–10.

again. I studied the Fathers and the Councils, always seeking to elucidate the Roman idea. I searched these same sources for a concept of faith during the controversy between Fr Gerbet and Fr Rozaven. I read the treatise *De fide* by Suarez, but could not decide easily between the two adversaries. This was because I had not received any proper teaching about the natural and the supernatural orders during my formation. This was the scourge of that era, and it is still far from remedied.

I wanted to master the Italian that I had started during my time at the bishop's palace, and so I applied myself to this by reading Manzoni's *Fiancés*[395] and, later on, Pellico's *Prisons*[396] in the original. I soon mastered this language, at least for prose, and I translated St Alphonsus Liguori's little book entitled, *La Voie du Salut*.[397] I sold my translation to the Bricou bookshop, who published it as a small 18° volume.

I was also very busy with ancient and modern ecclesiastical history. I saw Fr Bouvier every day, who took an interest in my work. One day, I ventured to tell him that there was a post that his seminary was lacking, the chair of ecclesiastical history, and that I would gladly take on the responsibility of filling it. He liked the idea at first and promised that he would think about it. A few days later he told me that the project was not feasible, but that I could do something better. This was to prepare a printed course for use in seminaries. 'By this

[395] Comte Alessandro Manzoni (1784–1873), Italian author who wrote mainly poetry, but also historical works, as well as the novel to which Guéranger refers. His *I Promessi Sposi, storia Milanese del secolo XVII*, Milan, 1827, was one of his most popular works and was translated into many languages. See Vapereau, *op. cit.*, p. 1328.

[396] Silvio Pellico (1789–1854), Italian poet and literary figure. The original of the work to which Guéranger refers, *Le Mie Prigioni*, recounts the story of Pellico's imprisonment for nine years first in Venice and then in Speilburg, Austria, after he was arrested and sentenced to death (from which sentence he was later pardoned), in 1820. Guéranger is mistaken in believing that he read the work at this time since it was not published until 1833. See Vapereau, *op. cit.*, p. 1562.

[397] Guéranger's translation may be found in A. Liguori, *Oeuvres complètes*, Paris, 1834–42, v. 1.

means,' he told me, 'you will have more influence than if you were to lecture in a single post.' Basically, knowing my ideas as he did, he was too embarrassed for me to be seen amidst his seminarians.

In Le Mans, I had daily contact with several young priests who were my contemporaries: Fr Morin,[398] the curate at the cathedral, who was devout and intelligent; Fr Gilbert,[399] a schoolmaster at *La Psallette*, who was excellent and yet very simple; Fr Bouvert,[400] professor of philosophy at the college where he became principal, and who then became parish priest of La Suze, who was intelligent and devoted to Roman principles; and Fr Gontier,[401] a curate at La Couture, who was a witty, caustic Gallican. Fr Saint-Martin,[402] a former examining magistrate in Laval who became a priest in 1830, joined us, and we were delighted by his verve and sparkling wit. Later on, I shall mention two other priests.

I did not see the bishop very much, who was a rather stiff, albeit good man. The cathedral dean, Fr Bureau, treated me very well. The second vicar general, Fr Bourmault, the former mayor of Évron, was a very stupid man and did not like me because of my doctrinal views. Fr Bouvier was the principal vicar general and, as I have said, he was very kind. There was an old canon on the Chapter whom Bishop de La Myre had made an honorary vicar general, and whom Bishop Carron had kept on as such; he was called Ménochet[403] and was not very

[398] Fr Morin (1810–1835), curate of the cathedral of Le Mans and then of Pontlieue from 1833. See the archives of the diocese of Le Mans.

[399] Person currently unidentified.

[400] René-Pierre-Jean Bouvert (1805–1871), professor of philosophy and then principal of the college in Le Mans; he became the parish priest of Foulletourte in La Suze. See the archives of the diocese of Le Mans. The name of La Suze changed to La Suze-sur-Sarthe in 1894.

[401] Augustin Gontier (1802–1881), ordained priest in 1828; became a curate in Niort and then at Notre-Dame de la Couture; parish priest of Changé-lès-le-Mans (1842); appointed an honorary canon of Le Mans in 1859. See *Le Chapitre*, pp. 100, 122, 136.

[402] Person currently unidentified.

[403] Philippe Ménochet (1766–1834), ordained priest in 1788; curate in Saint-Vénérand and then Houssay; honorary canon of Luçon; appointed an honorary canon of Le Mans in 1827. See *Le Chapitre*, p. 44.

favourably disposed towards me, again due to my principles. Fr Morin and I devised a plan to make these old Gallicans kneel down in front of the papal tiara and keys. When the feast of Corpus Christi came around we made an altar of repose near the cathedral, and we placed large-scale pontifical emblems in heavy relief in front of the flower-laced altar. It was a very beautiful work and was a great credit to our helpers. On approaching this altar with the Chapter, Canon Ménochet said: 'It is obvious that Fr Guéranger has erected this altar of repose.' Among our workers, we had a young man called Beaufreton,[404] who has become a foreman mason. He is the same man who built the vaults of the new choir in the abbey in 1864.

At that time, we were living in a state of heightened agitation surrounding the publication of *L'Avenir*. This journal, which was often very bold politically speaking, was irritating the Legitimists by its distain for their opinions. Nevertheless, it cannot be denied that the pride with which it defended religious liberty made an impression on the new government. Moreover, the adherence of many people from every rank and station to this doctrine had been a great help in preventing the government from meddling in spiritual matters. The result of this was that the re-foundation and public establishment of religious orders became relatively easy, and there was almost unlimited freedom to attack Gallicanism via publications.

The school bearing the name of Fr de La Mennais was generally taken in by his theories opposing Christian law,[405] and the encyclical of 1832 was very much needed.[406] Along-

---

[404] Person currently unidentified.

[405] Guéranger means that de La Mennais was defending freedom of political opinion and the total independence of Church and State. This is in opposition to the traditional ideal of the State governed by Christian law, according to the model of the divine right of the monarchy, as being the only legitimate model for Church and State.

[406] The encyclical *Mirari vos* of 15 August 1832, in which Gregory XVI (1765–1846; pope from 1831) disputed the need for a 'regeneration of the Church' extolled by de La Mennais, and showed how indifference was at the root of the various freedoms that he was demanding (freedom of education, freedom of the press, freedom of association, etc.). For further information, see Levillain, *op. cit.*, pp. 767–73, esp. pp. 771–2.

side this, Gallicanism was totally defeated since it could not hold out against the awakening of Catholic sensibility. The Middle Ages were becoming fashionable, Christian archaeology was on the horizon and historical scholarship based on the sources was about to make its appearance. Nevertheless, many people were not even aware of or the slightest bit concerned about this revolution, which would vindicate the Church by bringing into its fold many people who would have remained Voltarians[407] were it not for this movement. Picot, the inept editor of *L'Ami de la Religion,* was unwittingly helping the school of de La Mennais by showering abuse on it, stirring up prejudices and overexciting unhealthy emotions among the remnants of another age.[408] However much I held out for Christian law and lacked enthusiasm for the philosophical system of common sense, my ardent Ultramontanism meant that I was regarded as the leader of Mennaisianism in the diocese.

I had been given all the necessary faculties for sacred ministry, but my youthful appearance meant that from my return to Paris until my entry at Solesmes I did not hear a single confession. On the other hand, I was frequently invited into the pulpit. At the cathedral, Fr Morin, whom I liked very much, often relied on me at the parish Mass. In La Couture, Fr Gontier sometimes invited me to stand in for him. In Pré, the two curates, Fr Forget,[409] who has since become parish priest of Bonnétable, and Fr Sargeul,[410] who

---

[407] The followers of François-Marie-Arouet Voltaire (1674–1778), philosopher and historian. As a philosopher, Voltaire was a deist who opposed the personal God of Christianity and the dogmatic content of Christian Revelation. In this respect, he was especially critical of the Catholic Church. As a historian, he was convinced that humanity was marching towards progress independently of divine providence and military or diplomatic advances.

[408] The Gallican era.

[409] Joseph Forget (1799–1873), ordained priest in 1825; curate at Notre-Dame du Pré; parish priest of Lassy (1833); archpriest of Bonnétable (1846); appointed honorary canon of Le Mans in 1857. See *Le Chapitre,* p. 94.

[410] Michel Sargeul (1803–1868), was parish priest of Saint-Denis d'Anjou from 1847. See the archives of the diocese of Le Mans.

has since become the parish priest of Saint-Denis d'Anjou, were both contemporaries of mine at seminary. They could both have done well had they managed to work seriously, and they were very close to me through our common Roman doctrines. Their excellent parish priest, Fr Croissant-Morinière,[411] very often invited me to preach in his church. Lastly, Fr Le Baillif,[412] the chaplain at the Sacré-Coeur convent, invited me into his fold, and on Sunday afternoons I used to instruct the boarders. It was then that I got to know Mademoiselle Euphrasie Cosnard,[413] who was being educated there. This gave me the opportunity to make the acquaintance of her father, who lived in Sablé. At his insistence, I decided to spend a few days with him in my home town, something that was to have immense consequences for my future. God knew what he wanted to do, but I was completely ignorant of his will.

My reputation as a preacher always ready to talk about any subject opened up the cathedral pulpit to me for the major sermons preached before the Chapter. In 1831, I preached the sermon for the feast of the Sacred Heart. I had agreed with my friends to talk about Belgium and Poland in this sermon, and, to the great amazement of the old canons, I kept my word. Belgium was of great interest to the Roman school on account of the victory just carried off there by the Catholics, who had broken the Dutch yoke. The brave attempt of Poland to escape from the Muscovite yoke roused the hearts of all the faithful, who welcomed the double failure thereby inflicted on the treaties of 1815.[414] I brought

---

[411] Augustin Croissant-Morinière (d. 1832), parish priest of Pré. See the archives of the diocese of Le Mans.

[412] Jean-Baptiste Le Baillif (1793–1865), ordained priest in 1818; curate at Pré and then at Mayenne. He was appointed chaplain to the Sacré-Cœur convent of Le Mans and became an honorary canon of Le Mans in 1825. He then became parish priest of Saint-Benoît (1841–1861), and was made a titular canon of Le Mans in 1861. See *Le Chapitre*, pp. 40, 102, 104, 108.

[413] Euphrasie Cosnard (1809–1879). She did not marry.

[414] Guéranger is referring to the successful Belgian and the unsuccessful Polish uprisings of 1830. He wrongly assumes that the cause of Catholic freedom was the only factor involved in these conflicts, which

Belgium into my introduction by mentioning Blessed Juli-
enne, who had initiated the feast of Corpus Christi, just as
Blessed Margaret Mary prepared for the institution of the
feast of the Sacred Heart. I paid tribute to Poland, the first
country to obtain from the Holy See the favour of celebrating
the mystery of the Heart of Jesus with a feast. There were no
comments, and people continued to invite me. The following
year, I preached on Passion Sunday and gave the sermon for
All Saints.

---

were also motivated by economic concerns. In Belgium the uprising
led to the declaration of independence from Holland on 4 October
1830, with Léopold de Saxe-Coburg assuming control of the country.
This provoked the Russian tsar Nicholas I to promise military aid to the
Dutch king William I. This news indirectly provoked the insurrection of
Poland against the Russian powers in November 1830. The Poles were
ultimately unsuccessful in their attempt, and were beaten at Ostrolen-
ska in May 1831.

The Priory of Solesmes

In the spring of 1831, the newspapers carried an advertisement for the sale of the priory of Solesmes, which they described as an abbey. This monastery was bought in 1791 by Monsieur Le Noir de Chantelou,[415] who lived in La Flèche. In 1829 it had passed into the hands of Monsieur Salmon, a rich landowner in Sablé; Monsieur Thoré from Le Mans and Monsieur Emmanuel La Fautrardière from Sablé had also been involved in the acquisition.[416] These good men had bought the monastery for 32,000 francs, hoping to make a profit by investing in this property. They had thought of starting a minor seminary, but the buildings were not sufficient for this and Précigné was in any case expanding. It seemed to them that their desired outcome would be achieved via an industrial use. Among other ideas, it was suggested that the monastery could be used as a glassworks factory, but this idea was just as unsuccessful as the others. The purchasers were therefore reduced to putting Solesmes up for sale by means of the newspapers.

---

[415] Solesmes was sold to Louis Le Noir, sieur de Chantelou, on 4 April 1791. See C. Girault, *Les Biens d'Église dans La Sarthe à la fin du XVIIIe siècle*, Laval, 1953, pp. 140–4.

[416] Guéranger has made a mistake in recording the date of this transaction. Solesmes was sold to Pierre Thoré-Cohidet of Le Mans, René-Joseph Salmon and Emmanuel Lefebvre de La Fautrardière of Sablé in December 1825. *Ibid.* The first two of these co-owners were involved in a company that was formed in 1824 to exploit local anthracite mines.

This news made a deep impression on me. I was worried that this beloved monument from my childhood would perhaps pass through strange vicissitudes and that those beautiful statues would change owners, and maybe even perish under the blows of the black gang.[417] For want of a better idea, I thought of Fr de La Mennais, who already had several establishments, and wrote to Fr Gerbet, asking him to suggest this acquisition to his leader. In his reply, he thanked me but added that Fr de La Mennais did not have funds for such a work.

The advertisement that Solesmes was up for sale continued to appear in the newspapers, which proved that no buyers were coming forward, and the idea of saving this house and putting it to some use would not leave me. Suddenly, around June, I thought that if I could gather together a few young priests then we could re-establish the order of St Benedict there, with the divine office and studies. My service of the bishop and my time in Paris had put my seminary dreams on hold. Suddenly, they gained renewed impetus and have never left me since. I confided this to Fr Heurtebize, who listened gladly to me. I also spoke about it to the two curates in Pré, Frs Forget and Sargeul, and to the cathedral curate, Fr Morin, suggesting that they join the project. They were coming around to this idea, but none of them had decided firmly enough for me to be completely certain that I could count them as associates. Divine providence was guiding everything, however, and the year would not pass before an encounter occurred that made me put my desire into action.

I had promised Monsieur Cosnard that I would pay his family a visit in Sablé, and the fact that I wanted to see Solesmes again was one more reason for me to make this little trip. I reached my hosts on 22 July, the feast of St Mary

---

[417] The black gang was a group of speculators who trafficked in goods that had previously belonged to the Church and which were taken over by the State during the 1789 Revolution. The gang exploited historic buildings by dismantling them and trading in their component parts. See Larousse, *op. cit.*, v. 2, p. 150.

Magdalene. Monsieur Cosnard,[418] a former solicitor in Saint-Denis, Anjou, had settled in Sablé and was for the time being living with his sisters, Mademoiselles Manette and Perrotte Cosnard.[419] He had two daughters: Mademoiselle Euphrasie, about whom I have already spoken, and Mademoiselle Marie who, like her sister, had been raised in the Sacré-Coeur convent in Le Mans. Monsieur Cosnard was remarkable for the intensity of his political enthusiasm for the Legitimists. He was still influenced by the July catastrophe and could not talk about anything else. He was a very honest, Christian man, but his mind was as narrow as could be and his obstinacy was unparalleled. His sister, Mademoiselle Manette, extremely intelligent and of lively disposition, was very placid about politics. As for the gentle Mademoiselle Perrotte, she was even less bothered about current affairs.

This family had a close friendship with Fr Fonteinne,[420] the curate in Sablé. I had known this young priest at seminary, where he was in the class above me, but I had had until then only very fleeting dealings with him. He had been in his curacy for about two years and his parish priest was Fr Paillard,[421] the former principal of the college in Ernée, who was not particularly kind to his curate. He will feature in this account again.

An hour after I arrived in Sablé, Fr Fonteinne came to visit the Cosnard family. I was glad to associate with him, and I soon understood the moral situation of this household into which I had been received as a welcome guest. Fr Fonteinne subscribed to the *L'Avenir,* and he used to pass it on to

---

[418] René-Louis Cosnard.

[419] Marie-Anne (Manette) Cosnard (1789–1855); Perrine (Perrotte) Cosnard (1778–1850). Neither of these sisters married.

[420] Auguste Fonteinne (1804–1889), ordained priest 1828; curate in Sablé and then briefly parish priest of Asnières-sur-Vègre. He was one of Guéranger's first companions, making monastic profession on 21 November 1837. He became the first cellarer of Solesmes. See des Mazis, *op. cit.,* 172.

[421] Fr Paillard (1796–1847), became parish priest of Sablé in 1831. See *La Province du Maine,* 51 (1847): 401–2. This source does not give Fr Paillard's Christian name.

Monsieur Cosnard's sisters, who enjoyed the tone of this newspaper. Their brother, noticing that this reading was far from reinforcing their Legitimist ideas, was quite annoyed with Fr Fonteinne, especially since he feared that the infection would soon spread to his daughters. He wanted to sound out my political ideas, and I felt bound to state that the cause of the senior Bourbon line seemed completely lost to me. I said that in my opinion the only cause that could now rally Catholics was that of the Catholic Church.

From the very evening of my arrival, I expressed a desire to visit Solesmes as soon as possible, and Fr Fonteinne offered to join us. Early the next day, I made my way there with him and the entire Cosnard family. Seeing again the ancient monastery, the sheltered road that then led to it, the arid *poulie*, and the rocks on the other bank of the river Sarthe was for me an experience that was as pleasant as it was intense. Nevertheless, nothing could equal the emotion I felt as I beheld once again those expressive statues that had so caught my eye as a child, and which might be about to perish under the blows of the black gang. The emotion I had felt in the ruins of Marmoutier came back to me, and I got Fr Fonteinne to unite his fine, beautiful voice with mine in singing the first three verses of the *Rorate*. I then asked him to join me in adding the last two verses of Psalm 50, *Benigne fac*, and *tunc acceptabis.*[422] Those with us were moved, but they were far from suspecting the predestination that was mysteriously heralded at this solemn moment.

I went back to Solesmes several times during the ten days that I spent in Sablé, and always with Fr Fonteinne. On 29 July, the feast of St Martha, I joined him and the Cosnard family on a country outing that took place at Vrigné, the beautiful farm belonging to the Juigné family. It was then run

---

[422] *Benigne fac, Domine, in bona voluntate tua Sion, ut aedificentur muri Ierusalem. Tunc acceptabis sacrificium iustitiae, oblationes et holocausta; tunc imponent super altare tuum vitulos* (Ps 50:20–1). ('Deal favourably, O Lord, in your goodwill with Sion; that the walls of Jerusalem may be built up. Then shall you accept the sacrifice of justice, oblations and whole burnt-offerings; then shall they lay calves upon your altar', Douai Bible).

by the respectable Monsieur Marçais, the brother of Madame Gazeau,[423] whom I had known in my childhood and who was the cousin of the Cosnard sisters. This wonderful woman, who was the hand of providence for the poor people in Sablé, cared for the new Solesmes until her death with a concern that was demonstrated through all manner of service.

On 29 July, my friendship with Fr Fonteinne became much closer, and our mutual fondness for one another deepened. I got him to recite the office of the day in the Roman breviary with me, something to which he readily agreed. Nevertheless, the time was not yet right and I still did not feel drawn to reveal my thoughts to him. I shared some of them with Mademoiselle Manette Cosnard, but for the time being this was of no consequence.

I finally left Sablé and my hosts after staying for about a week and returned to Le Mans, although not without promising to come back in the autumn. I left feeling glad to have seen Solesmes again, and had an ever greater desire to realize in this former monastery the plan that was increasingly on my mind. My youthfulness, the complete absence of temporal resources, and the limited understanding of the project on the part of those to whom I suggested joining me did nothing to stop me. I was not even thinking about things, and yet I felt compelled to go forwards. I asked for God's help with all my heart, but did not even think of asking to know his will for the planned work. The Church's need seemed to me so urgent, and ideas about true Christianity in both Church and lay circles to be so false and half-hearted, that I could not think of anything other than the urgent need to found some sort of centre that would seek out and revive the pure traditions. My prayer was humble and fervent, and I venture to say that desire for any form of show had no place at all in my thoughts.

I resumed my studies, acquaintances and preaching, and thus reached the month of October. I had decided to make

---

[423] Marie Gazeau (née Marçais) (d. 1848).

my retreat at the Trappist monastery of Port-du-Salut,[424] and I carried out this plan. I was given as my confessor an old Flemish priest, a former parish priest, who did not seem up to much. Nevertheless, I still made my retreat as best I could. I then set out for Sablé, where I arrived in time for All Saints' day. I was once again with the Cosnard family, and I resumed my daily contact with Fr Fonteinne. Naturally, trips to Solesmes were very frequent, and I usually made them with Fr Fonteinne. Something within me was driving me to tell him about my plans, and I sensed that I would not resist for long. Finally, after a few days, I went to sit with him on the *poulie* before going into the monastery. As I was showing him the building as seen from the garden, I said to him: 'Look at this house and how beautiful it is; I want to establish here a house of prayer and study. I am thinking of re-establishing the Benedictines in this former monastery, and several priests from Le Mans would join me.' These words were welcomed with keen interest, and the conversation did not progress long before Fr Fonteinne told me that he would offer himself to be part of this work. He added modestly that he could not be of much help in terms of intellectual projects, but that he might be some use in providing the temporal care without which no house can survive. I accepted the offer gratefully, and on returning to Sablé I informed Mademoiselle Manette Cosnard of my conquest. She was very devoted to Fr Fonteinne, and from then on she committed herself wholeheartedly to the project. I told them that I first needed to speak to the bishop, without whose agreement I could not do anything like this. After staying in Sablé for a week, I returned to Le Mans and was delighted with my new recruit.

A few days later, I left for Paris. One of my first visits was to the office of *L'Avenir*. I was anxious to see Frs de La Mennais and Gerbet to tell them about my plans. The overly political and liberal leanings of *L'Avenir* were worrying me more and

---

[424] A monastery of Trappist monks from Darfield (Westphalia), who took over the former Augustinian priory of Port-Ringeard in the diocese of Le Mans in 1815. See Cottineau, *op. cit.,* v. 2, p. 2340.

more. Yet I trusted the Catholicism of these men, who seemed to be more carried away by events than taken in by doctrines that I sensed were in total contradiction to the Church's tradition. Fr de La Mennais looked very worried, but he listened to me kindly all the same. He agreed that nothing could be done without the religious orders, adding that he had thought about this need for a long time and had even tried something similar in his attempt to set up a 'Congregation' at La Chênaie. I replied that I was not thinking of anything new, but simply of re-establishing a Benedictine house. He objected that this order had the choir office. I replied that this was precisely the reason for which I was choosing it, and that my associates were attracted for the same reason. In short, his advice was kindly, as was Fr Gerbet's; both of them, however, had other things to think about at this time.

I had arrived during the crisis at *L'Avenir*. This newspaper had exhausted the funds from its shares. Moreover, it was experiencing strong opposition, although less as a result of its very advanced political ideas than due to the way in which it had quarrelled openly with the Legitimist party, and for its imprudent demand that the clergy should give up the subsidies they were receiving from the State.[425] Since he was about to go under, Fr de La Mennais announced in the final edition of the newspaper that he was leaving for Rome to ask the Sovereign Pontiff if *L'Avenir*'s doctrines were also his own, promising to renounce all ideas of which the Holy See disapproved. This was rather a clever climb-down. In the event of success in Rome, *L'Avenir* could be republished successfully; if the opposite outcome were to occur, the matter would be dropped. The only problem this raised was for the shareholders, who would lose everything. This is what happened, to the particular disappointment of Fr Bouvier, who lost the three thousand francs he had risked by trying to make a fortune in an area that would bring him anything but happiness. Fr de La Mennais left for Rome a few days after my

---

[425] The paper was making this demand since it supported the complete separation of Church and State.

arrival in Paris, either followed or preceded by Fr Lacordaire and Monsieur de Montalembert.

During my stay in Paris, I saw Monsieur de Coux, a learned economist and one of the editors of *L'Avenir*; I consulted him about procedures for acquiring Solesmes. Since we did not have the funds available to buy, he advised me to take out a lease with the owner on condition that we would be able to buy for a price fixed in advance when the lease expired. This compromise was what we later did, but we were still a long way from being able to carry it out.

I also saw Monsieur de Montalembert before his departure. He was very taken with my plan, and apologized for being unable to contribute to the work with a large donation since his very limited means at that time did not permit him this pleasure. He took me to the house of his friend the marquis de Dreux-Brézé,[426] who immediately promised a gift of 500 francs as soon as the foundation began. A year later, he was completely faithful in keeping his word.

I returned to Le Mans. During my absence, Fr Fonteinne had got in touch with Monsieur Salmon, the main owner of Solesmes, about the house. He told him that he had been entrusted by a private individual, who was not from this region, to negotiate for the house. Monsieur Salmon first suggested the price of 40,000 francs. He said that the general council to be held in January would also deal with Solesmes, and that the university wanted to buy it to establish a teacher training college. As far as his asking price was concerned, he told Fr Fonteinne that Monsieur Huet and Monsieur Dubignon,[427] acting on behalf of the black gang, had recently offered him up to 35,000 francs. Their intention was to demolish everything and sell the materials. The deal had not been successful because Monsieur Salmon had wanted to keep some tables and panelling from the refectory, as well as

---

[426] Henri-Léonard, marquis de Dreux-Brézé (1766–1829), principal master of ceremonies for France. He fled to Italy at the Revolution, but was reinstated as principal master of ceremonies in 1814 and appointed a peer of France in 1815. For further information, see Robinet et al., *op. cit.*, v. 1, p. 660.

[427] Persons currently unidentified.

some cupboards and a table from the kitchen. The buyers, who wanted these objects without any extra cost, broke off negotiations. Fr Fonteinne, to whom I had written from Paris about Monsieur de Coux's idea, ventured a few words about a lease prior to purchase. He discovered that Monsieur Salmon was very reluctant about this proposition. Therefore, this first conversation with the owner of Solesmes was fruitless. Fortunately, it was not our last conversation.

I felt that making an overture towards the bishop was a matter of some urgency, to see if we could count on his approval. I went to the bishop's palace on 29 November and informed the prelate of my project. He listened to me kindly and with interest, and did not appear alarmed by the difficulties of those times. He pointed out that he himself was not afraid of taking risks, notably in the case of the Carmelite foundation in Le Mans. Nevertheless, before giving me a definitive reply he asked for time to reflect, and put me off until 7 December. Bishop Carron was a man of great loyalty, firm in his resolutions and very much filled with zeal for the Church's freedom. His mind was nothing special and his knowledge was limited, which is precisely why it would have been difficult to exert much influence over him. Taken early from his diocese by a premature death, it is not easy to predict what his feelings for Solesmes would have been during subsequent events.

I had an audience with him on 7 December. He told me that he had thought about my project, and that it was clear to him that this foundation at Solesmes would end up as a school. He said that my personal dealings with Fr de La Mennais would soon give this school a reputation that many people would find reprehensible. Furthermore, although he personally was far from being hostile towards the school of Fr de La Mennais he was, as the youngest bishop in France, still loath to appear biased in the discussion that had been generated; this would inevitably happen when people saw that an establishment run according to Mennaisian doctrines was opening under his authority. I tried to respond to the prelate, giving the truth of the matter. His decision had been made, however, and he concluded by saying that since the

editors of *L'Avenir* were in Rome to obtain apostolic judgement on their ideas, a solution could not fail to be reached.
We would then finally know which direction to take, and his
sentiments would always be those of the Holy See, whatever
they turned out to be. He would see if it was appropriate to
follow up my plans, but until that time he could see no other
course of action than to wait.   .

   Such was the episcopal audience of 7 December, which
checked my haste but did not demoralize me. I wrote immediately to Fr Fonteinne, who visited Monsieur Salmon
without delay. Firstly, he said that the person who was thinking of buying Solesmes to start an institution was now having
a few problems. This being the case, this person was pulling
out, but these obstacles would be removed before 1833. This
was the sense in which I had written to Fr Fonteinne. He
thought that he should add, and I later agreed with him, that
the obstacles had come from the bishop, who had decided
that he should wait before giving permission for the establishment. This provided a very plausible excuse and at the
same time showed that the planned establishment was of a
religious nature, something that had not yet been articu-
lated. Monsieur Salmon seemed annoyed and told Fr
Fonteinne that he planned to demolish the cloister and the
bakery buildings if the offer was not kept.

   As can be seen, things did not get very far and we had to
resign ourselves to the will of God. Before going any further,
however, a few words should be said about the impression
made on certain people in the locality by my two trips to
Sablé. At the presbytery, Fr Paillard, who was parish priest of
the town and who was later opposed to Solesmes, was not
very favourably disposed towards Fr Fonteinne, his curate.
He was not pleased about the contact I had formed with him,
even though he was far from suspecting our plans. His close
friend was Fr Bellenfant, the rector of the minor seminary of
Précigné, a respectable priest but very narrow-minded. The
two friends could not understand my situation in the
diocese, being quite incapable of thinking that a priest my
age could be anything other than a parish curate. The
thought crossed their minds that I was looking for a position,

and that I was planning to teach. Since my father and brother had followed this career, they thought it entirely natural for me to be attracted to it myself. Starting from this supposition, Fr Bellenfant, whom I had visited in Précigné, was convinced that I was hanging around his minor seminary with the intention of one day replacing him. This preposterous idea tormented him until I settled at Solesmes, and I must admit that I have had a good laugh about it on more than one occasion. Notwithstanding the ridiculousness of such a hypothesis, these two men instinctively alienated themselves from me. Ensuing events showed that the devil had wanted to make the most of the friendship between them in order to prepare an opposition to Solesmes that would yield the most miserable of fruits.

In Search of Resources

The year 1832 began inauspiciously. I had confided my lack of success with the prelate to Frs Bouvier and Heurtebize, and they shared my concerns. I had expressed something of this to the young priests on whom I was relying in Le Mans. This did not do much to encourage them, and I should have already realized that they would prove completely unreliable when the time came for action. Yet since I was far from feeling discouraged, I pursued my recruitment plans. A young deacon from the Mayenne region, Monsieur Le Boucher,[428] whom I had met in passing in Le Mans and Sablé, seemed suited to the work. I confided in him and found him to be of very good disposition. He assured me that I could count on him. I was deluding myself about his intellectual and moral value, but at that time I was far from possessing the experience that is gained by frequent dealings with people. The fact is that he was to persevere, and although he had to withdraw later on this was only after he had spent three years at Solesmes.

My mind was working away, and I was wondering how I could reverse the problem of the bishop's opposition. Finally, in the first half of January, I thought that I had found the solution. I decided to write in the strictest secrecy to the Holy

---

[428] Julien Le Boucher, ordained priest in 1834. He began his novitiate at Solesmes in 1833 when he was already a deacon, but left in 1836 after a disagreement with Guéranger over quinquennial vows. He later entered the 'Congrégation de Sainte-Croix' and was sent to Algeria. See the archives of the abbey of Saint-Pierre de Solesmes.

Father, informing him of my project and asking him to tell me that it pleased him. In this way I would get one over on the bishop, who was not rejecting the idea, and in his submission to the Holy See would even be glad to obey without incurring any responsibility. In my complete simplicity, I could think of no better way to proceed than to send the letter to Monsieur de Montalembert, who was in Rome with Fr de La Mennais, asking him to present it to the Holy Father.

I began to write this letter immediately and dated it 18 January, the feast of the Chair of St Peter in Rome.[429] There is no need for me to add that I accompanied this effort with the most fervent prayer for its success. God granted my prayer by not allowing the good bishop to ever learn of what I had tried to do in order to evade his resistance. Here is the content of my letter: *Beatissime Pater* ...[430]

While this letter was making its way to Rome under the cover of Monsieur de Montalembert, I was invited by the Visitation nuns to preach the panegyric for St Francis de Sales in their church on 29 January.[431] On the appointed day, I gave this discourse, which was appreciated by the nuns of this monastery and which inaugurated my ever closer and fruitful dealings with them.

I was continuing to study assiduously, and was especially occupied with the book I had planned about the reform and renewal of ecclesiastical studies. I was not to finish this work, but its preparation was very interesting for me and gave a focus to my activity. Finally, I received a first letter from Monsieur de Montalembert in reply to my message. It was dated 9 February and, after informing me of the obstacles that Fr de La Mennais

---

[429] At the time when Guéranger was writing, the feast of St Peter in Rome was kept on 18 January. The ancient date for this feast (22 February) was kept as the feast of St Peter in Antioch, recalling the fact that St Peter went to Antioch during the first years of the spread of Christianity beyond Palestine. The current Roman calendar has restored the feast of St Peter in Rome to its ancient date of 22 February and suppressed the feast of St Peter in Antioch.

[430] See the appendix on p. 245 for the Latin text followed by an English translation.

[431] His feast day was formerly 29 January but is now 24 January.

and his companions were encountering from the French and Russian ambassadors to the Holy See, Monsieur de Montalembert told me that he had delivered my book entitled *L'Élection des Évêques* to Cardinal Pacca,[432] as well as the letter presenting the book in homage to the pope; His Eminence had agreed to take charge of presenting both of them to the Holy Father. He had taken the trouble to read the book and had been satisfied with it. This was to no purpose, however, since the Holy See ended up accepting the episcopal nominations presented by the July government. This was an acknowledgement that the Concordat of 1801 still existed, and that the serious change introduced in the constitutional *Charte* in 1830 had not changed any of the rights of patronage of the head of state over the bishops. It followed that I could not expect to receive much sympathy from Cardinal Lambruschini,[433] Gregory XVI's secretary of state, when my great plan was submitted to him.

Monsieur de Montalembert thought it inopportune to speak about the matter to Cardinal Pacca straight away, although His Eminence was kindly disposed towards my book and to my first letter. He wanted to sound things out beforehand, so as not to jeopardize anything. While he was waiting he told Fr Ventura,[434] the superior general of the Theatins,[435] about my project, who replied that the Roman court at that time enjoyed so little freedom of activity that it

---

[432] Bartolomeo Pacca (1756–1844), Italian statesman; apostolic nuncio in Cologne and then Lisbon. Made cardinal in 1808, he became pro-secretary of state in 1808. See Larousse, *op. cit.,* v. 12, pp. 3–4.

[433] Luigi Lambruschini (1776–1854), Italian statesman. He became bishop of Sabina, archbishop of Genoa, papal nuncio in Paris, and was appointed cardinal in 1831. See Larousse, *op. cit.,* v. 10, p. 112.

[434] G.-D. Joachim Ventura (1792–1861), Italian preacher and theologian. He became superior general of his order in 1824. For further information, see Larousse, *op. cit.,* v. 15, p. 874.

[435] Theatins (order of clerks regular), founded in Rome in 1524 by St Gaétan de Thienne and three companions. Their aim was to reform the Church via the sanctification of the clergy, and they were especially devoted to preaching and working with the poor and the sick. A French foundation was made in Paris in 1648. For further information, see Jacquemet, *op. cit.,* v. 14, pp. 958–9.

would not venture a single written word about such matters unless it was via the recognized and diplomatic channel of official powers. The time was therefore not ripe to count on any support from Rome for the re-establishment of a religious order in France.

A new letter that Monsieur de Montalembert wrote to me from Monte Cassino, dated 30 April, revealed the outcome of this matter and confirmed the futility of my attempt. He told me that around the end of March he had got in touch with Dom Vincent Bini, the abbot of St Paul's[436] and, after convincing him that my project had no connection with Fr de La Mennais', had obtained reassurances that it would be considered favourably. Bini had even invited him to dinner with the community at St Paul's. At this meeting, Monsieur de Montalembert had encountered a great deal of sympathy for my project among the young religious, but at the same time not much interest among the seniors, who kept on stressing the recent destruction of the abbey of Melleray.[437] Nevertheless, Bini promised his support with the Congregation of Bishops and Regulars, in the event of Cardinal Lambruschini considering the project after he had been informed of it.

---

[436] The Benedictine monastery of St Paul-outside-the-walls in Rome. It was restored by Gregory II in 714, became a Cluniac house around 950, and joined the Cassinese Congregation in 1425. See Cottineau, *op. cit.,* v. 2, p. 2521.

[437] On 28 September 1831, the monks of Melleray were the object of an expulsion order on the grounds that their religious association was illegal. Although this was technically true, the order was in reality motivated partly by the political sympathies for the Bourbon family of their abbot, Antoine Saulnier de Beauregard, and partly by the jealousy of local tradesmen against competition from the flourishing monastic industries at the abbey. In November 1831 the monks were expelled, and approximately seventy Irish and English monks were sent back to their respective countries. These expelled monks founded the abbeys of Mount Melleray in Ireland and Mount Saint Bernard in England. Nevertheless, Dom Antoine and a group of about thirty elderly French monks soon returned to Melleray and resumed some form of discreet monastic life. For further information, see Michaud, *op. cit.,* v. 38, pp. 47–50.

Monsieur de Montalembert could not and would not seek
to have dealings with His Eminence, who was hostile to both
him and Fr de La Mennais, and who was under the influence
of the Russian and French diplomatic service. He therefore
fell back on the excellent Cardinal Pacca, who was very interested in the matter. He promised his assistance provided that
Lambruschini was also favourable, which was far from
hopeful. On this occasion, Pacca told Monsieur de
Montalembert that the pope had received my book kindly
but had announced his decision not to read it. This was
because such a book was a protest against the position he
had just taken by accepting the bishops appointed by Louis-
Philippe. Some time afterwards, Monsieur de Montalembert
learnt via Fr Bini that, on being informed of my project,
Lambruschini had definitely rejected the idea of getting the
pope to intervene, even very indirectly, in its execution. His
Eminence regarded it as an imprudent and vain attempt, and
had given the pope to understand that the slightest sign of
encouragement given to me would jeopardize his position in
the eyes of the government, and that he should therefore be
very careful.

Such was Fr Bini's report to Monsieur de Montalembert,
who wanted to accomplish the mission with which I had
entrusted him. He returned to see the kindly Cardinal Pacca
and finally delivered my letter addressed to the Holy Father,
asking the cardinal to give it to him himself. His Eminence,
who had already told Gregory XVI about this letter, promised
to deliver it and also to inform Monsieur de Montalembert of
the reception that it received. It was not received favourably,
and indeed it could not be, given the scale of the moral weakness that then characterized the Roman court. My first dealings with Rome were thus marked by powerlessness, and
such was the failure that Pacca, who was a much stronger
character than those around the poor pope, withdrew into a
deep silence towards Monsieur de Montalembert, as though
after an unsuccessful business venture.

I received this distressing news in the first half of May, and
found myself helpless in the face of the deadline that the
bishop had imposed on me. I transmitted this news to Fr

Fonteinne, who still had Monsieur Salmon on his hands. In order to explain the delay in reaching a deal, he ventured to tell him that the person concerned had wanted to consult the pope about the planned establishment at Solesmes, and that the reply was not forthcoming on account of the customary slowness of the Roman court. During this time there was an increasing risk that Solesmes would be sold to someone else, and even demolished. Monsieur Huet came again; other buyers attracted by the advertisement, which was republished from time to time in the newspapers, were also making offers. It was at this time that Victor Hugo,[438] who had demonstrated in *Notre-Dame de Paris* that he was an amateur Christian art enthusiast, was gathering information about the building of Solesmes and had the vague desire to buy it.

These cruel uncertainties made me rethink the whole thing. I would not give up on an idea that I felt to come from God, but I began to think that the Benedictines might be better established in Le Mans. Fr Heurtebize encouraged this idea, as well as giving me more than a hope that he would join us. I was still confident that the bishop's inertia would give way at any time. He welcomed Fr Moreau's project to found a secular Congregation, and yet Fr Moreau was considered to be just as much, if not more than me, a partisan of doctrines that were still awaiting pronouncement from the Holy See.

---

[438] Victor-Marie Hugo (1802–1885), a writer who was at the forefront of the Romantic movement. His historical novel *Notre-Dame de Paris* was published in 1831. For further information, see Prevost et d'Amat, *op. cit.*, v. 17, pp. 1453–9.

The Précigné Episode

In this situation, my project was still as dear to me as ever; I was waiting patiently on events and God was holding Solesmes for me. I was to experience several jolts in a row, after which God's hand would show itself unmistakably.

The first blow was with regard to the Legitimist uprising that had suddenly weakened several *départements* in the West, notably the territory comprising the diocese of Le Mans.[439] The conduct of some clerics in La Sarthe and La Mayenne was very imprudent. They hired men for the uprising, and their attitude in these circumstances had been more or less sustained by the belief that they matched the quite openly expressed Legitimist feelings professed by Bishop Carron. The prelate was in Laval[440] when the uprising in the *département* of La Sarthe was alarming the government. He was told not to leave the town, which was under siege, as was the whole *département* of La Mayenne.

At the same time, visits to private homes were taking place, especially to the homes of several clerics. The town of Sablé was very worked up by its extreme loathing for the Chouans. The bourgeoisie at this time were even more stupid than

---

[439] An unsuccessful attempt at a Bourbon Restoration mounted by the duchesse de Berry in 1832. The duchesse was eventually arrested at Nantes in the same year, having spent several months in hiding. See *Les Dates*, p. 157.

[440] The *département* of La Mayenne was then part of the diocese of Le Mans.

they are today. Men were riding through the countryside with their hunting rifles, with the idea of bumping into the Chouans and pitting themselves against them. In the midst of this turmoil, Fr Fonteinne received a visit at the presbytery from Monsieur Pillerault,[441] the Justice of the Peace, who summoned him in the name of the law to hand over his papers and correspondence. Fr Fonteinne owed this visit to the foolishness of the Sablé bourgeoisie who, on hearing that he felt more strongly than other priests in Sablé and being unable to understand the school of Fr de La Mennais, had taken *L'Avenir* to be a Legitimist newspaper. If they had gone to the trouble of asking Monsieur Cosnard, the most ardent Legitimist in Sablé, for information then they would have heard angry anathemas against Fr Fonteinne that would have opened their eyes.

Monsieur Pillerault, who was second to none in his praise of the Orléanists, took a file of correspondence containing my letters from Fr Fonteinne's house. He found them to be very mysterious, but was especially struck by two terms that he could not fathom. I kept on talking about 'Monsieur What's-his-name' and a certain 'little place'. These innocent terms referred quite simply to 'Monsieur Salmon' and the 'priory of Solesmes'. After racking his brains in vain, the worthy Justice of the Peace thought that he had got hold of the outlines of a conspiracy. He went to Fr Fonteinne's house and demanded to know officially the identity of 'Monsieur What's-his-name' and the 'little place'. Fr Fonteinne replied that he could not explain these letters from a friend, who had written as he had thought fit. Monsieur Pillerault declared the correspondence to be suspicious. One of the letters, where the use of 'Monsieur What's-his-name' and 'little place' seemed particularly mysterious to him, was sent to the public prosecutor's office in La Flèche. Soon afterwards, it was returned from there safe and sound and unexplained.

This was simply amusing, but at that very moment events

---

[441] Auguste Pillerault (1797–1882), qualified in law and worked as a solicitor in Pontvallain (1824–1830). He served as Justice of the Peace for the canton of Sablé from 1830–1868. See the departmental archives of La Sarthe.

of the utmost gravity were taking place in the minor seminary of Précigné. The vice-rector of the establishment, Fr Bouttier,[442] who later became the rector and who was an extremely virtuous man, was a Legitimist to the hilt. He had really fired up the pupils, and most of the teachers were just as fanatical. People talked of nothing but the Chouannerie, and the only thing the pupils from the senior classes wanted to do was to take up their muskets and answer the call of the duchesse de Berry. Meanwhile they were practising during their walks, using sticks instead of rifles. One day, the foolishness of these young people, aided by the imprudence of their leaders, drove them to remove the tricolour flag sported from the Pincé steeple. The Legitimists from Le Mans made frequent visits to the seminary, visiting both the Tessé and Saint-Vincent,[443] and the conversations were aimed at recruitment.

The vicar general, Fr Bouvier, was carrying the burden of the administration on his own at this critical time. The bishop was interned in Laval on account of his political sympathies, but the vicar general had found a way to be on the best of terms with the prefect of La Sarthe, Monsieur Tourangin.[444] This was a smart move, and it earned Fr Bouvier the favour of the government. It could also be said that it was a wise and pastoral gesture since the Legitimist attempts could not but end in their own defeat. Furthermore, by trying to compromise the clergy in a lost cause, they were making themselves culpable before God and his Church. Fr Bouvier went to the

---

[442] Thomas Bouttier (1805–1894), taught in the minor seminary before his ordination and became its vice-rector in 1832. He became the rector in 1845, when he was also appointed an honorary canon of Le Mans. He was chaplain to the Little Sisters of Jesus in Précigné when he died. See *Le Chapitre*, pp. 73, 159.

[443] The major seminary, which was founded in 1815 in the buildings of the former Benedictine abbey in the Congregation of Saint-Maur. For further information, see Charles, *op. cit.*, pp. 59–61.

[444] Denis-Victor Tourangin (1788–1880), studied law and became a lawyer in Bourges in 1814; he served as prefect of La Sarthe (1830–1833). See R. Plessix, 'Les Préfets et les Sous-Préfets de La Sarthe – 1800–2000', in *La Province du Maine*, 18 (2005): 171–383, esp. 207–8.

Tessé and told the pupils that he would denounce and hand over to the authorities the first one of them who showed signs of unrest; he spoke in similar terms at Saint-Vincent. The bishop must have been displeased to learn of this initiative from his vicar general; Fr Bouvier, however, considered himself as entrusted with some sort of tyranny derived from the urgency of the situation.

Suddenly (we were in June), a letter from Fr Bellenfant, the rector of Précigné, informed him that the authorities had raided the minor seminary.[445] He said that the police had taken all the professors and lecturers and detained them at La Flèche; he also said that he would already have suffered the same fate if, in the interests of the pupils and their families, he had not asked for sufficient delay to write to the bishop's palace and hand over the house to the ecclesiastical authorities. After receiving this letter, Fr Bouvier sent someone into town to fetch me. Summoning Fr Heurtebize and me into his room, he appealed to our trustworthiness and asked us to leave for Précigné the following morning. He wanted us to examine the moral state of the minor seminary, giving us the power to begin the holidays immediately if we thought that the pupils were too aggravated to resume their classes. He also charged Fr Heurtebize and me to stay on as rector and vice-rector respectively if we thought it best to keep the house going until the usual holiday period.

We were both taken aback at receiving such a mandate, but the situation was so critical that there was no question of refusing. Fear that such an abrupt change of position would have unforeseen consequences for me was something that troubled me greatly. My plans could be turned completely on their head, and I wished with my whole heart that the situation at Précigné was such that there would be nothing for us to do other than to show up and return the following day. I

---

[445] The minor seminary of Précigné was raided on 3 June 1832 by the president of the tribunal of La Flèche, two divisions of infantrymen and about a dozen policemen. They claimed that guns and gunpowder were hidden in the house and proceeded to dissolve the house and imprison the academic staff. This was a false claim. See F. Pichon, *Essai Historique sur les séminaires du Mans, 1802–1875,* Le Mans, 1879, pp. 178–80.

entrusted Solesmes to God, and Fr Heurtebize and I arranged to meet at 5.00 a.m. the following morning. Fr Bouvier had arranged for a coach to be made ready for us, and had procured a pass for us from the prefecture; this is because we would need to pass through several towns that had been authorized to take up arms in order to oppose the uprising.

We left as planned the following day, and as early as Le Grand Saint-Georges[446] we were stopped by the National Guard and led to the post. The peasants hardly seemed to take any notice of our pass. In Saint-Léonard[447] they stopped our horses by crossing their bayonets in front of them. In Chemiré-le-Gaudin[448] and Fercé[449] the welcome was scarcely any better. At Noyen[450] we were led into an old church that was being used as a market and shown into the attic (which had been transformed into a room), where three town councillors were sitting. The walls of this vile hovel were plastered with old rifles and rusty swords. We were received with suspicion, but the prefect's pass was enough to ensure that we suffered no violence. We were asked what we were planning to do in the town, to which we replied that we were going to say Mass. We took our leave and went to the parish church, where we found the parish priest; he informed us of his unpleasant situation at this time of unrest. He took us to have lunch in the presbytery after we had celebrated our Masses. We were barely halfway through the meal, when a fusilier appeared in the dining room to tell us that the town councillors were requesting us to leave the town as soon as possible. This strong message was soon followed by a second, and then by a third that was even more insistent.

[446] Saint-Georges-du-Plain, a commune 9km from Le Mans. See Charles, *op. cit.,* p. 374.

[447] Saint-Léonard-des-Bois, a commune in the canton of Fresnay, 50km from Le Mans. *Ibid.,* p. 379.

[448] A commune in the canton of La Suze, 20km from Le Mans. *Ibid.,* pp. 314–15.

[449] A commune in the canton of Brûlon, 23km from Le Mans. *Ibid.,* p. 331.

[450] A commune in the canton of Malicorne, 30km from Le Mans. *Ibid.,* p. 359. Its name changed to Noyen-sur-Sarthe in 1962.

After the third message we got into our coach, in spite of the polite pleas of the parish priest, whom we did not want to get into trouble by our presence.

From Noyen to Sablé we were not stopped by the National Guard, but after Parcé[451] we encountered a squad of front-line troops who jeered at us rudely, but confined their insolence to this. We thought that we ought not to get out of the coach while crossing Sablé, and went straight to the minor seminary of Précigné. The rector was waiting for us, and the prefecture had informed the mayor.

Firstly we listened to Fr Bellenfant's report, which recounted the scenes that had taken place; he told us that he was awaiting our arrival in order to go to prison. He gave an eloquent account of the violent frame of mind of the young people, of the concern of the families who had come from all over to collect their children, and of the impossibility of re-establishing sufficient order in the house to resume lessons. We remained silent and told the good rector that we planned to visit the mayor, Monsieur Rigault,[452] who had asked us most insistently to visit his home. A new scene awaited us there. Monsieur Rigault had been the enemy of the minor seminary. His avowed Orléanism made the townsfolk think that the misfortune afflicting the establishment was due to his activities. Sending the pupils home more than two months before the usual time would become a source of murmuring among the people, who were to be defrauded of the profit they would have made in what was to become a barren period for them. Monsieur Rigault was as eloquent in demonstrating that the academic year should be continued as had been Fr Bellenfant in begging us to begin the holidays straight away. Madame Rigault went one better than her husband, and did not skimp on complimenting us so as to ensure the success of his plea. After listening to everything,

---

[451] A commune in the canton of Sablé, 38km from Le Mans. *Ibid.*, pp. 360–1. Its name changed to Parcé-sur-Sarthe in 1933.

[452] Louis Rigault (b. 1774), served as mayor of Précigné from 1814–1821. Guéranger appears to be mistaken in recording that Monsieur Rigault was the mayor of Précigné at this time. See the departmental archives of La Sarthe.

we withdrew gracefully and did not let on about our decision.

When we returned to the minor seminary we had supper. The rector kept us company, and pressed us to find out the decision we had made. He did not hide his own opinion and desire, and wanted us to announce the immediate closure of the academic year. It was easy to see that my being entrusted with this mission had confirmed his prejudice that I was planning to supplant him at Précigné. He had no doubt that I had wanted it, and yet God knew what a burden it was for me. We did not think it appropriate to satisfy his eagerness. We told him that we needed to reflect and to consult with one another, and that we would give him a definitive answer the following day. Once we had said this, we took our leave and retired to our room.

When we were alone, it was easy for us to agree on the position to be taken. It was not prudent to revive a house that would inevitably collapse. The harm had been done, and the only thing to do was to let these young people (who had been let loose so foolishly) go off on their holidays. We could also leave, to complete their year of major seminary,[453] the poor students promised to us by Fr Bouvier, as a replacement for the young, scatterbrain teachers who were now atoning for their foolishness at La Flèche.[454] In any case, their incarceration was very soft. They were imprisoned in the presbytery, which was vacant at that time, where they found themselves in the company of the marquis de Juigné[455] and several other decent people, whom the government had the good sense to release along with them after about two weeks of captivity.

The following morning, after celebrating Holy Mass, we informed the rector of our decision over breakfast: namely,

---

[453] Students from the major seminary had been offered as replacement professors in the minor seminary in a bid to keep the academic year open.

[454] A town situated 43km from Le Mans. For further information, see Charles, *op. cit.,* pp. 237–47.

[455] Jacques-Marie-Anatole Le Clerc de Juigné (1788–1845), squadron leader of the National Guard under the Bourbon Restoration and a peer of France from 1826.

after mature reflection, to announce the end of the academic year. He welcomed this decision with obvious satisfaction. Fr Heurtebize then announced it to the young people whom we had assembled, and said that this measure seemed to us entirely satisfactory. Fr Bellenfant told us that he was going to La Flèche during the day and, after bidding him farewell, we got into the coach and rejoined the road to Le Mans, thanking God for having saved us from a situation that neither of us had enjoyed. The return was more peaceful than the outward journey. It is true that we stopped off at the 'auberge du Lion d'Or' so as not to cause any trouble to the good parish priest of Noyen. It was run by a man called Desnois,[456] who was very elderly but who was delighted to put us up, together with our horse and coachman. When we returned to Le Mans, our first priority was to give an account of our mission to Fr Bouvier. He was somewhat annoyed at the decision we had felt obliged to make, but nevertheless agreed that it would have been difficult to act otherwise.

[456] Person currently unidentified.

New Incidents

Just when I was feeling reassured after the worry caused by a mission whose outcome could have been so detrimental to my plans, a new incident brought me another problem. Bishop Carron had finally managed to leave Laval and return to the town of his episcopal see. When he arrived, he held a meeting of his council and filled the vacant posts. On 22 June, Fr Fonteinne received news from the bishop's palace that he had been appointed to the parish of Asnières.[457] This measure was going to distance him from Solesmes, and it could have been a serious setback to our wonderful plans. In being distanced from Sablé, Fr Fonteinne could no longer keep an eye on the situation so directly, or continue his negotiations with Monsieur Salmon. Moreover, if the day were to arrive when the establishment could finally be opened, could anyone be sure that the bishop would willingly give us one of his parish priests, especially just after his installation in a parish? This event troubled me greatly, particularly since it was causing Fr Fonteinne a great deal of anguish. He attributed this abrupt change to the influence of the parish priest of Sablé, whose dealings with him were far from praiseworthy.

Another incident soon complicated the situation. Fr Mortreux,[458] the chaplain to the Visitation monastery in Le

---

[457] A commune in the canton of Sablé, 39km from Le Mans. See Charles, *op. cit.,* p. 302. Its name changed to Asnières-sur-Vègre in 1936.

[458] Pierre-Joseph Mortreux (1802–1866), ordained priest in 1825; vice-rector of the minor seminary at Précigné (1824–1830); parish priest of

Mans, had just been appointed to the parish of Bouère.[459] Fr
Bouvier thought of suggesting my name to the bishop for
this post of chaplain, and put forward the particular advantages for me of such a position: I would remain in Le Mans
with my family, and this ministry would leave me with spare
time for study. If I were to accept it, I would have to give up
my beloved plans. As Fr Bouvier replied, however, were
these plans feasible? In speaking like this, Fr Bouvier did not
know of the failure I had experienced in Rome, or else he
would have been even more insistent. On the other hand,
what if I were to refuse? I was not being guaranteed anything
by my bishop. I was not focusing on anything else, and was
not even thinking about other difficulties. As I have said, if I
refused and my project did not materialize, I was missing out
on the chance to land myself an enjoyable and advantageous
position. I had not solicited anything, nor had I desired it,
but it had happened to me of its own accord. Surely this was
God's plan, made clear when Fr Fonteinne left Sablé?

The divine goodness did not keep me in suspense for long.
It was July, and the prisoners of La Flèche had been freed. One
of them, Fr Boulangé,[460] had returned to his family in Le Mans.
Out of courtesy to the Visitation monastery, Fr Bouvier
thought (and the bishop agreed with him) that it would be a
good idea to offer two candidates to the nuns, and I was therefore joined by Fr Boulangé in this interview. The community
turned me down as being too young and asked for Fr
Boulangé, who was a year younger than me. It is true that,
exteriorly, I looked even younger than I was. This providential
solution settled my course for ever; I saw in it the will of God
and it was not difficult for me to pick up my plans again, which
had never really been broken off by this strange incident.

Clermont (1830–1833); parish priest of Bouère (1833–1866). See the
archives of the diocese of Le Mans.

[459] A commune in the canton of Grez-en-Bouère, 18km from Château-
Gontier. See Joanne, *op. cit.,* v. I, p. 529.

[460] Théodore Boulangé (1806–1883), ordained priest in 1829; made an
honorary canon of Limoges in 1843 and of Le Mans in 1858. For further
information, see *Le Chapitre,* pp. 96, 139.

The seminary holidays were imminent. Fr Heurtebize suggested that I speak about the Solesmes project to two seminarians whom he thought quite suited to the work. One of them was called Audruger[461] and the other Daigremont.[462] They did not seem able to understand the project, and still less to dedicate themselves to it, so my efforts on that score came to nothing. On the other hand, I saw Fr Bouvier, who was still interested in the project. In my distress, I felt trapped in a dead end. I asked Fr Bouvier if he would agree to give the bishop a report that I would write to explain my motives for wanting to re-establish the Benedictines. I also wanted him to urge the bishop to grant the much sought permission. Fr Bouvier agreed to take on the role of private advocate in this matter, and I began composing the report immediately. I completed it, but it was not presented due to circumstances that rendered it useless and even superfluous.

August came around; I left Le Mans and went to Asnières and the home of Fr Fonteinne, who very much wanted to see me. We spent a happy week together, during which we talked about Solesmes almost constantly. We were not full of hope, but neither were we disheartened. The providential moment was approaching, but it was still hidden from us. As for firm candidates, I was assured only of Fr Fonteinne and Monsieur Le Boucher. Solesmes could have been bought at any moment by some bidder or other, and I did not have a penny to buy it myself.

After spending several weeks in Le Mans, I agreed to make a trip to Angers to make the acquaintance of a very distinguished priest whom I had often heard recommended by Fr Morel, an honorary canon[463] and my old college friend. This

---

[461] Firmin-Léon de La Motte Audruger (b. 1809), parish priest of Niafle in the diocese of Le Mans (1852–1867). See Angot, *op. cit.*, v. 3, p. 165.

[462] Léandre Daigremont (1804–1878), ordained priest in 1829; curate at Saint-Germain-les-Fouilloux; chaplain of the hospice in Craon; parish priest of Saint-Erblon and Beaulieu. He did later enter Solesmes and made profession in 1868. See the archives of the abbey of Saint-Pierre de Solesmes.

[463] There is no mention in the archives of the diocese of Angers of Fr Jules Morel being an honorary canon.

priest was called Banchereau[464] and was parish priest of Montreuil-Belfroy near Angers.[465] He had been entrusted with several seminarians, to whom he taught theology in his presbytery. I found in him great devotion combined with perfect understanding of theological matters, and also a commitment to Roman doctrines that was as enlightened as it was profound. We became friends and I told him about my plans. He was taken with them, and gave me some hope that he would join us. After my departure, a regular correspondence developed between us.

After spending several days with Fr Banchereau, I returned to Angers and the home of Fr Morel, who put me up. It was there that I read the famous encyclical of Gregory XVI, *Mirari vos*, which had been published in Rome on 15 August, and which reached France via the newspapers for September. Immediately, I realized that several paragraphs of this vast document were dealing with Fr de La Mennais and his school, even though it included no names. I did not have to make much of a sacrifice in the light of this decision, which was fighting against doctrines for which I had little attraction and which I had even fought against myself, although I had excused certain applications of these theories. I was truly glad to give complete assent to the teachings of the Holy See, which were finally being explained.

Having fulfilled my Catholic duty of submission insofar as I was bound, I thought that such an event would either jeopardize my project or work to its advantage. After imploring God's help, I thought that I should write immediately to Bishop Carron from Angers. I reminded him of the reason for the delay he had imposed on me: the fear he had expressed of appearing to be getting involved with the school of Fr de La Mennais by approving an association that many people would find suspicious, on account of my connection with

---

[464] Joseph Banchereau (1790–1839), ordained priest in 1820; appointed chaplain to deaf-and-dumb Catholics in Angers; became parish priest of Montreuil-Belfroy in 1824. See the archives of the diocese of Angers.

[465] A commune about 8km from Angers. For further information, see Port, *op. cit.*, v. 2, p. 718.

him. I then pointed out to the prelate that since he wanted to re-establish unity with regard to what was the object of so many controversies, the time had come when his wish was to be granted. Furthermore, I said that the encyclical would bring about peace through the submission that it demanded. I said that I welcomed the encyclical from the depths of my heart, and that none of those who had lost could be sorry about a defeat that was re-establishing peace in human hearts.

A few days after my return to Le Mans I received the prelate's reply, dated from Laval. It was couched in very friendly terms. The prelate was delighted with the solution that Rome had just given to the questions referred to its tribunal. He congratulated me for the sentiments I had expressed with regard to the encyclical, and ended by telling me that he would be willing to listen to my plans when he got back to Le Mans.

This was a big step forward. The crisis provoked by the apostolic judgement was bringing about the founding of Solesmes, which could not be anything other than an institution devoted to the Holy See. After a year of trials, I was coming into port. I shared this happy news with Fr Fonteinne straight away, and he was as delighted about it as I was.

View of the priory of Solesmes from a distance in 1833 (anonymous nineteenth-century pencil drawing).

Two views of the priory church of Solesmes in 1833 (anonymous nineteenth-century pencil drawings).

9 février 1860.

Facsimile of the opening page of Guéranger's autobiography.

1833 194

Facsimile of a page of Guéranger's autobiography – the first part of
a letter to Guéranger from Dom Claude Perrot, monk of Eiseldeln.

Facsimile of a page of Guéranger's autobiography – describing some of the Roman liturgical customs observed at Solesmes.

Elaboration of the Constitutions and Approval by the Bishop of Le Mans

The time had come to think about drawing up a body of rules for the association, so as to be in a position to present it for the bishop's approval should my negotiations prove successful. I had already been reflecting for a long time on the form of life that could appropriately be established at Solesmes, and had decided on the fundamental points. These were to organize the conventual observances according to the spirit of the Rule of St Benedict, so as to get through the trial period without the influence of other ideas, and to prepare for the future by assimilating everything essential to a Benedictine institute. I asked for God's help, and then started to write on loose sheets of paper. I confided my plan to Fr Boulangé, who had been successful against me at the Visitation monastery and who felt very drawn to Solesmes. He was willing to transcribe the articles into the notebook that would be submitted for the bishop's approval.

This collection of rules was therefore drawn up with the idea of gradually leading those who followed them into the practise of the Rule of St Benedict, allowing for certain modifications of form required by current customs and the circumstances of the times. In principle, I proclaimed that the Patriarch of Western monasticism would be the patron of the association. His Rule would be read in public every day at Solesmes and, as far as the prescribed observances were concerned, I had decided on the following form: The divine office celebrated in choir in its entirety, according to the Roman rite. Since we were not yet Benedictines, we did not have the right to use the monastic office, but the adoption of the Roman liturgy would already set us apart from the diocese. There would be abstinence during Advent, on Wednesdays throughout the year, on Mondays from 14 September and also on the vigils of certain solemnities; there would be fasting on the Wednesdays and Fridays of Advent, and on Fridays from 14 September; Matins at 4.30 a.m. in summer, and after Compline in winter; for a habit, the cassock without bands[466] and the cincture; in choir the Roman surplice, with a black, hooded cloak over this in winter; work focused mainly on study; reading in the refectory and serving at table for a week in turn; strict silence during the night; during the day (outside of recreation) permission required to speak for more than five minutes; a weekly walk between lunch and Vespers, except in Advent and Lent; an hour of recreation after lunch and supper, except on Fridays in Lent and on Ash Wednesday; a spiritual conference every day.

In essence, this was the level of observance that I thought could be imposed on the life of the new aspirants to Benedictine life. All of the conventual observances in the Rule of St Benedict were included, albeit in mitigated form, and the mind of the holy legislator could be understood and appreciated in the daily public reading of his direct teachings. Four years later, this collection of rules was presented to the Holy See, with very slight modifications, and obtained apostolic approval. Nevertheless, two things were missing: perpetual abstinence from meat and the night office. It seemed to me that recruitment to the association would be impossible if this double condition was not modified. Subsequent events have shown that most of the candidates whom the Spirit of God has led to Solesmes would not have been able to persevere in their vocation if the abstinence had not been mitigated, and if they had been obliged to break their sleep

---

[466] Two strips of cloth (usually black and edged with white) that hung from the front of the collar, and which were formerly worn by Catholic clerics. They were gradually replaced by the white Roman collar that is worn by Catholic clerics today.

during the night for Matins. Nevertheless, I am conscious of the weight of responsibility that I bear before the divine majesty in settling these major questions, and I beg God to forgive my temerity in his merciful knowledge of my weakness and lack of virtue, and also of the need I had to organize the new institute using something that is in itself as ancient as it is venerable.

We soon encountered a new cause for concern. One day during October, Fr Fonteinne was travelling from Asnières to Sablé and, casting his eyes over the monastery, he noticed that demolition work had begun. He went onto the site and saw that the bakery buildings and the chapterhouse that overlooked the cloister had been knocked down, and that men were in the process of tackling the vaults on this side of the cloister. He made enquiries and learnt that the uncertainty shown to Monsieur Salmon with regard to the acquisition, as well as the limited success of the advertisement in the papers, had led Monsieur La Fautrardière to ask his co-owners to demolish the house. Monsieur La Fautrardière had only tied up 3,000 francs in the acquisition of Solesmes, whose purchase price had risen to 32,000 francs. He lamented the block on his funds, however, and had finally managed to get his shareholders to begin this odious work of destruction; these men hoped to recover their stake via the sale of materials. Firstly, it had been decided to tackle the section of the cloister leading into the chapterhouse and the bakery; the hammer would then be turned on the church, knocking down the nave and the tower before stopping temporarily before the transept, whose chapels with their sculptures would be saved for a new campaign. Lastly, the conventual building itself would be tackled if buyers had not been found.

It was time to act and press ahead, but what could be done while the bishop was absent from Le Mans? He was expected to return at the beginning of October, but on 1 November he had still not arrived. One of his sisters, who had come from Rennes to see him in Laval, had become seriously ill during her stay and the prelate had not wanted to abandon her. This lady had only just begun to convalesce when the chambermaid who had been looking after her was struck by the same illness. This meant that the mistress of the house was waiting for her servant to get better, and the prelate, who wanted to return to Le Mans with his sister, was detained indefinitely. He finally arrived in Le Mans a few days after All Saints' day. As soon as I had been informed of this, I thought of visiting him to ask for the benefit of the promise he had made to me when he replied to my letter from Angers.

On Thursday 8 November, after entrusting myself to St Benedict and St Scholastica, I had an audience with the prelate. I had visited him in his drawing room the previous day, and knew that he had passed on my letter and talked about his response during the first council meeting he had held on his return. I brought up the question straight away, reminding him of his commitment to listen to me favourably, and told him that Solesmes was being demolished. On hearing this news, he quickly told me that I should run and stop the hammer blows and pursue the negotiations, as I had planned to do. He then asked who my collaborators were. Firstly, I mentioned Fr Boulangé. The bishop objected that he had agreed to be posted to the Visitation monastery. I replied that he had only done this because the project had been postponed somewhat indefinitely, and that in the uncertainty he needed to take up a post. Moreover, the Visitation nuns were aware of his intentions. The prelate agreed to give me Fr Boulangé, but not with good grace.

I then mentioned Fr Fonteinne. This surprised the bishop even more. I knew that he had seen a letter from Mademoiselle Manette Cosnard to Fr Bouvier, in which she had harsh words to say about the appointment of Fr Fonteinne to the parish of Asnières. The bishop added that Fr Fonteinne did not have a very good relationship with the parish priest of Sablé, and that the Cosnard ladies thought Fr Fonteinne was causing him trouble. I tried to re-establish the facts, and the bishop then asked me what I would do with Fr Fonteinne. I replied firmly that I would make him the monastic cellarer, a job for which he possessed rare qualities. This candidate was given to me. I then spoke about Fr

Daubrée,[467] Fr Banchereau and Monsieur Le Boucher, ending my visit by telling the prelate that I would come back two days later to present the constitutions of the new monastery for his approval. He agreed with this plan, and I felt happy when I left him.

I wrote to Fr Fonteinne straight away, asking him to visit Monsieur Salmon and tell him that plans for the acquisition were at last underway and that the demolition should be stopped. At the same time, I got Fr Boulangé to complete the transcription of the constitutions. Everything was summed up in 149 Latin articles, and I had an audience with the prelate on 10 November, who received me with the same kindness. He promised that he would read this manuscript carefully, and indicated a day in the near future when he would receive me. I informed him of one of Fr Fonteinne's ideas, who had thought that a letter from the prelate to the marquis de La Porte de Ryan,[468] the owner of the château in Sablé, might induce him to make a sizeable offering for the future establishment at Solesmes. Fr Fonteinne was resting his hope on the marquis' previous gesture at the bishop's request: a gift of 10,000 francs to the *Bureau de Charité*[469] in Sablé. The prelate told me that he did not think it appropriate for him to get personally involved to this extent. If Fr Fonteinne wanted to write to the marquis de Ryan, however, then the bishop was giving him permission to exploit the episcopal approval given to the work, and said that as bishop he would be willing to give a very favourable report should the marquis call on him to do so.

---

[467] Léon Daubrée entered Solesmes in July 1833 but left five or six months later. See the archives of the abbey of Saint-Pierre de Solesmes.

[468] Guy-François-Henri Porte de Ryan (or Riant), the marquis de Sablé, assumed ownership of the lands around Sablé in 1808. See R. de Linière, *Armorial de La Sarthe*, v. 1, Le Mans, 1948, p. 347.

[469] The *Bureaux de Charité* were created in 1796, each consisting of five members appointed by the minister of the interior, charged with distributing public financial assistance given to the local population. There was a *Bureau de Charité* in each canton, and several of the larger communes also had one. *See Annuaire du département de La Sarthe 1824–1825*, Le Mans, 1824, p. 193.

I conveyed this news to Fr Fonteinne, urging him to write directly to the marquis de Ryan and to go and see Monsieur Salmon. He duly saw him, and they both went to Solesmes. Fr Fonteinne said that the offer was serious and severely reprimanded the demolition, to such an extent that Monsieur Salmon stopped the workers on the spot. Nothing was firmly decided during this conversation, in which both of them sounded one another out.

At Fr Fonteinne's request, I had written the draft of the letter that he was to write to the marquis de Ryan. He sent the letter, and soon received the reply in the marquise's hand, although it was signed only by her husband. It did not grant anything, spoke snidely about the plan to open a monastery in Solesmes, and used as an excuse the charitable works to be carried out in the region of Nogent-le-Rotrou,[470] which were absorbing all his resources. It was the first disappointment in this realm, which was followed by many others. When God is moving things forwards, however, nothing can stop them.

I wrote directly to Monsieur de Chateaubriand, although I was not expecting any direct assistance from him since I was well aware that his business affairs were in a bad state. I reminded him of what he had said in the preface to his *Études historiques* about the work of the Benedictines and the need to re-establish this school.[471] I informed him of the plan for Solesmes, and asked him straight out if he would not think it beneath him to bring out a brochure about this since he knew how to produce them. I also asked him if he would be generous enough to devote the proceeds to a work that was so bold as to count on his sympathy.

[470] A commune in the Eure-et-Loire region. See Joanne, *op. cit.*, v. V, pp. 2985–6.

[471] 'Let us first pay resounding homage to this school of the Benedictines, which will never be replaced by anything else. If I was not now a stranger in the land that witnessed my birth, and if I had the right to suggest something, I would be so bold as to request the re-establishment of an order that so deserved its renown. I would like to see revived the Congregation of Saint-Maur in the abbey of Saint-Denis.' See F.-R. Chateaubriand, preface to *Études historiques* (1831) in *Oeuvres complètes* Paris, 1836, v. 4, pp. 17–18.

He sent a kind reply, but did not give me what I asked for. I later published it, although I cut some lines. I give it here in its entirety:

Paris, 11 October 1832

Dear Father,

Your letter sent to Geneva was forwarded to me in Paris, and reached me when I was ill. I still cannot write myself, so I am dictating a few random words to express both my gratitude for your confidence in me, and also my good wishes for your planned work. I do not, however, have a penny to my name and although I have both rich and poor friends, the former would not give me anything and the latter would have nothing to give me. I too have dreamt of re-establishing the Benedictines and I wanted to locate the restored Congregation at Saint-Denis, with its empty tombs and empty library. Time alone would not have failed to fill the tombs, and I would have relied on the work of my new Mabillon[472] to fill the library. Nevertheless, man proposes and God disposes; my dreams are passing away like my life, which will soon be over. Since you are young, make your dreams better than mine. Since we are both Christians we shall in God's good time reach the all-knowing Eternity, which is the only unchanging reality. There we will find the Benedictines of old to be much more learned than they were on earth. This is because they were men of virtue as well as learning, and they now see the origin of things and the antiquity of the universe with their own eyes.

I ask you to include me in the company of the honorary

---

[472] Jean Mabillon (1632–1707), a monk of the Congregation of Saint-Maur. After pursuing brilliant studies in rhetoric and literature in Reims, he was clothed in the monastic habit in 1653 at the abbey of Saint-Rémi in Reims. He was ordained priest in 1660, and sent to the abbey of Saint-Germain-des-Prés, Paris in 1664. He travelled extensively in Europe, visiting libraries in order to gather material for his critical editions of the works of St Bernard, St Augustine, and the acts of the Benedictine saints. He was greatly esteemed in literary circles, and became a member of the 'Académie Royale des Inscriptions' in 1701. For further information, see Larousse, *op. cit.*, v. 10, p. 843.

Benedictines of Solesmes. I will find you twenty francs and send it to you at once if you ask me; even forty francs if I really think about it and work out all my resources.

Addictissimus et humillimus Servus
Frater de Chateaubriand, e Neocongregatione Sancti Mauri

I informed Monsieur de Montalembert of the situation. He could not do anything personally, but obtained five hundred francs for me from his friend the marquis de Dreux-Brézé. This was the first money that providence provided me with for the work, and it is only right to honour its memory. At the instigation of Monsieur de Montalembert, Monsieur de Brézé was our first benefactor.

I sent additional letters to various people who might help me, either themselves or via their influence. I appealed to Fr des Genettes, my former parish priest. He was arriving from Fribourg, and had just received the parish of Notre-Dame-des-Victoires. He was as poor as Job; he did not even have a silver cutlery set for his table and was trying to avoid being noticed. He could not promise or give me anything. When I went to Paris the following spring, he put himself out to place two hundred francs into my fund. It was only several years afterwards that the Blessed Virgin raised this venerable priest from his humiliation, showing the merciful power of her Immaculate Heart in the abandoned church of Notre-Dame-des-Victoires.[473]

Monsieur de Cazalès,[474] who was then a layman, took a

---

[473] This church was ransacked during the riots in Paris after the July 1830 Revolution. In 1836 Fr des Genettes founded the 'Archconfraternity of the Blessed and Immaculate Heart of Mary', which earned his church considerable renown and financial assistance.

[474] Edmond-Louis-Marie de Cazalès (1804–1876), studied law and worked as a judge (1827–1829). In 1835 he became professor of literature at the Catholic university of Louvain, but returned to France in 1837. He was ordained priest in Rome in 1843, and co-founded the *Correspondant* in the same year. He became rector of the minor seminary of Nîmes in 1845, and of the major seminary of Montauban in 1847, when he also became honorary vicar general of this diocese. He was elected a *député* for Tarn-et-Garonne in the National Assembly of 1848. He

great interest in the letter that I wrote to him about the work. He was not very rich, but I had been counting on his relatives. His reply was rather discouraging, but he promised to visit Solesmes and wanted to be personally involved in the foundation.

On the advice of the Visitation nuns in Le Mans, I sent a request to a rich English Catholic called Mr Cox,[475] a relative of one of the nuns; this was unsuccessful. I wrote to Fr Coëdro,[476] the superior of the missionaries in Rennes, who had been portrayed to me as being very benevolent towards works like ours, and of having a great deal of influence in his town. He replied that he had no means to help me, despite all his sympathy. Madame de Vaufleury[477] from Laval was full of goodwill, but she could not do anything for the time being.

I made a request to Monsieur Bailly de Surcy,[478] the editor of the *Tribune catholique,*[479] to whom I had sent several

---

became an honorary canon of the dioceses of Versailles and of Perpignan, before being appointed honorary vicar general and a titular canon of Versailles in 1859. See the archives of the diocese of Versailles.

[475] Person currently unidentified.

[476] Pierre-Louis-François Coëdro (1788–1840), ordained priest 1812; became a professor and then vice-rector of the minor seminary in Rennes; parish priest of Montauban from 1818–1823. He was superior of the diocesan missionaries in Rennes (the Congregation of Saint-Méen) from 1821 until his death. He was also vicar general of the diocese of Rennes. See the archives of the diocese of Rennes.

[477] Françoise Berset de Vaufleury, (née Letourneurs-Mouette). See Angot, *op. cit.,* v. 2, p. 679.

[478] Emmanuel Bailly de Surcy (1794–1861), a philosophy teacher who began various educational initiatives for disadvantaged young people in Paris. He founded the Catholic paper *Correspondant* in 1829, which was succeeded by *La Tribune catholique* in 1832. This paper was in turn replaced by *L'Univers catholique* in 1833. Bailly de Surcy founded the first 'Conference of Charity' with six companions on 23 April 1833. This was the beginning of the St Vincent de Paul Society, which was directed by Bailly de Surcy until 1844. See Jacquemet, *op. cit.,* v. 1, p. 1165.

[479] The *Tribune catholique* was a Catholic daily paper launched in January 1832 by Emmanuel Bailly de Surcy, who became its editor. It was intended to unite both liberal and traditionalist Catholics after the collapse of *L'Avenir.* Its moderate position meant that it never attracted a strong following, and it merged with *L'Univers* in October 1833. *Ibid.,* v. 15, p. 328.

articles. He conducted a boarding school in Paris for students of law and medicine, and could be regarded as the father of Christian youth in our day by means of his foundation, the 'Conférences de St-Vincent-de-Paul'. He was far from rich, but when he received the letter I sent him he replied immediately, saying that I could count on him for five hundred francs. The marquis de Régnon,[480] a courageous defender of the freedom of the Church, to whom I wrote in Nantes, told me in his reply that he was placing five hundred francs at my disposal, which I received from his hands the following January.

I am omitting other less substantial donations, which were promised and given during the first months of 1833. The total figure was far from considerable, however, and most of the letters that I wrote during November and December 1832 were without effect. I shall add here that the marquis Anatole de Juigné gave one thousand francs to Fr Fonteinne, and that Fr Bouvier promised me the same sum, which he paid the following spring. All this was not much to start such a great work, but God sustained my trust and I never doubted that we would be successful. I returned to Le Mans, where some significant events took place.

[480] The marquis de Régnon (1795–1863), did much to defend the rights of the Cistercian monks of Melleray when they were forbidden to wear the religious habit and to ring their bells. He was arrested and briefly imprisoned for his actions. See *Revue de Bretagne et de Vendée*, III (1863): 487–8.

Acquisition of the Priory of Solesmes

The time had come to rouse the enthusiasm of the potential friends of the project both near and afar, since the bishop was not very encouraging about the idea of asking for help from the diocese. This was a blessing. It is impossible to be a prophet in one's own country, and later on I came to understand this. On the other hand, Fr Fonteinne could at any time have struck a deal with Monsieur Salmon, and although we had agreed that we needed to begin with a lease this still involved paying out money. We also needed enough money for repair work and for adapting the monastery to our own purposes.

Fr Boulangé talked constantly about my plan to the Visitation nuns, with whom he was cultivating a very good relationship for me, and he told them of the work's need for immediate temporal assistance. Madame de Clanchy[481] (the superior) and I agreed that the monastery would make a novena to the Blessed Virgin to obtain her protection. The novena would begin on 7 December and end on 15 December,

---

[481] Marie-Madeleine de Chantal Clanchy (1769–1840), professed at Blois in 1801. She fulfilled many offices in the community (including assistant infirmarian, sacristan, novice mistress, and bursar), before being elected superior in 1818. After her re-election as superior in 1821, she transferred the community from Blois to Le Mans. She was elected superior of the Visitation monastery in Annecy in 1824, and re-elected in 1827. She was then elected superior of the monastery in Le Mans in 1830, and re-elected in 1833. After another spell as novice mistress, she was again elected superior of the community of Le Mans in 1838. See the archives of the Visitation monastery, Nantes.

the octave day of the Immaculate Conception. This is the mystery for which Mary herself had inspired me with faith and trust.

During the first days of this novena, I was praying in the chapel of the Visitation monastery. Deep within me, I felt called to consecrate the work of re-establishing the Benedictines in France to the Sacred Heart of Jesus, to which I had consecrated myself in the chapel of this monastery on Holy Thursday in 1823. I made a solemn promise to ask the bishop for the favour of Benediction of the Blessed Sacrament in honour of the Sacred Heart on the first Friday of every month when we were established, and to build an altar of the Sacred Heart in our monastery church if we were in a position to continue the work three years after the day of our installation. Let us give thanks to almighty God, who approved the novena and the promise, and who has given tangible signs of the favour he bestowed on me of appreciating, after so much initial resistance, the mysteries of the Heart of Jesus and the Immaculate Conception of the Queen of Heaven.

Fr Fonteinne and I considered that we needed the sum of 6,000 francs to begin; for the time being we had only the five hundred francs of disposable capital from the marquis de Brézé, which I could access as much as I wished. God spoke to the heart of Mademoiselle Manette Cosnard, who with the agreement of her sister Perrette told Fr Fonteinne that we could count on 6,000 francs. She had received this money from her cousin, Monsieur Marçais,[482] a farmer from Vrigné who was also the brother of Madame Gazeau, whom we shall mention later. In view of the modest fortune of the two Cosnard sisters, this offering was very substantial and was extremely significant for us. It served only as the prelude to many more generous gifts from these ladies, and also from their niece Mademoiselle Euphrasie, which meant that the work could get off the ground. The two Cosnard sisters made their decision during the novena. Help from on high appeared once again to stave off what could have been a very serious danger. Fr Moreau was looking for a suitable house

---

[482] Person currently unidentified.

to establish his proposed work. He was scouring the whole of the Sablé region and was making us very worried. We knew that he had a considerable sum at his disposal, and that if he got on the right side of Monsieur Salmon he would immediately oust both us and our plans for leasing; he could pay upfront to ensure the acquisition of Solesmes.

I therefore urged Fr Fonteinne to bring things to a swift conclusion. On 12 December an agreement was finally reached between him and Monsieur Salmon. A three-year lease had been agreed in return for 1,000 francs per year, which would be paid for three consecutive years. On expiry of this term, the house would remain ours for the sum of 36,000 francs. This was a great success. Fr Fonteinne hurried to inform me of it in a letter written the same day, urging me to come to Sablé quickly, lest these clauses, which had been agreed only verbally, be changed.

I received the letter in Le Mans the following day, 13 December. I immediately ran to reserve a place on the stage-coach from Sablé that was leaving at 1.00 p.m., so as to arrive during the daytime. After a quick lunch at mid-day, I lost no time in going over to the coach. I was told that it would not be leaving due to the poor state of the road. I was very disappointed. Since I mentioned lodging a complaint, the manager told me that a horse had been saddled for me, and that I could make the journey with the boy who was about to leave for Sablé with the mail. There were thirty-six miles[483] to cover on horseback over snow-covered ground.

I decided to go on account of the urgency, and was led to my steed. He was a rehashed veteran from the armed cavalry, and must have been ridden by some cuirassier or other in his day. His skin was torn in more than one place, but even worse than this was his height, which meant that when I raised my foot it barely reached the stirrup. Also, his girth meant that a man of my height could only just mount him properly. As far as his character was concerned, I saw instantly that, perhaps due to his age, he was naturally placid, but also that his trot would not be very gentle.

---

[483] Guéranger's text says 'twelve leagues'.

Moreover he was, as one would expect, roughshod.

The time had come to leave, so I heaved myself up onto this beast and crossed the streets of Le Mans in the company of the post-boy, who was carrying the mail in a leather bag slung across his shoulder. He kept urging me to strike the animal or else we would not get there; I achieved something of a trot using this method, but my arm was getting tired. We reached the market town of Le Grand Saint-Georges[484] when a woman called out to me from her doorway: 'Father, you are on a very poor mount for a priest! What a bloody awful horse you have between your legs!' The rude remark cheered me up a bit. The conversation with my companion during this ride was nonexistent, and so I was left entirely to my own thoughts. I had a strong sense that I was entering an unknown future, and entrusted myself to God.

Throughout the entire journey, almost from when I left Le Mans, I was haunted by a text from the Gospel that kept occurring to me, and with such force that I could not stop myself from speaking it aloud perhaps fifty times. It was the following passage from St Luke: 'For which of you, desiring to build a tower, does not first sit down and count the cost, whether he has enough to complete it? Otherwise, when he has laid a foundation, and is not able to finish it, all who see it begin to mock him, saying, "This man began to build and was not able to finish"' (Lk 14:28–30).[485]

I then repeated the other comparison: 'Or what king, going to encounter another king in war ...' (Lk 14:31 *seq.*). Finally, I reached the conclusion to which Our Lord leads us: 'So, therefore, whoever of you does not renounce all that he has cannot be my disciple' (Lk 14:33). Somewhat anxiously, I

---

[484] Guéranger has made a slight mistake here since the commune was formerly known as Saint-Georges-le-Grand. Its name changed to Saint-Georges-du-Bois in 1952.

[485] Guéranger quotes from the Latin Vulgate edition of the Bible at this point, and in the two subsequent quotes below. The quotations given here are from the *Revised Standard Version* (Catholic Edition), London, 1966.

asked myself what God wanted to teach me by this sentence. I was poor and did not possess anything. What was I to renounce in order to be a disciple of Jesus Christ? Ensuing events taught me the successive renunciations that God was asking of me in return for the honour of being associated with his work. I say *his* work since in 1837 it appeared as such via the solemn approval given to it by the apostolic see.[486]

On reaching Noyen I changed horse, but apart from its colour the second one was similar in every respect to the first. I was already so exhausted that I needed to climb onto a boundary stone to reach the stirrup and mount the saddle. I trotted like this with my companion until Parcé. The bridge on the river Sarthe did not then exist, so one had to cross the river by ferry. I got off the horse, but after reaching the other bank my courage gave way. I had done nearly thirty miles by horseback on two hopeless mounts, and I no longer felt strong enough to brave this sort of effort. I told the boy to take my horse to Sablé with his own, and to inform the two Cosnard sisters that I was finishing the remainder of the journey on foot.

I arrived exhausted around 8.00 p.m., but was sorry to find that Fr Fonteinne was no longer there; not expecting me to arrive so quickly, he had returned to his parish of Asnières that afternoon. The following day, 14 December, someone was sent to fetch him first thing in the morning, and he arrived without delay. Monsieur Salmon was soon informed, and came to the home of the two Cosnard sisters. The terms decided on by him and Fr Fonteinne were maintained, and a private agreement drawn up by Monsieur Cosnard (who had been a solicitor in Saint-Denis, Anjou) was signed by me and Monsieur Salmon, who was answering for his co-owners.

We paid him the rent of 3,000 francs for the three years and Solesmes was in our hands. The next day was 15 December, the octave of the Immaculate Conception and the last day of the novena. This was the first supernatural help to

---

[486] In a brief entitled *Innumeras Inter,* of 1 September 1837, Gregory XVI formally approved the Congregation of France, the erection of Solesmes as an independent abbey and the appointment of Guéranger as its first abbot.

come to the Congregation of France, which dates from this day. The name of Mary Immaculate must therefore be engraved at the beginning of these annals.

I returned to Le Mans without delay, and on 19 December I had an audience with the bishop. I told him what I had just done, and he congratulated me heartily. I then asked him if he wished to approve the constitutions. He replied that he had liked them very much and would indeed sanction them. Then, taking a quill, he wrote and signed the approval.[487] This was the first sanction given to the work by the Church, and I thanked God for it from the depths of my heart.

I then asked the prelate to release Fr Fonteinne so that he could join me as soon as possible. He granted this with good grace, allowing him to leave the parish of Asnières straight after Christmas. I had not banked on such complete success and cannot but view it as one of the effects of the novena. I took leave of the bishop, expressing my gratitude to him. It was a solemn day for him. By virtue of his authority, he was contributing to the re-establishment of the order of St Benedict in France via this indispensable preliminary stage. At the same time, he was preparing more remotely for the restoration of the Roman liturgy by giving us permission to use it publicly in a church of his diocese.

News of the acquisition of Solesmes and of the imminent gathering of a religious community in this house soon spread throughout the town and diocese. It was welcomed quite well, but was poorly understood; it was such a long time since the monks had disappeared. In addition, I was a very young priest, as was Fr Fonteinne, and both of us were from the diocese. I remember that before leaving Sablé, on the very day of the acquisition, Fr Fonteinne and I both went to visit Fr Paillard, the parish priest of Sablé, to inform him courteously of what we had just done. He received our news

---

[487] The title of the first constitutions, formally approved by Bishop Carron on 19 December 1832, was *Regulas Societatis regularis, in dioecesi Cenomanensi existentis, favente et auspice Illustrissimo ac Reverendissimo D.D. Episcopo.* See des Mazis, *op. cit.,* 180.

politely, but added that it would be regrettable if religious from Solesmes wanted to exercise their sacred ministry, especially to hear confessions, since this could only be detrimental to the parish of Sablé. Fr Paillard was all the more worried since Fr Fonteinne, who had left the curacy of Sablé just six months ago, was still held in affection by many people in the parish. It was only to be expected that discord would prevail between the monastery and the Sablé presbytery during the lifetime of such a parish priest.

The bishop held his council on 21 December and informed them of the forthcoming vacancy of the parish of Asnières, as well as the permission he had given to Fr Fonteinne to join me. There were no comments, except from the old Canon Ménochet, who muttered: 'They will make it into a Lamennaisian refuge.' No one paid any attention to his words, and for the time being the matter was closed.

After establishing the dwelling of the future monks, we also needed to prepare a library for their studies. Fr Lamarre[488] was a venerable priest who had died a holy death not long before, and Fr Bouvier (the executor of his will) gave me a bound copy of the Lebel edition of Bossuet and a chalice for Solesmes, both of which had belonged to this devout cleric. He gave me permission to take any duplicates to be found in the seminary library. Generally speaking, one does not find many important works in this category, but I was nevertheless able to put aside *Les Conciles* by Labbe[489] and some other items. We had the whole lot valued by Monsieur Richelet,[490] the town

---

[488] Pierre Lamarre (1756–1832), ordained priest 1780; made an honorary canon of Le Mans in 1808; parish priest of Mareil-en-Champagne; assistant priest at the cathedral. See *Le Chapitre*, pp. 21, 51.

[489] Philippe Labbe (1607–1667), Jesuit who published extensively in many areas of scholarship. His seventeen-volume compilation of the acts of the various church councils, *Sacrosancta concilia ad regiam editionem exacta*, Paris, 1671, was completed and published by Fr Cossart. See Vapereau, *op. cit.*, p. 1145.

[490] Charles-Joseph Richelet (1803–1871), curator of the library in Le Mans (1826–1836); distinguished literary figure and archaeologist, as well as a printer and bookseller. See F. Legeay, *Nécrologie et Bibliographie contemporaines de La Sarthe – 1844–1880*, Le Mans, 1881, pp. 368–70.

bookseller, and, for the sum of a thousand francs paid over ten years, I managed to find more than six hundred volumes there. Added to my own more choice collection, and that of Fr Fonteinne, we reached the figure of more than twelve hundred books.

There was something tempting me more than anything else as the foundation of our literary store: the acquisition of the Bollandist volumes. For a month I had known about a very complete set (fifty-three volumes) on sale at Méquignon-junior's in Paris. I had even spoken about this to Fr Fonteinne, giving him to understand that I would prob-ably buy it. The price was 1,200 francs.[491] It was certainly not an expensive copy, but we could not break into the 3,000 francs that remained after Monsieur Salmon had been paid. I was focusing on the promised donations from Monsieur de Brézé and Monsieur Bailly, who were still in Paris. I was even counting on a few hundred francs that might be donated in this region in order to complete this sum. I told Fr Fonteinne about my planned attempt as though it was imminent, and I was waiting from day to day, worried that someone might walk off with the work.

On Christmas Eve, I finally wrote to Méquignon, telling him that I was reserving his copy of the Bollandists, that he should send it to me immediately and that he would be paid in Paris as soon as I received it. I wrote this letter in the evening and took it with me as I went to Matins in the cath-edral, so as to make up my mind before God. After the *Te Deum*[492] I left my stall, placed the mozetta and the aumusse in the sacristy and, with my mind fully made up, ran to the post office and slipped my letter into the box. I felt pleased with what I had done and asked God's friends, whose virtues and wonders are recounted by the *Acta Sanctorum,* to acknowledge the sacrifice that had been offered for them

---

[491] This sum was more than the annual rent for the priory of Solesmes.

[492] A chant of praise and thanksgiving, probably of fourth-century origin, that is sung at the end of the night office and at certain other liturgical functions, such as the blessing of a new abbot or abbess. The first line is: *Te Deum laudamus: te Dominum confitemur* ('We praise you, O God; we acknowledge you to be the Lord').

and shower their protection on Solesmes. The fifty-three volumes soon reached me in Le Mans. I sent them on to Sablé, from where we took them triumphantly to Solesmes in a tipcart.

Two days after Christmas I had gone to Sablé, where I found Fr Fonteinne at the home of the two Cosnard sisters. He had left Asnières for good, but without saying anything to his parishioners except to the de Lorière family. Since his successor, Fr Naveau,[493] had not arrived in time for Sunday, Fr Fonteinne asked me to take the services at Asnières. I had to ascend the pulpit and make his farewells to the parish. He was greatly loved by the people, and the arguments I used to console his parishioners at his departure were not very effective. I had dinner at the château and then returned promptly to Sablé.

[493] Person currently unidentified.

The Year 1833:
Preparations for the Restoration

I returned to Le Mans without delay and went to Laval a few days later, with the intention of collecting donations for the work. I was not very successful, and barely collected six hundred francs. Fr de Hercé,[494] parish priest of La Trinité and later bishop of Nantes, welcomed me kindly. Fr Coulon,[495] who has since become the archpriest of La Flèche, introduced me to various households. I was well received everywhere, but the donations were not significant.

I went to visit the Jesuits. Fr Thomas,[496] superior of Saint-Michel, gave me two six-franc pieces. This was more than he had to do, but I must say that people in this house were initially hostile to us. It was made up of old Fathers of the Faith, the curtest among whom was Fr Gloriot.[497] I knew that

---

[494] Jean-François de Hercé (1776–1849), English teacher; married in 1804 and lived in Laval with the title of mayor of Oeun-des-Vallons; mayor of Laval (1814–1829); widowed in 1826; ordained priest in 1830; parish priest of La Trinité in Laval 1831; made honorary canon of Le Mans in 1832; ordained coadjutor bishop of Nantes in 1836 and assumed full control of the diocese in 1838; resigned in 1848 due to poor health. See Angot, *op. cit.,* v. 2, p. 428.

[495] Pierre Coulon (1805–1882), ordained priest in 1827; professor of philosophy at the Tessé, and then Laval; parish priest of Grazay in 1833; of Château-du-Loir in 1837; archpriest of La Flèche in 1857. See *Le Chapitre,* pp. 94, 138.

[496] Antoine Thomas (1753–1833), entered the newly revived Jesuits in France in 1814; solemnly professed in 1819. See the Jesuit archives at Vanves.

[497] Charles Gloriot (1768–1840), refused to take the constitutional oath and was ordained priest in Fribourg in 1792. He was incorporated into

he had said when speaking about the future Benedictines: 'They are sectarians.' Annoyance against Fr de La Mennais and his school had reached a peak in this house, and they continued to think that we were Mennaisians and to treat us as such. This hostile attitude towards Solesmes persisted in this house for a long time. It reached such a point that the malicious words continued even after the canonical erection of the Congregation; in 1838 I was forced to write about it to the superior general, Fr Roothan.[498] He agreed to write to the various houses of the order in France, asking that they henceforth speak well of Solesmes. He was good enough to write to me about this, and I know from several Jesuits that the circular was actually sent and that it met with due obedience. Since then there have been no more hostile words against Solesmes from this quarter.

I shall add something about the hostility that goes back to this year, 1833. I was told that a lady from Lyons had planned to offer Solesmes a substantial sum after she heard about our foundation and the approval that it had obtained from our bishop. She had been dissuaded from this by a member of the Society of Saint-Sulpice,[499] which was very influential in Lyons, on the pretext that Solesmes would undoubtedly be a hotbed of Mennaisianism.

---

the Sacred Heart Fathers and then the Fathers of the Faith, and worked on various missions. He returned to France in 1800 and entered the Jesuits in 1814. From 1816–1840 he resumed his work of preaching and leading missions, although he also became superior of the Jesuit house in Besançon in 1833. He was not a member of the community at Laval, but could easily have been staying there during Guéranger's visit. In 1833 the community at Laval comprised six priests and five brothers. See the Jesuit archives at Vanves.

[498] Jean-Philippe Roothan (1785–1853), a Dutchman who entered the Jesuits in Russia. Ordained priest in 1812; worked as parish priest in Russia, then in 1823 he became principal of a college in Turin after the Jesuits were expelled from Russia. He became provincial vicar of Italy in 1829, and superior general of the order a few months later. For further information, see Larousse, *op. cit.,* v. 13, p. 1374.

[499] The 'Société de Saint-Sulpice' grew out of a seminary founded by Fr Jean-Jacques Olier near the church of Saint-Sulpice, Paris in 1642. For further information, see Jacquemet, *op. cit.,* v. 14, pp. 574–6.

Be that as it may, I returned from Laval to Sablé, bringing the proceeds of my humble collection to Fr Fonteinne. The work to be carried out at Solesmes to prepare the house for its purpose would soon consume this feeble assistance. We found the house to be in a fairly good state, but it needed numerous repairs that were incumbent upon the tenant. Our sellers had completely replaced the windows on the river side, and had carefully maintained the roof of the conventual buildings since they were hoping to sell the house. In return, they had let the church roofing go to ruin; it took three annual campaigns for us to restore this important roof to a good state of repair. The vaults had suffered greatly from this abandonment. Shortly before we had full use of it, lightning struck the bell tower and came right into the house, knocking a considerable hole in the staircase used for Matins. This was one of the first repairs that we had to carry out.

It was not long before we suffered a new disaster. During a violent storm around 20 January, wind entered the church tower through the lower bays and pushed against the roof with such violence that it burst open; the blast violently ripped off an area of more than twenty square feet, the whole of which (rafters, laths and slates) fell into the cloister courtyard, having first damaged the roof of the cloister itself. We had to repair this damage, which seemed to come from evil forces. In order to prevent it happening again, Fr Fonteinne had the great bays of the church tower covered in such a way that they would henceforth break the force of the wind.

We had to unblock the great window above the entrance door in the church. It had been walled up to avoid maintaining a stained-glass window. Restoring this window was a great expense for us. The sacristy was in a miserable state. Not only grass, but also bushes were growing there. The wooden panelling on one side had been eaten away by damp, and on the other side three cupboards made of strong oakwood had been wonderfully preserved. On the top shelf of the third cupboard, we found laurel branches that had been blessed on Palm Sunday in 1790. Their lack of material value meant that they had been overlooked during the various lootings of the house. I kept them for Ash Wednesday in 1834, when we burnt them and thus used them for their purpose after more than forty years.

The church statues had suffered numerous defacements of their fingers and other minor parts, a large number of which we restored. Moreover, on the whim of some eighteenth-century prior[500] their eyes had been painted. This gave them a haggard appearance, which had made a great impression on me during my childhood and which vanished as soon as we had etched out those vile pupils. We found a marble main altar that must date from 1720, when the Maurists had completely changed the choir of their church. The iron bar that supported the hanging pyx was still fixed to this altar, which had never had a tabernacle. As for the pyx itself, which was made of copper, it was said in the town that it had been removed and taken to Château-Gontier during the Revolution. We got rid of the iron bar, which no longer served any purpose. It was only in 1838 that the former support method was restored. Until then the Blessed Sacrament was kept on an altar in the right transept, in a wooden tabernacle that I had ordered in Laval during the trip that I mentioned earlier.

We no longer had the two black marble side altars, or the two statues of St Peter and St Paul, which were modelled on the white marble ones in the church of La Couture in Le Mans. Neither did we possess the last of the bells, which dates from 1503 and which has such perfect pitch. At the request of the parish priest of Solesmes, these objects had been given to the parish by a widow, Madame Le Noir de Chantelou, two years before our arrival. We had to replace

---

[500] This procedure appears to have been known in the sixteenth century: 'The eyes of all the statues had been brightened up with a black dot. The effect produced was very questionable … We would willingly believe that this application is original to the monument. This is because our sculptors also used black paint very discreetly in order to highlight two decorations in the coronation scene, beneath the text, *O virtutes* … which would not be seen without it. The need to colour graven inscriptions on cartridges might have led them to this method.' See M. de La Tremblaye, *Solesmes, Les Sculptures de l'église abbatiale (1496–1553)*, Solesmes, 1892, p. 162.

the two altars with two others that were very mediocre, which we came across in Monsieur Landeau's place.

To furnish the house, apart from the choir stalls we found refectory tables, a kitchen table, a large dresser in the kitchen and another smaller one in the guest room, four huge upholstered armchairs, half a dozen old chairs and a completely worm-eaten four-poster bed. Fr Fonteinne had his own furniture (which was new and very suitable) brought from Asnières. He ordered an oak chest for the sacristy, in which to store vestments, and two large cupboards made of white wood for the library. When they were ready, I stored our books in them, which amounted to about fifteen hundred in total, including the Bollandists and the Vatican edition of St Ephrem.

The Cosnard sisters gave us a lot of help to complete and organize the housework. They were ably assisted by their cousin, the widow Madame Gazeau, a very devout woman who was dedicated to good works and who was greatly esteemed in Sablé through her reputation for ardent, imaginative charity; she had been the hand of providence to the poor people in the town for the past thirty years. She was very devoted to Fr Fonteinne and directed all of her enthusiasm on Solesmes. For the remaining fifteen years of her life, she gave continual service to the monastery in all its temporal concerns. We needed an odd-job man, and Fr Fonteinne found one in a boy called Pierre,[501] who was a domestic at the hospital in Sablé. He was very hard-working and could come immediately, even offering to enter as a lay brother. He moved in with us on 11 July, but a month later a serious fault in his behaviour forced us to dismiss him straight away.

The parish priest, Fr Jousse, regarded the establishment of the work very kindly. He was a real peasant and very ignorant, but he gave us a good welcome. Later on, when war was declared by the parish of Sablé, he held out for us against his dean, and only declared his opposition to us in 1838; he stayed like this until he left the parish.

---

[501] Pierre Hureau, was installed with Guéranger on 11 July 1833 as a lay brother, but did not persevere. See L. Soltner, 'Les premiers compagnons de Dom Guéranger' in *Lettre aux Amis de Solesmes*, 4 (1983): 15.

Monsieur Enjubault La Roche,[502] mayor of Solesmes and former captain of the lancers in the wars of the Empire, was no less of a yokel than the parish priest. He was very narrow-minded, knew nothing of the world and thought that our plan to re-establish monks at Solesmes was a bad idea. He had the most ludicrous argument with me about this subject, in which he naively demonstrated his firm conviction that monks could be nothing but bad news and that they would cause him a lot of trouble in terms of supervision. It was impossible to get him to give way, and the notion was so entrenched in his mind that when he later saw how we were living he kept on saying that we were not monks. Fresh proof of the hostility that society had felt towards religious orders at the end of the eighteenth century would be encountered in the total lack of welcome that the plan to restore the monks met with among the old people in Sablé, who still carried out their religious duties. They could not understand why anyone was thinking of resurrecting a useless, superfluous institution whose passing they did not lament in the slightest. We could count on friendship only from the new generation, since a study of the past would gradually show what eighteenth-century Christians had forgotten: the holiness of the monastic state and the services rendered by monks.

A few months later, when the Catholic newspapers were discussing the work that was to be started at Solesmes, the civil administration (the government, the police and the king's public prosecutor) made no objection. Yet we were still very close to the events of Melleray. The court of Nantes, which had judged the trial, had not failed in its preamble to present all the legal clauses against religious bodies from the Constitutional Assembly, and from subsequent governments, as being legitimate. The impetus for freedom stemming from the 1830 Revolution, the increased boldness of the religious press, the words 'freedom of association' mentioned in the new *Charte*, the recognition of the right to protest, and a certain appeasement of the irreligious passion that had

---

[502] Augustin-Grégoire-François Enjubault La Roche (1774–1843), mayor of Solesmes from 1825 until his death. See http://www.vinotyvues.free.fr.

fermented during the Restoration were all giving me confidence. It was unlikely that a denouncement or even a complaint would come from the neighbourhood. It was clear that the establishment was ensuring the conservation of the monument of Solesmes, which was dear to people in the whole region; they loved these beautiful stone saints and beheld them with admiration. The bourgeoisie of Sablé, who were then extremely irreligious and backward in everything, spouted all sorts of nonsense for a long time afterwards, but things were limited to that and no one thought of complaining to the administration.

Nevertheless, I felt bound to establish that we would not at first wear the religious habit, but simply the cassock without bands. In choir we would wear the Roman surplice, so as to separate us from the secular clergy and to be in harmony with the liturgy that we were going to use. Only in winter would we wear over this a large black cloak with a monastic-style hood. This outfit sufficed for us until 15 August 1836, and it had been so effective that we were able to start wearing the Benedictine habit on that day without provoking the slightest surprise among the local people.

In accordance with the accepted custom at that time for evading the red tape that the administration could have created for us, it was agreed that in the event of a legal challenge we would completely avoid mentioning that we were monks. We would reply that we were French citizens living as we thought appropriate, under the rights of common law and without any mitigation or privilege. It was for this reason that I had had written on the church collection box the clause about benefactors of the *establishment* and not of the *monastery*. Since then, events have moved on, and it would no longer be possible for us to refuge to acknowledge the titles of 'monks' and 'Benedictines' before the law; the regime of the Second Empire is significantly different from the 1830 *Charte*.[503] Later in these memoirs, we shall see the outcome of events relating to the legal aspects of Solesmes.

---

[503] During the Second Empire (1852–1870) the enforcement of the law of
1790 suppressing most religious orders and banning monastic vows

Journey to Nantes and Visit to the Abbey of Melleray

I now resume my story. We urgently needed money at Solesmes, and we had to try new means of procuring it. I thought that a trip to Nantes would be more productive than the one to Laval. The marquis de Régnon strongly urged me to go there, and I also hoped to obtain the bishop's permission to preach a sermon appealing for money in aid of the work.

I left around 20 February. The marquis de Régnon gave me a perfect welcome. He had obtained the prelate's permission for me to stay in some sort of ecclesiastical house that was dependent on the bishop's palace. I was received there without charge and treated with consideration. The bishop (Micolon de Guérines[504]) invited me to dinner and was very gracious. I saw immediately that he was completely under

---

was tightened. Nevertheless, monasteries continued to be founded in France by means of legal loopholes and the benevolence of the authorities, who did not enforce the full rigour of the law. For example, when the priory of Ligugé was re-founded by Guéranger in 1853, the bishop of Poitiers had the foundation ratified by the ministry of religion as a 'house of assistant priests'. See L.-J. Bord, *Histoire de l'Abbaye Saint-Martin de Ligugé, 361–2001,* Paris, 2006, p. 179, n. 17.

[504] Joseph-Michel-Jean-Baptiste-Paul-Augustin Micolon de Guérines (1760–1838), vicar general of Clermont until forced into exile in Switzerland during the Revolution. He later returned to France and was consecrated bishop of Clermont in 1802. He was appointed bishop of Castres after the 1817 Concordat, but was unable to take possession of this see. He was transferred to the see of Nantes in 1822. See Michaud, *op. cit.,* v. 28, pp. 258–9.

the influence of his secretary, Fr Vrignaud,[505] whom I did not like very much. I could see that my extremely youthful appearance was not doing much to help me, even though Bishop Carron had written in my favour to his colleague in Nantes.

Nantes is a charitable town, but all the resources of its rich Christian families were directed towards feeding the hundreds of peasants in hiding all over the place who had been mobilized for the unfortunate Legitimist expedition of the previous year. I shall add that the marquis de Régnon was not the right man to get me into the drawing rooms of the Nantes' aristocracy; he had been closely involved with *L'Avenir* and was therefore suspicious to the Legitimist camp.

I saw immediately that I would only collect a few donations. The marquis de Régnon enabled me to make the acquaintance of Fr Fournier,[506] the curate of Saint-Nicolas, who has since become parish priest of this large parish. I was welcomed very well there. He introduced me to several of his friends, who were excellent Catholics and who agreed to make their donation. Everything that I received from this quarter, in addition to the 400 francs given to me by the marquis de Régnon, was far from reaching a thousand francs, and I needed much more. It was then that I placed my final hope on the sermon in aid of the work, to which the marquis de Régnon and Fr Fournier thought I would attract enough

---

[505] Charles-Pierre Vrignaud (1800–1850), ordained priest in 1823; made an honorary canon of Nantes in 1825; appointed bishop's secretary in 1826, and remained in this post until his death, in the service of three successive bishops. He became a titular canon in 1832 and vicar general of Nantes in 1836. See the archives of the diocese of Nantes.

[506] Félix Fournier (1803–1877), ordained priest in 1827; appointed curate in the parish of Saint-Nicolas, and became the parish priest there in 1836; it was there that he founded one of the first conferences of the St Vincent de Paul Society outside of Paris in 1837. He was elected a *député* for Loire-Inférieure in the National Assembly of 1848, but soon resumed his ecclesiastical and intellectual activities, becoming president of the 'Société Académique' of Nantes in 1857. He was consecrated bishop of Nantes in 1870. For further information, see *L'Épiscopat*, pp. 400–1.

people to obtain a worthwhile collection. I had planned to visit Dom Antoine Saulnier de Beauregard in his abbey of Melleray, where he and about thirty monks had finally returned, although without the habit and the conventual observances.[507] I had known this great abbot at the bishop's palace of Le Mans, where he spent several days with my bishop each year on his way to Paris. I wanted to ask him if he could give or lend us a few lay brothers. This trip would only last a few days, after which I would return to Nantes and ask at the bishop's palace for permission to give the sermon in question.

I made this trip, and spent two whole days under the roof of this venerable man. He promised me some help, and shortly afterwards he sent me a lay brother on loan; later on, he sent a non-priest choir monk called Br Gérasime. I hardly saw them, and since they were completely useless we did not keep them; they had already left by the time of our installation.

My conversations with Dom Antoine were very interesting. I did not weary of listening to this old octogenarian monk, whose mind had remained so fresh and active. Firstly, he wanted to know the fundamental basis of the planned foundation. He was sorry that I had not prescribed perpetual abstinence from meat and Matins during the night, even though he agreed that it would have been difficult if not impossible to recruit candidates under such conditions. Nevertheless, he stressed the danger of a foundation in which all the members start out at the same time. He assured me that the authority of the superior could not be established under such conditions, and told me in very strong terms that he was predicting major disagreements as a result of the original equality between members of the work. The stress he placed on this issue worried me somewhat, all the more so since he later wrote me a letter in which he returned to the same subject with great insistence. I had no answer in the face of such an experienced man. The way he presented the problem encouraged me to drop everything and yet, in all honesty, I could no longer do

---

[507] See footnote 437, p. 147. For further information, see F. Benoist, *Notice sur l'Abbaye de Notre-Dame de La Trappe de Melleray*, Nantes, 1884.

this. I called on God to help me and tried to reassure myself.

Apart from these monastic conversations with the venerable abbot, I had the benefit of listening to him at length during the two days that I spent with him. He told me about the attack on his monastery and the dispersal of his monks.

It was clear to me that jealousy on the part of the Nantes' shopkeepers had been the sole cause of this; were it not for commercial rivalry, the abbey would have remained standing, even though it was under suspicion of being not entirely impartial during the recent civil war crisis. The abbot was greatly esteemed at Court under the Restoration, and he went there every year. During the insurrection of the previous year, he had known everything; papers found in his room proved as much. He was not fooled by anyone, so much so that when he was talking about the rumour spread about by the government that the duchesse de Berry, imprisoned in Blaye, could be pregnant, he told me without batting an eyelid that, knowing the princess as he did, this disgrace was entirely possible. The truth of this rumour was confirmed before I had returned to Nantes.[508]

Dom Antoine had had some difficulty in understanding the system of defence of religious houses by appeal to the right to ownership and the right to a home. By that time, however, he had completely mastered it and was feeling strong. A few years later, he was able to reopen his monastery thanks to this principle, although he still had to give up the various industries that could have competed with the inhabitants of Nantes.

Far from sharing Abbot de Rancé's[509] ideas about monastic

[508] The duchesse de Berry gave birth to a daughter in prison in May 1833. This event forced her to admit that she had secretly married the comte Lucchesi-Palli during her Italian exile, and had thereby deprived herself of the title of Regent. For further information, see Larousse, *op. cit.*, v. 2, p. 611.

[509] Armand-Jean Le Bouthillier de Rancé (1626–1700), ordained priest in 1651, and became a canon of Tours; refused to become the coadjutor bishop of Tours and entered La Trappe in 1662. From 1666 he was at the forefront of a movement to reform La Trappe towards strict discipline and mortification. For further information, see A. J. Krailsheimer, *A.-J. de Rancé, Abbot of La Trappe*, Oxford, 1974.

studies,[510] he expressly praised the aim of our work, adding that he regretted being too old to try to reform ideas about this important subject at La Trappe.[511] He also deplored the fate of monasteries that appoint superiors who are deficient in doctrine. He spoke about the rigorism that was then still in vogue in church moral teaching, and opined that there was an urgent need for improvement in this area. He said that the influence of St Alphonsus Liguori's theology would be beneficial, and was sorry that he still did not know about this himself.

I eventually left this venerable witness of monasticism and returned to Nantes. I quickly got in touch with Fr Vrignault about the plan for a sermon. As I have said, he controlled the bishop and it was he more than anyone who had to be won over. I explained my desire and soon saw that he was opposed to it. The reason he gave was that since the government was ill-disposed towards the Church, the plan to establish a monastery of men would be considered illegal and would lead to complaints, especially after the violent destruction of Melleray. Furthermore, he said that the recent insurrection in Brittany[512] had made the clergy particularly odious to the civil

---

[510] For example, in a letter of 5 October 1680 de Rancé states: 'Erudition is the reef on which humility founders, and vanity, the most common result of study, has often caused a thousand fatal wounds in a scholar's heart.' Quoted in A. J. Krailsheimer, *The Letters of Armand-Jean de Rancé – Abbot and Reformer of La Trappe*, (v. 1), Kalamazoo, 1984, p. 227. In a later letter of 7 March 1691, de Rancé claims that the only reason monks take up study is, 'to try to gain distinction for knowledge, having lost it for strictness of discipline, regularity and holiness of life.' *Ibid.*, (v. 2), p. 167. Ironically, de Rancé himself had been a brilliant student of classical languages in his youth.

[511] The monastery of La Grande Trappe, founded in 1122 in the diocese of Séez, in the commune of Soligny-la-Trappe. In 1140 it was given to the Congregation of Savigny, and became a Cistercian house in 1147. It was reformed by Abbot de Rancé in 1662, suppressed at the Revolution and restored in 1816. See Cottineau, *op. cit.*, v. 2, pp. 3201–2.

[512] The 1832 Legitimist uprising in Brittany led by the duchesse de Berry; the clergy were suspected of being sympathetic to the Legitimist rebels. Nevertheless, the situation was more complicated than this, and the anti-clerical publication *L'Ami de la Clarté* of 17 June 1832 noted that priests in Riaillé attended to the wounded and gave food to the patriots.

and military authorities. He also said that in this situation it would be better to win them over, rather than propound the sort of ideas that I represented. This language made me very indignant, but all of my replies were useless. I was therefore forced to withdraw; the whole point of my trip to Nantes had failed.

Among the people whom I got to know in this town, I must mention Dom Le Comte,[513] a Benedictine monk of the Congregation of Saint-Maur and a venerable old man, who welcomed me with kindly interest. He studied my project with great earnestness, was very encouraging towards me and finished by asking if he could end his days at Solesmes. This prospect delighted me, and Dom Le Comte strengthened my hope in all sorts of ways until my departure. After the installation he wrote to me in the most encouraging terms, and would certainly have carried through his plan were it not for the opposition of two of his sisters who lived with him; they were all too eloquent in pointing out the difficulties that his age and infirmity posed to his decision. Dom Le Comte died a few months after our establishment at Solesmes.[514] He had thought that the planned constitutions were wise and truly Benedictine; this approval from a learned and devout religious seemed to me a good omen. I gathered precious teaching about the spirit of the Congregation of Saint-Maur in its last years from the mouth of Dom Le Comte. Philosophers, pleasure-seekers, Jansenists and true monks were all to be found there. Among the latter, Dom Le Comte told me that the camp opposed to Jansenism was gaining ground towards the end. Personally, he had always accepted the papal bull *Unigenitus*.[515] I cannot forget the venerable characteristics of this veteran from the order of St Benedict who, far from being

---

[513] Louis-Dominique Le Comte (1760–1841), professed at Saint-Germer in 1781. See *Matricula*, p. 176.

[514] Guéranger appears to be mistaken in believing that Dom Le Comte died as early as 1833.

[515] A bull promulgated by Clement XI in 1713, which condemned Jansenism, especially as manifested by several contemporary Jesuit writings, as being false, heretical and blasphemous. The bull was controversial in France; the archbishop of Paris and seven other bishops refused to accept it. For further information, see Larousse, *op. cit.*, v. 15, p. 650.

shocked by my extreme youthfulness, had accepted this precarious work from the very beginning, to the extent of considering devoting himself to it personally.

Among those who were interested in the work, I shall also mention Madame de La Ferronnays,[516] the superior of the Visitation monastery, who was very kind and gave me a white vestment and some church linen for Solesmes. Canon Angebault,[517] who has since become the bishop of Angers and whom I shall discuss later, got someone to tell me that he did not want me to visit him at home. In return for this, he sent a copy of the Vence Bible,[518] an eighteenth-century edition, and the great historical work by Lenglet-Dufresnoy[519] (both of which were in poor condition) to the house where I was staying. Essentially, the worthy canon did not owe me anything.

When I got back to Le Mans, I dealt with the issue of personnel for the foundation, and this is how far I had got at that time: Fr Morin, the cathedral curate, decided firmly and he was great

---

[516] Marie-Antoinette de La Ferronnays (1782–1841), professed at Nantes in 1812. She taught in the boarding school before being elected superior in 1821. She served as superior four times before her death, as well as acting as novice mistress and bursar during periods when she was not superior. For further information, see the archives of the Visitation monastery, Nantes.

[517] Guillaume-Laurent-Louis Angebault (1790–1869), ordained priest in 1815; became pro-secretary to the bishop of Angers (1817); secretary (1819); honorary canon (1819); titular canon (1825); honorary vicar general (1830 and 1838); he was consecrated bishop of Angers in 1842. For further information, see *L'Épiscopat*, pp. 51–3.

[518] Henri-François de Vence (1675–1749), Hebraist. The *Bible de Vence* was the name acquired by an edition of the bible by Calmet (1748–1750) that was reprinted in Avignon (1767–1773), and which included Vence's six-volume *Analyses et des dissertations sur les livres de l'Ancien Testament*, as well as his two-volume *Analyses ou explication des Psaumes*. A new edition of this bible was begun in 1827. See Vapereau, *op. cit.*, p. 2025.

[519] Nicolas Lenglet-Dufresnoy (1674–1755), first studied theology but abandoned this for diplomacy and politics. He published a large number of theological, geographical and historical works, but Guéranger is probably referring to his *Méthode pour étudier l'histoire avec un catalogue des principaux historiens*, Paris, 1713, (2 vols). See Vapereau, *op. cit.*, p. 1227.

bonus for the work. He was devout, intelligent, in good health and had a character made for cloistered life. He was kept on the staff of the bishop's palace until 1835, when his death took him from us. Fr Boulangé seemed to be holding firm, but his family's need for him prevented him from carrying out his plan for the time being. Fr Heurtebize had given me great hopes, but his indecisive character kept me uncertain for a long time. In the end he withdrew, although tentatively as usual. He had pointed out to me two young priests whom he thought suited to the work: Frs Audruger and Daigremont. The former bowed to his family's opposition, while the second thanked me but did not think he was suited to the work. Nevertheless, God destined him to it in his final days.[520] My old friends from Le Mans, on whom I had counted, were no longer thinking about it. As far as candidates from the diocese were concerned, I still had Fr Fonteinne, as well as Fr Jouanne, a young priest from Sablé and the curate in La Mayenne, who was ready to join for the installation day.

As far as the Anjou region was concerned, Fr Banchereau gave up after he had given me the greatest hopes, and I was left with just Monsieur Le Boucher, a young deacon who was installed with us but who would later leave. Finally, following a long correspondence, it looked as though I could count on Fr Daubrée, a young priest who was living at the college in Juilly. He was extremely devout and had a very cultivated mind since he had spent some time at La Chênaie with Fr de La Mennais when the latter was still with the Church. He was also installed with us on 11 July, but did not stay.

The work, which was so devoid of financial resources, was thus even more limited with regard to personnel. Humanly speaking, it seemed doomed. Nevertheless, God kept me from taking any notice of this and pushed me forward. The feast of St Benedict on 21 March was drawing near. I decided to celebrate it at Solesmes with Fr Fonteinne. For this

---

[520] Given that Léandre Daigremont did not make monastic profession until 1868 (see footnote 462, p. 160), this is clear evidence that the final text of Guéranger's autobiography was still being written after this date, which is around five years later than the traditional date of 1864–1865 given for the completion of his text.

purpose, I brought a large silver ciborium, a red vestment, and a de Plantin missal from the Visitation monastery, which was always so kind to us. I wrote to Monsieur Le Boucher, inviting him to take part in the feast, and he came. Monsieur de Cazalès, who had promised to visit me, happened to be present for 21 March, although he did not know about the feast and was not expected.

With the permission of the parish priest (and in his presence), I sang the Mass in the parish church. Fr Fonteinne was at the lectern, where he was using an old folio Roman graduale (the Bordeaux edition) from the Elisabethine convent in Sablé. The former gardener from the hospice in Sablé served the Mass. Monsieur de Cazalès was in the nave, along with two or three women from the town. This was the first feast of St Benedict at Solesmes since 1790. Everyone was praying fervently at this small gathering that was filled with hope and trust. It was eighty years since the Roman liturgy had died out in the diocese of Le Mans under Bishop de Froullay[521] in the face of Robinet's liturgy.[522] It was making its first appearance in humility and isolation, but the great Patriarch of Western monasticism was receiving its first fruits. I think that this day was richly blessed.

Monsieur de Cazalès spent the day with me. He was very struck by the magnificence of the sculptures in the priory church. He studied them at length, not only in terms of the statuary but also in terms of their decoration and layout. He took the opportunity to write an article about them, which he published a few months later in the *Revue européenne*[523]

---

[521] Charles-Louis de Froullay (1687–1767), ordained priest (1711); king's chaplain and vicar general of Toulouse (1715); bishop of Le Mans (1723–1767). Although he strived to combat Gallicanism in his diocese, he unwittingly gave way to its influence by introducing the Gallican liturgy. For further information, see Angot, *op. cit.*, v. II, pp. 236–7.

[522] Urbain Robinet (1683–1758), a canon from Paris who was the author of the breviary of Rouen (1733) and, in 1744, of a *Breviarum ecclesiasticum* intended to compete with the breviary of Paris.

[523] *Revue européenne* (juin 1833): 443–4. The title *Revue européenne* was the new name assumed by the *Correspondant* in 1831, a Catholic journal published from 1829–48 that promoted the cause of religious freedom.

and where he also talked about the Mass on 21 March. This encounter did to a certain extent rekindle his vague desire to join us at some stage.

He talked to me a great deal about the *Douloureuse Passion* by Catherine Emmerich,[524] which Brentano[525] had just published in Germany. He confided to me that he was going to prepare and publish a translation of it. This has enjoyed great success in France and has done a lot of good to souls.

I confided to Monsieur de Cazalès that I was preparing to make the journey to Paris with the aim of collecting charitable donations for the work, and asked for his support among his acquaintances. He told me that he knew of only one person who could become interested in such a project: a Russian lady called Madame Swetchine.[526] He wrote a letter of introduction for me immediately, and took his leave after he had given it to me. He returned to Solesmes several years after the foundation and was very kind, but God had not called him to the religious life. Later on he took up the ecclesiastical state, and his name is dear to Catholics in France.

The feast of Easter was drawing near, and on Easter Monday we began to worry for the peace of the town of Solesmes. A rather noisy gathering was held on this day. It originated from the crowd that used to assemble during the exposition and veneration of the relic of the sacred thorn of

---

[524] Catherine Emmerich (1774–1824), Augustinian canoness of the convent of Agnetenburg, Dulmen in Germany. The French translation of her visions, *La douloureuse passion de Notre Seigneur Jésus d'après les méditations d'Anne-Catherine Emmerich*, was first published in 1835.

[525] Clément de Brentano (1777–1842), German poet. For further information, see Larousse, *op. cit.*, v. 2, p. 1230.

[526] Anne-Sophie Soïmonoff (1782–1857), married Nicolas Swetchine, who was some twenty-three years her senior, in 1799. She converted to Catholicism in 1815. In 1816 the couple left Russia and eventually settled in Paris in 1826. For further information, see M.-J. Rouët de Journel, *Une Russe Catholique: La vie de Madame Swetchine*, Paris, 1953. See footnote 573, p. 219.

Christ, which had been preserved in the reliquary since the twelfth century.[527] The Revolution had momentarily deprived this precious relic of its cult, but the gathering on Easter Monday had continued all the same, becoming more and more secular. The site chosen for the dances was the monastery, and its acquisition for a religious work would not fail to irritate a crowd of people who would no longer find a place at Solesmes for their games during their forthcoming gathering. We were worried that they would kick up a fuss.

I had to return to Le Mans for Holy Week. I wrote to Fr Fonteinne to enlist his presence, along with some trustworthy men, at the monastery on the afternoon of Easter Monday, so as to keep watch and ensure that we were not invaded. A group of individuals who had challenged the fact they were not allowed in tried every possible trick to cause uproar in the town. The boldest among them installed themselves in front of the door opening onto the square, where for a long time they stood on chairs and sung vulgar satirical songs to the accompaniment of violins. After this they returned to Sablé in the evening, not failing to drink in vast quantities. The following year, when Easter Monday came around again, the community was up and running and there was no trouble or reaction. People resigned themselves to dancing in the taverns.

I was about to leave for Paris, but I wanted to see the bishop beforehand. I found him to be cold and embarrassed. A lot of hot air had been made in my respect. His vicar general, Fr Bourmault, and the older members of the Chapter generally, were not favourably disposed towards me. It should also be said that I was very young, and that my Roman ideas seemed very strange to them. The thought that I was going to take Fr Morin from the cathedral curacy also

---

[527] The relic of the sacred thorn of Christ was brought from the East by Robert IV of Sablé and offered to the ancient priory of Solesmes. It was hidden by the inhabitants of Solesmes during the Revolution, and was eventually returned to the abbey of Solesmes in 1859. Guéranger restored the custom of venerating this relic on Easter Monday, a custom that continues to this day. See L. Soltner, *Solesmes and Dom Guéranger (1805–1875)*, Solesmes, 1974, p. 90.

offended the administration. In the end, the prelate was not very friendly but he did not go back on what he had authorized. Perhaps his lack of welcome should be attributed to his suffering. Be that as it may, he agreed that we could say Holy Mass in the house and reserve the Blessed Sacrament. I wrote to Fr Fonteinne straight away, and appointed the guest room to serve as a temporary church.

Sojourn in Paris

With this accomplished, I left for Paris around 12 April, having first entrusted myself to Our Lord for the success of this trip. I took my former lodgings in the seminary of the 'Missions Étrangères', and soon began my excursions. One of my first visits was to Madame Swetchine, for which I had a letter from Monsieur de Cazalès. On 16 April I went to her home at 73, rue Saint-Dominique. This encounter was quite an event for me.

I found myself before a woman of fifty years of age, who was short, rather stocky, with a foreign face, cross-eyed and somewhat brusque in her movements, although the overall effect was tempered by rare distinction and an expression of sweetness and goodness that I have rarely encountered to the same degree. She was moved with emotion as she read the letter from Monsieur de Cazalès and then turned towards me with obvious interest, wishing to hear me talk about the work planned for Solesmes. When she heard that this work was to be founded on prayer and divine praise as its principal aim, she shed tears of joy. It was not difficult for me to recognize in her a holy and generous woman who had sacrificed all worldly attachments for God. She then listened rapturously as I told her about the works of religious erudition to which we devoted ourselves in the order of St Benedict, and soon promised to help the work in whatever way she could. In no time, we became close friends. I promised to see her as often as possible, and she indicated a time when I would always be received.

I was no longer alone. From the very outset, Solesmes had found a strong friendship in this noble and holy soul. Madame Swetchine, the close friend of Joseph de Maistre, was the most beautiful conquest over the Greek schism that the Church has made in our time. My dealings with her could not fail to bring me many benefits, which would make me better able to understand life, people and events. Her drawing room, one of the most important in Paris, would give me the opportunity to see and understand many things of which a man from the provinces was hardly aware.

As in Nantes, I was aspiring to give a sermon in aid of the work at Solesmes in a Parisian church. I was expecting some publicity from this, and also financial assistance from the collection that would accompany the sermon. God had decided not to support this plan in Paris anymore than he had in Nantes. In order to make a success of it, I needed help from Archbishop de Quélen. The prelate had withdrawn to live in various different communities, having refused to accept the house that the city of Paris had assigned to him in compensation for his archbishop's palace being vandalized during the popular riots.[528] He lived by turns in the convent of the 'Dames de Saint-Michel' and in the Sacré-Coeur convent. I kept trying to get an audience, which Monsieur de Cazalès would have obtained for me immediately if he had not been detained outside Paris by a rather serious indisposition. Madame Swetchine herself did a lot to get me an interview. Finally, I was received by the prelate on 29 April. He listened to the plan to re-establish the order of St Benedict with great interest. He praised the work effusively, promising his own kind assistance and giving me permission to use his name as a patron. I then dared to mention the sermon. On this point he was not encouraging, and immediately pointed out the difficulties that might ensue with the government. I

---

[528] Archbishop de Quélen's attachment to the senior Bourbon line made him very unpopular with the people after the 1830 July Revolution. In 1831, his episcopal palace was ransacked by the people and his books and furniture were thrown into the river Seine. See Larousse, *op. cit.*, v. 13, p. 513.

did not understand this objection very well, and when I left the archbishop I was very happy but determined to return to the attack.

The fact is that the political side of the Solesmes foundation had never bothered me until then. I had made the most of my time in Paris to get a prospectus printed about the work, not thinking that the authorities might find this reprehensible. As it happened, it did not attract attention at that time. Later on, when the Dominicans returned from Italy after their profession and established themselves in France, the government took measures against them. Since the authorities did not want to go as far as persecution, they eventually left things alone. For my part, I had drawn up my prospectus as early as 1833, without thinking that I was thereby attacking a dormant legality. I could not imagine that a sermon preached in a church in Paris, in aid of the reestablishment of an institution suppressed by the law, was anything other than a perfectly legitimate act originating from the freedom won in July 1830.

I saw the archbishop again on 7 May. He was kind but tried to dissuade me from the idea of a sermon, claiming that it would produce only a minimal result. He again stressed the illegality of religious orders, at the same time as deploring this fact. I felt that there would be no possibility of help from him if the government was to ask for explanations, or even if it was planning to oppose us. I submitted, but it took another thirty years and a change of political regime before I understood the situation. I can now see that in 1833 the government was being indulgent towards us.

Monsieur Bailly de Surcy was very friendly to me throughout my stay in Paris. On several occasions I had sent a few articles from Le Mans to his *Tribune catholique,* which was the predecessor of *L'Univers*. Right from the beginning, he had helped me financially, although he was far from rich. During my time with him he acquired a printing press, which led both of us to look into whether he could in due course transfer his printing patent to Solesmes, where the monks would work as typographers. Later on Monsieur Bailly came to study the matter on site, and we realized that it was not possible to carry out this idea. On the one hand, we were not big enough to provide sufficient material to supply the press as authors, and on the other hand, with our divine office and conventual observances, we would not have enough time to carry out the job of typesetting with any profit. Getting workers to come from Paris and set up in the house was not realistic, and would the government have allowed the Bailly printing press to be transported to the countryside?

During my stay, Monsieur Bailly devoted himself to procuring contacts and resources for me, but without much result. He lent me the sum of 1,000 francs to send to Fr Fonteinne, which I reimbursed before I left from the donations that I had collected. He was always a most devoted friend to Solesmes.

It is to him that I owe my acquaintance with several young people from the schools, who were lodging in his house and whom he was training to defend the principal interests of religion and public morality in talks that were partly open to the public. These discussions were led with real talent, and the speaker was often brilliant. It is there that, among other people, I got to know Monsieur Ozanam,[529] who was already looking very promising.

Monsieur Bailly introduced me to Monsieur Prosper de Charnacé,[530] one of his boarders, who was thinking of taking

---

[529] Blessed Antoine-Frédéric Ozanam (1813–1853), born in Milan to French parents. He grew up in France and obtained doctorates in both law and letters. He then became a teacher at the Stanislas college and titular professor at the Sorbonne, Paris. Profoundly conscious of the needs of young people and the poor, he was one of Bailly de Surcy's original companions in 1833 and is often considered to be the founder of the St Vincent de Paul Society; it is more accurate to say that he played a pre-eminent role among the group of original founders. He was beatified in 1997. For further information, see Jacquemet, *op. cit.*, v. 10, pp. 364–6. For a discussion of the origins of the St Vincent de Paul Society, see P. Jarry, *Un artisan du renouveau catholique au XIXème siècle: Emmanuel Bailly – 1794–1861,* unpublished doctoral thesis, Université Catholique d'Angers, 1971, pp. 380–6.

[530] Prosper de Charnacé (1811–1888), studied theology at Solesmes from October 1833. He became an honorary canon of the diocese of Laval. See the archives of the abbey of Saint-Pierre de Solesmes.

up the clerical state. This young man, who belonged to one of the best aristocratic families in Maine and Anjou, wanted to study theology at Solesmes and prepare for holy orders there. It was agreed that he would obtain the consent of the bishop of Le Mans and return to Solesmes for All Saints' day if the prelate was favourable. Everything turned out successfully, and Solesmes later gained a table companion in this young man who carried out his studies as agreed.

A most interesting incident demonstrates my relationship with Monsieur Bailly at this time. One day he asked me to accompany him to a house in rue du Petit Bourbon-Saint-Sulpice. There I found eight of his best young people,[531] one of whom was Monsieur Ozanam, assembled around a table covered with a cloth. Monsieur Bailly exhorted them to visit the poor and relieve their suffering. He assigned each of them a destitute family to assist and comfort; this was the beginning of the St Vincent de Paul Society. The following year I came back to Paris, but the cramped room I had seen was no longer sufficient; two years later the institution spread far beyond Paris. Having started the work and guided its members as their leader, Monsieur Bailly finally handed it over to Monsieur Gossier,[532] who was succeeded by Monsieur Baudon.[533] It would, however, be a supreme injustice to fail to recognize Monsieur Bailly as the founder of the St Vincent de Paul Society. This has actually been done, even though he presided over it and managed it for more than two years in sight of the whole of Paris. I am anxious to record my testimony here, thanking God for permitting my presence at the beginnings of a work that has

---

[531] Guéranger appears to be mistaken in recalling the number of students present at this gathering. Monsieur Bailly and the following six young men were present at this first meeting, making a total of seven: Paul Lamache, Felix Clavé, Auguste Le Taillandier, Jules Devaux, Frédéric Ozanam, François Lallier. Two more members joined shortly after this first meeting, which accounts for the popular belief that there were eight students at the first meeting. See A. Foucault, *La Société de Saint-Vincent-de-Paul – histoire de cent ans*, Paris, 1933, p. 19.

[532] Person currently unidentified.

[533] Person currently unidentified.

given rise to innumerable charitable acts throughout the
entire world, so to speak, and which has merited persecution by the Church's enemies.

During this time in Paris, I often saw my former parish
priest, Fr des Genettes, who was taking a keen interest in
Solesmes. In his poverty, he helped me with donations and
obtained several gifts for me. The main thing he did for my
mission in Paris, however, was to put me in touch with a
former Maurist, Dom Groult d'Arcy,[534] who was living in a
beautiful local fort in Vaugirard, and from whom the excellent parish priest was expecting significant assistance for the
future Benedictines.

Dom Groult was still a very young religious at the time of
the Revolution. I do not know how he got through this critical period, but under the First Empire he established quite a
successful boarding school. When I got to know him, he had
withdrawn to his house at Vaugirard, leading a secular life
and not wearing clerical dress. He did not say Mass, even
though he was a priest, but I know that he recited the divine
office using a breviary from the Congregation of Saint-Maur
drawn up by Dom Foulon.[535]

He held considerable assets. Apart from the house in
Vaugirard, which was solid, vast, well-built and with huge
grounds, he owned the abbey of Saint-Vincent in Senlis, the
former Génovéfain house,[536] and also had considerable sums

---

[534] This may be Nicolas Joseph Groult (1763–1843), professed at Fleury in
1784. See *Matricula*, p. 179.

[535] Nicolas Foulon (1742–1813), professed at Vendôme in 1759. He was
charged with renewing the breviary of the Congregation of Saint-Maur,
and this was published in 1787. It proved to be an eccentric work that
was refused approval by the superior general and which was never officially adopted by the Congregation. For example, Foulon eliminated all
Jesuits from the list of saints, changed the authorized prayers without
permission and introduced feasts for various false prophets. For
further information, see Prevost et d'Amat, *op. cit.*, v. 14, pp. 679–80.

[536] An abbey of Canons Regular of St Augustine of the Congregation of St
Géneviève, founded in 1059. See Cottineau, *op. cit.*, v. 2, p. 3005. For
further information on the Génovéfains, see Y. Breton, *Les
Génovéfains en haute-Bretagne en Anjou et dans Le Maine aux XVII
et XVIII siècles*, Paris, 2006.

of money under his control. I could not ascribe even an approximate figure to these sums. The lion's share of this fortune was a deposit that had been entrusted to him by Dom Verneuil, the last prior of the abbey of Saint-Denis, on condition that these resources be used for the re-establishment of the order of St Benedict should this become possible.

In 1817 Dom Verneuil, a worthy religious, had felt that the time was right to revive his Congregation. He thought that the re-establishment of the former royal dynasty was the sign to restore the Maurist institution, which had been held in such esteem. He was counting on help from the royal author-ities, in whom he placed all his hope. He therefore recalled all the former Maurists whom he considered suitable for re-establishing the institution. He obtained the agreement of some of them, who were exercising various roles in the secular clergy and in education. In order to gather together these religious, he acquired the abbey of Saint-Vincent in Senlis, which I have mentioned. Then, via Fr de Montesquiou,[537] one of the government ministers, he obtained an audience with Louis XVIII; he was presented to him along with two of his former companions whose names I do not know.

The king received these respectable monks very well, prais-ing their plan and promising to consider it with the greatest of interest. Dom Verneuil then saw Fr de Montesquiou and asked what needed to be done to bring the project to fruition. Fr de Montesquiou tried to get him to understand that since the

---

[537] François-Xavier-Marc-Antoine, duc de Montesquiou-Fezensac (1757–1832), statesman. Ordained priest and elected president of the house of clergy in 1789; elected president of the assembly in 1790, but opposed the suppression of religious orders, the civil constitution and the oath of allegiance. He sought refuge in England in 1792, but later played a key role at the Bourbon Restoration. He became minister of the interior in 1815, then minister of state and a member of the Chamber of Peers. Louis XVIII gave him the title of 'comte' in 1817 and 'duc' in 1821. He resigned from the Chamber of Peers in 1832, and died shortly afterwards. For further information, see Larousse, *op. cit.*, v. VI, p. 504.

208 *In a Great and Noble Tradition*

religious orders had been suppressed in France by a law,[538] a law was needed to re-establish them. He added that there would certainly be less opposition to the Congregation of Saint-Maur than to any old religious order. Nevertheless, they could not expect any authorization to reunite from the government, and he suggested that the only thing for them to do was to make this reunion spontaneously, which would serve as a basis for the ministry to raise the matter favourably before the legislative chambers.

Dom Verneuil informed his colleagues of the advice he had received from Fr de Montesquiou, and soon saw that the project would not be successful. The government wanted the reunion to occur before proceeding to request approval in the chambers. They could not promise this approval for certain, and the Benedictines thought that in sacrificing their positions they were running the risk of jeopardizing their future if the project did not obtain legislative support. Therefore they all remained in their posts. These elderly men from the *Ancien Régime* were quite incapable of understanding a project that had not received legal sanction, and still more incapable of running the risk. Dom Verneuil was thus reduced to a few former monks who did not hold any positions, who gathered together at Saint-Vincent, where they spent a year or two. There was only one novice, a young man who turned up by chance and whom Dom Verneuil rescued. Among the former Benedictines who had offered themselves for the work of restoration was Dom Barbier, an excellent monk and the former prior of Évron, who was living in this town. He did not go to Senlis. He was a friend of the Heurtebize family, and it was he who raised the venerable priest whose name I have already mentioned more than once, and inspired in him the attraction for the order of St Benedict that he has retained throughout his life.

Dom Verneuil's project was not successful, and this holy religious did not last long after this attempt. As I have said, he

---

[538] Religious orders other than teaching and nursing orders were suppressed by the government on 13 February 1790, as was permission to make solemn monastic vows. See *Les Dates*, p. 135.

left Dom Groult a considerable sum in deposit to be used for re-establishing the Benedictine order, should providence lead to this possibility in the future. Dom Groult had combined this money with his own assets, and yet was living quite simply on what remained.

He received me with interest and listened gladly. As for helping the work financially, he told me that he would not do anything at the moment. He had good intentions for the future, if the work was successful. Nevertheless, he added that he was willing to give me Saint-Vincent in Senlis immediately. This house was bringing in nothing but tax burdens for Dom Groult, and he admitted that 20,000 francs needed to be spent immediately to repair the roof. Neither the location nor the house was suitable for me, but it was easy to see that if I had accepted then he would have felt partially disassociated from his commitments with Dom Verneuil. I politely refused this house, which was in an area where I had no contacts and where we were unknown. The work would be carried out at Solesmes or nowhere. This house in Senlis was sold after Dom Groult's death, and has since become a Catholic boarding school.

Dom Groult did not much appreciate my idea of establishing pure monastic life at Solesmes. He wanted teaching and a boarding school; he was very afraid that I would introduce overly monastic customs into the house. It was clear that he no longer had the Benedictine spirit, if he had ever had it. In any case, he was glad to see me and invited me to dinner several times during my stay in Paris. I shall give the sequence of our dealings with one another as they occurred.

I remained in Paris for about two months, and was within easy reach of many people. I had frequent dealings with Monsieur de Montalembert. He took me to the home of the marquis de Dreux-Brézé, whom he had interested in Solesmes and who received me graciously. I also saw Monsieur de Carné,[539] who introduced me to Monsieur de

---

[539] Louis-Marcien, comte de Carné (1804–1874), one of the founders of the *Correspondant* who also worked on its successor, the *Revue européenne*. He was a elected a *député* in 1839 and became the minister for foreign affairs in 1847. See Jacquemet, *op. cit.*, v. 2, p. 585.

Chateaubriand, whom I had to thank for his letter. The great man lodged in the Marie-Thérèse Infirmary. Ten years previously, meeting the author of the *Martyrs* would have had a great effect on me. I must admit that in 1833 I was not very impressed. Chateaubriand was not an imposing figure, and his indecisive ideas about religion had already been distressing me for several years. I found his manner to be very superficial, which was shown in his undying boast to be a man of the moment. He congratulated me on the work and, like a bankrupt lord of the manor, paid me the forty-franc contribution that he mentioned in his letter. He had a secretary working for him, who was present during the visit, but I did not see Madame de Chateaubriand.[540] I had included his letter in the prospectus about the work. It was reprinted in the newspapers, and many honest people took literally the title of honorary Benedictine that Chateaubriand assumed there, to such an extent that they were convinced he was going to live at Solesmes.

I also had dealings with Fr Lacordaire, but we were not close. Victor Pavie[541] was then in Paris, and he often met up with me. I saw Sainte-Beuve again with him, for whose conversion he was hoping to some extent. He wanted to introduce me to Victor Hugo (who was then a friend of his), but he was not at home and I had better things to do than go back there. Through Madame Swetchine, I made the acquaintance of Monsieur Dugas-Montbel,[542] the translator of Homer, who

---

[540] Céleste-Buisson de Lavigne (1775–1847), the wife of the vicomte de Chateaubriand. She founded the Marie-Thérèse Infirmary in Paris in 1819. This charitable work was staffed by sisters of St Vincent de Paul, and cared for elderly and infirm priests, as well as local ladies. For further information, see *Les Contemporains*, 495, 6 avril 1902.

[541] Victor Pavie (1808–1886), a printer from Angers who studied law in Paris. He was also an author who was part of the Romantic movement. See www.cadytech.com/dumas/personnage.

[542] Jean-Baptiste Dugas-Montbel (1776–1834), Hellenist who devoted himself to translating the poetry and prose of Homer. His two most famous translations are *L'Iliade*, Paris, 1815, and *L'Odyssée, suivie de la Batrachomyomachie, des hymnes, de divers fragments attribués à Homère*, Paris, 1818. He spent the rest of his life revising and improving these translations, which met with critical acclaim. See Vapereau, *op. cit.*, v. 1, p. 669.

received me kindly. Monsieur Pouqueville[543] from the 'Institut'[544] wanted to meet me, and he listened with great interest as I talked about Solesmes. He donated several interesting volumes, and every year until his death, for which he had to wait only a few years, he sent me books and articles that came his way in his capacity as a member of the 'Académie des Inscriptions'.[545] Naturally, I was welcome in the home of the marquis Anatole de Juigné, a neighbour of Solesmes who had been very interested in the work right from the beginning. I had many other dealings with seculars, but I cannot remember them. The idea of the foundation was generally well received everywhere, but people hardly knew what monks were any more.

I also saw a certain number of clerics, Fr Combalot[546]

[543] François-Charles-Hugues-Laurent Pouqueville (1770–1838), traveller and literary figure. His learned travel writings on Greece, Constantinople, Albania and other countries attracted the attention of the government, and he was appointed French consul in Janina and then in Patras. He was admitted to the 'Académie des Inscriptions' in 1827. For further information, see Firmin et al., *op. cit.,* v. 40, pp. 931–2.

[544] The 'Institut de France' was the body of scholarly associations that comprised the 1795 regrouping of the five learned academies in France: 'Académie Française', 'Académie des Inscriptions et Belles-Lettres', 'Académie des Sciences', 'Académie des Beaux-arts', 'Académie des Sciences morales et politiques'. For further information, see Larousse, *op. cit.,* v. 9, p. 724.

[545] The 'Académie des Inscriptions et Belles-Lettres' was originally formed in 1663 as the 'Académie des Inscriptions et Medailles', and was responsible for composing inscriptions for the monuments erected by king Louis XIV, and for medals issued in his honour. In 1701 it received its current title and gradually acquired a more academic role, promoting historical and archaeological scholarship and continuing the scholarly work of the Benedictines of the Congregation of Saint-Maur. For further information, see Larousse, *op. cit.,* v.1, p. 44.

[546] Théodore Combalot (1797–1873), ordained priest in 1820; curate and parish priest of Charavines for a few months after ordination; appointed director of studies at the minor seminary in Paris (1820), and then director of studies and professor of philosophy at the major seminary in 1823. In 1824 he attempted to enter the Jesuit novitiate in Montrouge, but was rejected on account of his attachment to de La Mennais. He broke with de La Mennais after the latter's condemnation by Rome in 1832, and went on to found several religious congregations of his own. For further information, see Prevost et d'Amat, *op. cit.,* v. 9, p. 354.

among others, who was then brimming with youthfulness and enthusiasm. He too hardly had a clue about what it meant to be a Benedictine, but he was a devout young priest and could not fail to approve of the work. I saw Fr Augé,[547] the principal of Stanislas college, a venerable old man who was very friendly to me. He had his deputy with him, Fr Buquet,[548] a kindly man who has since become the bishop of Parium. Fr Maret,[549] who has since become the bishop of Sura, came to visit me at the 'Missions' to hear me talk about the Benedictines. He was deaf and did not look very well; I have not seen him since. Fr Chatenay,[550] an elegant and starchy man who later took over editing *L'Ami de la Religion* after Henrion,[551] visited me with the same intention. I went to see Fr Caillau, with whom I had worked on the *Collectio Selecta SS. Patrum*. He did not receive me well, showing

---

[547] Antoine-Jean-Baptiste Augé (1758–1844), after priestly ordination in the diocese of Beauvais he became rector of the minor seminary in Boulogne, and then vicar general of this diocese. He was made a canon in 1800 and moved to Paris, where he founded Stanislas college with two fellow priests. He was principal of this college from 1813–38. He later became vicar general and principal archdeacon of Paris. For further information, *Ibid.*, v. 4, p. 488.

[548] Louis-Charles Buquet (1796–1872), principal of Stanislas college; became vicar general and vicar capitular of Paris; refused the bishoprics of Versailles and Troyes; appointed bishop of Parium *in partibus* in 1863, and made a canon of Saint-Denis in Paris. For further information, *Ibid.*, v. 7, p. 675.

[549] Henri-Louis-Charles Maret (1805–1884), theologian and prelate. He was professor of dogma on the theology faculty in Paris, as well as a canon of Notre-Dame and honorary vicar general of Paris. His Gallican liberalism meant that his appointment to the see of Vannes in 1860 was blocked by Rome, but he was appointed bishop of Sura *in partibus* in 1861. For further information, see Larousse, *op. cit.*, v. 10, pp. 1162–3.

[550] Charles-Frédéric Chatenay (1798–1857), ordained priest 1832; became an honorary canon of Montpellier; editor of *L'Ami de la Religion* (1843–1845); vicar general of Pamiers in 1849. For further information, see Prevost et d'Amat, *op. cit.*, v. 8, pp. 793–4.

[551] Matthieu-Richard-Auguste Henrion (b. 1805), religious writer who qualified as a lawyer before turning to a literary career. He was the editor of *L'Ami de la Religion* from 1840 until 1843. For further information, see Firmin et al., *op. cit.*, v. 24, p. 178.

point-blank his antipathy for the work and his crude Gallicanism. It was he, the former French missionary and later a Mercy Father, who produced such spiteful articles against the *Institutions liturgiques* in the *Bibliographie Catholique*.[552] During my stay at the 'Missions', I had the joy of meeting once again a friendly Scotsman called Fr Gillis,[553] whom I had known in 1830 and who had become a close friend. He was a very devout man, with a character that was entirely French; we lived together like two brothers. He took a great interest in the work, not just because he was my friend but because he understood it. He was certainly the most outstanding priest in the whole of the Scottish mission. Later on, the Holy See made him vicar apostolic of Edinburgh,[554] where he died before his time, leaving a memory that was cherished by the Church in those regions.

My sojourn in Paris was not to be very productive in terms of material assistance. With great difficulty, I collected a sum of about 2,300 francs. Furthermore, the trip appeared to be no more auspicious from the point of view of vocations. At

---

[552] The *Institutions liturgiques* was a comprehensive introduction to the study of liturgy, surveying its historical and doctrinal content and development, the role of the popes in fostering liturgical unity, and advocating the supremacy of the Roman liturgy over Gallican liturgies. The original plan for the work outlined in the first volume was never entirely realized, but Guéranger did produce three volumes: *Institutions liturgiques,* Le Mans-Paris, 1840; *Institutions liturgiques,* Le Mans-Paris, 1841; *Institutions liturgiques,* Paris, 1851. For a discussion of this controversy, see Johnson, *op. cit.,* pp. 190–243. For a more recent discussion of the *Institutions liturgiques* and aspects of Guéranger's liturgical spirituality, see Bowen, *op. cit.,* pp. 99–125. The *Bibliographie catholique* was a Catholic journal founded in 1841 that was published for fifty years. See Jacquemet, *op. cit.,* v. 2, pp. 19–20.

[553] James Gillis (1802–1864), was actually a native of Canada. He was ordained priest in 1827; appointed coadjutor vicar apostolic of the Eastern District of Scotland and titular bishop of Limyra in 1837; he succeeded to the position of vicar apostolic of the Eastern District in 1852. See www.catholic-hierarchy.org/bishop/bgilli.html.

[554] Guéranger is mistaken in calling him the vicar apostolic of Edinburgh. Gillis was officially entitled 'vicar apostolic of the Eastern District', which included the city of Edinburgh.

that time, I was encouraging an interesting young man from Monsieur Bailly's house to enter Solesmes. He was called Félix Clavé and was very talented and naïve. We stayed in contact for several years, after which I lost touch with him. I thought that I would have better luck with Fr Lafayolle,[555] the chaplain of the 'Hospice de la Charité'. He came to see me at the 'Missions' and we agreed about everything. He made moves at the archbishop's palace for his replacement, and when I left Paris we made an appointment at Solesmes for 11 July, the planned opening time as advertised in the prospectus for the work. When I had left his courage failed him, and he soon wrote to me to withdraw.

Fr Daubrée, who had finally submitted to his call, was persevering at Juilly. I could not fail to visit and encourage him. I therefore left on 26 May for this former Oratorian college, which had been made into a very famous Catholic boarding school. Fr de Salinis, who was previously one of the editors of the *Mémorial catholique* and who has since become bishop of Amiens and then archbishop of Auch, shared the direction of the house with his friend, Fr de Scorbiac.[556] These gentlemen received me with open arms, and the pupils gave me a very warm welcome. I saw the excellent Fr Daubrée for the first time, having until then only known him via his letters. I stayed one full day at Juilly, being in a hurry to get back to Paris.

In Paris I received frequent letters from Fr Fonteinne, with whom I had an assiduous correspondence, informing him of my successes and failures. He was continuing to make arrangements for the house, where he was living with Pierre,

---

555 Person currently unidentified.
556 Bruno-Casimir de Scorbiac (1796–1846), ordained priest in Paris in 1820; assistant chaplain at the lycée Henri IV (1820–1825); appointed university chaplain in 1825, a post that enabled him to lecture in various colleges throughout France. He joined his friend Fr Louis-Antoine de Salinis in reopening the college at Juilly in 1828, which they co-directed until 1840. He founded the *Revue de l'Université Catholique,* which was published from 1835–1865. Finally, he became vicar general of Bordeaux in 1841. For further information, see the family archives of the de Scorbiac family.

a lay brother from Melleray called Br Bertrand[557] and a certain Br Gérasime,[558] a non-priest choir monk who had also been sent by Father Abbot. Neither of these monks was there when I got back. They were getting bored, and Fr Fonteinne had had to send them back to Melleray. There were also two children, of whom I had once hoped to make something. One of them was from Asnières and was called Arsène,[559] the other one was from Solesmes and his name was Henri Tillé. It was not possible to keep either of them.

The work was far from making great strides, and yet God placed a simple trust in my heart that was undeterred by anything. I was praying a great deal, and very fervently, but my prayer was never disturbed by worries. I now recognize clearly that I was being sustained. However little I had thought about it from a human perspective, it was all too clear that I did not have the means at my disposal for such a work to succeed. I had a great devotion to visiting the Black Virgin, which was kept in the chapel of the sisters of St Thomas of Villanova. This is the same Madonna that was previously in the now destroyed church of Saint-Étienne des Grès, and at whose feet St Francis de Sales was delivered from a temptation against trusting in God. Before this revered image, I entrusted my labours to the Queen of Heaven and asked her to bless them. After this, I went on my way without ever feeling the slightest hesitation.

I had several opportunities to exercise my ministry in Paris during this time, and I did so gladly. The clergy had a little more freedom outside since the cholera epidemic. Nevertheless, in order to walk about in safety it was a good idea not to turn up in clerical dress wherever one went. I had brought my secular clothes from 1830 with me, and I often used them

---

[557] Br Bertrand was skilled in the fabrication of sandals and boots and in the husbandry of cows, but he left after two weeks due to an arm injury. See L. Soltner, 'Les premiers compagnons de Dom Guéranger' in *Lettre aux Amis de Solesmes*, 4 (1983): 16.

[558] Fr Gérasime did not arrive at Solesmes until after Br Bertrand's departure. He too seems to have had health problems. *Ibid.*

[559] Arsène Bouju was fifteen-years-old and was interested in becoming a lay brother. He stayed at Solesmes for just a few months. *Ibid.*

in the street. Fr des Genettes got me to give the sermon on Ascension Day in the church of Notre-Dame-des-Victoires. Fr Le Courtier,[560] his successor at the 'Missions', insisted on inviting me to give the first Holy Communion retreat to the children of the parish. I was glad to devote myself to this, and I must say that the children were very docile and attentive.

During this time, we kept ourselves busy publicizing the work via the press. Monsieur de La Noue, one of Monsieur Bailly's young people, submitted a good article to the *Tribune catholique,* which was reprinted in the *Union belge.* One after another, various Catholic journals were also talking about the work, the *Revue européenne* among others. Donations were sought, but not many materialized; public opinion was not at all prepared for a work like this. I therefore returned to Madame Swetchine, who had made plans in earnest to help me. First, I must talk about a ceremony that took place at her home.

Pope Gregory XVI had delivered a brief granting her a domestic oratory. On his own authority, the archbishop added to this the right to reserve the Blessed Sacrament; he came to bless the chapel on 20 May. Madame Swetchine invited me to the ceremony and to the lunch that followed it. The prelate was rather cold towards me. The chapel itself had been decorated very sumptuously, endowed with elaborate sacred vessels and elegantly embroidered vestments. Since then, I have had the opportunity to celebrate Holy Mass there during my various trips to Paris.

As far as helping Solesmes was concerned, Madame Swetchine had devised a plan for contributions of five francs per year, which was to be managed by several of her lady

---

560 François-Marie-Joseph Le Courtier (1799–1885), ordained priest in 1823; he was successively curate in the parishes of Saint-Roch, Saint-Nicholas-des-Champs and Saint-Étienne-du-Mont, before becoming parish priest of the 'Missions Étrangères' (1830–1840). He became a titular canon of Paris (1849); archpriest of Notre-Dame (1850); and preacher to the Emperor Napoleon in 1854. He was consecrated bishop of Montpellier in 1861, and was given the title of archbishop of Sebastia after his resignation in 1873. See *L'Épiscopat,* pp. 374–5.

friends who would collect this donation. We started immediately, but the contributions were so feeble and the benefactors so few that the annual figure could not be very great. In the first year it had great difficulty reaching six hundred francs, and it never rose to fifteen hundred as long as the work lasted. There were some windfalls of several hundred francs that Madame Swetchine had even solicited from abroad (for example from her friend the comtesse Essling in Odessa[561]), but overall the effort was rather feeble; there was a lack of interest. No one in the *faubourg* Saint-Germain was bothered about the Benedictines, and still less did they want their resurrection. This meant that the lady patronesses were wasting their time. They often found very rich people who agreed to give five francs out of consideration for them, but who refused any voluntary commitment other than to pay this contribution each year. These people said in all earnestness that this was the interest on one hundred francs. This fundraising work did not last beyond the year 1838.

The marquise de Pastoret,[562] a close friend of Madame Swetchine and a devout, respectable woman, was in charge of the lady patronesses. She showed great consideration towards me, and even invited me to dinner. I made the acquaintance of her husband, the old marquis de Pastoret,[563] who received me with great courtesy. In his capacity as a member of the 'Académie des Inscriptions', he had great esteem for the Benedictines. He had been a friend of Dom Brial[564] and Dom Poirier.[565] I got to know Fr Dupanloup[566] at Pastoret's house

---

[561] Roxandre-Skarlatovna Stourdza (1786–1844), the comtesse Essling. See M. Brecht (ed.), *Geschichte des Pietismus,* Munich, 1862, p. 134.

[562] Adelaïde-Anne-Louis Piscatory de Vaufreland (1765–1843). She married Claude-Emmanuel de Pastoret on 14 July 1789. See http://www.fr.wikipedia.org/wiki/Claude-Emmanuel.

[563] Claude-Emmanuel de Pastoret (1755–1840), lawyer, man of letters and politician. He served as a *député* in the legislative assembly; minister of the interior (1791); senator (1809); minister of state (1826); chancellor of France (1829–1830); peer of France; and president of the Chamber of Peers (1829–1830). For further information, *Ibid.*

[564] Michel-Joseph Brial (1743–1828), professed at La Daurade in 1764. See *Matricula,* p. 164.

since he was a regular visitor there. He looked very young then, but it was easy to see that if he did not achieve anything in life then this would not be through any fault of his own. The marquise de Lillers,[567] another friend of Madame Swetchine and more unaffected than Madame de Pastoret, was very devoted to the work. She arranged for me to have dinner with Bishop Guillon of Morocco, who offered to tell the queen about Solesmes in his capacity as her chaplain; she would certainly not fail to make her donation. Madame Swetchine did not consider it wise to pursue this avenue, for fear of offending the *faubourg* Saint-Germain.

There was also the duchesse de Rauzan,[568] who took the project to heart; the duchesse de Liancourt,[569] who is now the duchesse de La Rochefoucauld and the only one of these ladies with whom I have stayed in touch; the comtesse de Swistounoff,[570] a Russian convert whose kindness was cold but genuine; and Mademoiselle de Pomarey,[571] a devout, spiritual woman who took the work seriously. There were a few more lady patronesses, but not many; I did not know them personally and I have forgotten their names. Also at Madame Swetchine's home, I got to know a Russian convert called Monsieur Yermoloff,[572] who was extremely intelligent,

---

[565] Germain Poirier (1726–1803), professed at Saint-Faron in 1740. See *Matricula*, p. 139.

[566] Felix-Antoine-Philibert Dupanloup (1802–1878), ordained priest in 1825; curate at La Madeleine (1826–1834); curate at Saint-Roch (1834–1837); rector of minor seminary of Notre-Dame-des-Champs; canon of Notre-Dame and honorary vicar general (1845); bishop of Orléans in 1849. For further information, see *L'Épiscopat*, pp. 433–9.

[567] Ambroisine-Marie d'Estampes (1769–1861), married Charles, duc de Biéville, the marquis de Lillers, in 1789. See www.web.genealogie .free.fr/Les_dynasties.

[568] Claire-Henriette de Durfort-Duras (1799–1863), married Henri-Louis de Chastellux (1786–1863), duc de Rauzan, on 28 August 1819. See www.web.genealogie.free.fr/Les_dynasties.

[569] Zénaide Chapt de Rastignac (1798–1875), married François XIV de La Rochefoucauld (1794–1874) on 10 June 1817. See http://www.fr .wikipedia.org/wiki.

[570] Person currently unidentified.

[571] Person currently unidentified.

profoundly Catholic and whom I liked very much. As for General Swetchine,[573] already almost an octogenarian, I saw him in the drawing room several times. He was always polite and kind to me until his death. Even though he was completely indifferent to all religious ideas, he never hampered any of his wife's endeavours.

I did not go back to Solesmes without first making various purchases in Paris for our future church. Firstly, we needed to supply the choir with chant books. The only edition on sale had just been produced in Dijon according to Valfré's notation. I bought graduals, antiphonals and processionals. I purchased seven copes: two white and two red, of differing quality, then a green one, a purple one and a black one. We were not numerous enough to think about dalmatics. As for chasubles, I had assembled locally what we needed to begin with.

I bought a bronze-plated cross and the candlesticks for the main altar at Choiselat's. I also bought silver-plated copper furnishings for the two altars in the transepts. These two altars had been given to the parish priest of Solesmes two years ago by Madame Le Noir de Chanteloup, and were replaced by two old discarded ones that Fr Fonteinne found at Monsieur Landeau's place. Madame Le Noir had also given the parish the only remaining bell in the monastery, along with the two replicas of the white marble statues of St Peter and St Paul in the church of La Couture in Le Mans. I also bought at Choiselat's the processional cross, two thuribles and incense boats, the acolyte candles and the holy water bucket, all made of silver-plated copper. Finally, I bought the reliquary of St Peter, with its bronze statuette. We needed two bells: one in the church tower for the offices and the other above the chapterhouse for the conventual observances. I was talking about this in Dom Groult's home one day in the presence of the parish priest of Vaugirard, and

---

[572] Pierre Yermoloff (b. 1792).

[573] Nicolas Swetchine (1759–1850), remained Orthodox when his wife converted to Catholicism in 1815, although he was not a profoundly religious man.

expressed my desire to find a shop where I could purchase them. The good parish priest told me that he could show me an excellent place in the *faubourg* Saint-Martin. 'But,' he added, 'the shopkeeper has such a strange, ridiculous name that I am sure you will never have heard it before.' He searched for a long time without remembering. 'At last,' he exclaimed, a quarter of an hour later, 'the name has come back to me. He is called Hildebrand! Have you ever heard of a name like that?' Dom Groult and I had difficulty in suppressing a burst of laughter. After the initial mirth, I said to him gently: 'But, Father, has anyone *not* heard of the fiery Hildebrand or, in other words, St Gregory VII?'[574] My remark was lost on him since the good parish priest admitted naively that he had never heard of either of them. I went to old Monsieur Hildebrand's shop in rue Saint-Martin and bought my two bells; one larger and one smaller. They cost 130 francs for the pair.

As for literary works that we might undertake, I saw the Gaume brothers[575] on several occasions, who discussed with me their project to re-edit the Montfaucon[576] edition of St John Chrysostom, offering me responsibility for this task.

[574] Gregory VII (*c.*1025–1085), pope from 1073; he was canonized in 1606. Hildebrand was his baptismal name. For further information, see Farmer, *op. cit.*, pp. 232–3.

[575] Jean-Alexis Gaume (1797–1869) and Jean-Joseph Gaume (1802–1879). The elder brother was ordained priest in 1821 and became professor of moral theology at the major seminary of Besançon. He became the chaplain to the Carmelites in Paris in 1834, and was later canon (1840), vicar general (1842–1856) and vicar capitular (1848) of the diocese of Paris. His younger brother was ordained priest in 1825 and became professor of dogma at the major seminary in Nevers. He later became a titular canon (1828) and vicar general (1848) of this diocese; he resigned in 1852 and withdrew to Paris. For further information, see Prevost et d'Amat, *op. cit.*, v. 15, pp. 779–80.

[576] Bernard de Montfaucon (1655–1741), initially pursued a military career, but was professed as a monk of the Congregation of Saint-Maur in 1676 at Daurade, Toulouse. He began work on an edition of the Greek Fathers in 1687, and made extensive research trips to Italian libraries in aid of his work. His appointment as procurator general of the Congregation while in Italy interrupted his research, but on his return to France in 1701 he resumed work. His acclaimed editions of

This work did not appear until about ten years later.

Finally, my long sojourn in Paris came to an end and I arrived in Le Mans on 18 June. The bishop was no longer there. His health, which had been threatening him for a long time, had got worse and he had left for the waters. I was very annoyed not to find him in his town, all the more so since I had advertised in the newspapers that our small society would be installed at Solesmes on 11 July. In itself the agreed day could not be better, and it was no longer possible for me to defer it. I promptly went to Sablé to see Fr Fonteinne, and was able to assess the major preparations and repairs of all kinds that had occupied his free time during my absence. I soon returned to Le Mans, where I saw a lot of Fr Bouvier and whom I found kind as ever. I also saw Fr Heurtebize, who was as friendly as usual but less resolved than ever about joining the future Benedictines. Fr Boulangé was not making much progress and asked for more time. As for Fr Morin, he certainly would have come if the bishop had not kept him in his cathedral curacy, which he was to leave only for his eternal reward.

---

the works of St Athanasius and St John Chrysostom are but a small part of his numerous publications. For further information, see Larousse, *op. cit.,* v. 11, p. 506.

Inauguration of Monastic Life

July finally came around, and the installation day was imminent. The bishop wrote to Fr Bouvier saying that it would be impossible for him to be back in his diocese on 11 July, and that he was consequently entrusting Fr Bouvier to go to Solesmes in place of him for the installation of the new community. The prelate added that should the trip be impossible for Fr Bouvier, he was asking him to enlist Fr Bourmault, the second vicar general, or one of the honorary vicars general to stand in for him. The bishop then added these words that have remained with me: 'Finally, if none of these men wishes to undertake it, Fr Guéranger will have to install himself on his own.'

After passing on this letter to me, Fr Bouvier explained that to his great regret he could not preside over the ceremony on 11 July since the *viva voce* theological examinations took place in the seminary on that very day, which he would have to supervise. He went to Fr Bourmault straight away to inform him of the bishop's wishes. I did not enjoy much affection from Fr Bourmault, a great reader of *L'Ami de la Religion* who did not look kindly on the work of Solesmes, and he flatly refused. Fr Bouvier informed me of this expected refusal at my father's home, and we discussed what could be done to avoid Solesmes looking as though it had been brushed aside by the administration. I suggested that Fr Bouvier should try Canon Ménochet, whom Bishop Carron had kept on as a vicar general. He was not very keen on me, but he was a venerable man and a former confessor of the faith in Rochefort harbour.[577] Perhaps he would be flattered by this task, which was to consecrate the resurrection of a past institution.

Fr Bouvier left immediately, and headed for Canon Ménochet's home. Shortly afterwards, he returned with the news that the old man had gladly agreed to install the aspirants to the Benedictine Rule at Solesmes on 11 July. I hurried to thank him, and we made the arrangements for his task; soon after this I made my way to Solesmes.

Fr Daubrée arrived around 8 July, followed shortly afterwards by Monsieur Le Boucher; Fr Jouanne came last. As for Fr Lafayolle, after arranging his departure at the archbishop's palace in Paris, his courage failed him and he ended up writing me a letter of excuse. Including Fr Fonteinne and me, there were five of us in all. The lay brothers comprised Pierre,[578] a young cook from Le Mans called Garnier[579] (who was later known by the name *Tête de Bique*),[580] a young wheelwright called Joseph[581] who was also from Le Mans, and a fourth whose name I have forgotten.[582]

On the morning of 10 July, we went to the room that was to serve as the chapterhouse and proceeded with the election of a prior. I was elected by the brethren, and immediately announced that Monsieur Le Boucher was to be the sub-prior and that Fr Fonteinne was to be the cellarer. From then on we took the name 'Père', and even 'Dom' for

---

[577] During the Revolution, from 1794, a large number of priests were held prisoner in boats that were moored in Rochefort harbour due to a lack of prison space.

[578] Pierre Hureau. There is no information about this postulant in the archives of the abbey of Saint-Pierre de Solesmes.

[579] Pierre Garnier. There is no information about this postulant in the archives of the abbey of Saint-Pierre de Solesmes.

[580] Literally: 'Goat head'. This nickname was commonly used in the community at the time, and indicated someone rather unruly and thoughtless. See Soltner, *op. cit.,* 19.

[581] Joseph Piogé. There is no information about this postulant in the archives of the abbey of Saint-Pierre de Solesmes.

[582] There is no record of this fourth lay brother in the archives of the abbey of Saint-Pierre de Solesmes. None of these four original lay brothers persevered in monastic life.

priests; Fr Bouvier had thought that we should do this.[583]

The temporary chapel was still the guest room, and we reserved the Blessed Sacrament there until the installation. With Fr Bouvier's permission, it was there that I blessed the bell destined for the church and named it Marie-Pierre. Monsieur de Charnacé attended the very simple ceremony and the bell was placed in the tower immediately, where it still remains.

Canon Ménochet arrived around 4.00 p.m. We received him with ceremonial since he was representing the bishop, and escorted him to the temporary chapel while we sang the *Benedictus*. He was lodged in the priory, which we later called the *abbatiale*, and was very kind. We sang first Vespers of St Benedict and, in the evening, Compline according to the Roman rite, which was observed at Solesmes until first Vespers of Christmas in 1846. It was only from 1840 that we followed the monastic office in choir on major feasts of the order.

The following day, 11 July (the feast of the translation of the Holy Patriarch), we celebrated Matins and Lauds. After saying our private Masses, we waited for the hour to say Terce, which was to be the time of the ceremony. About thirty secular priests had gathered to witness it. Among them were Fr Boulangé and Fr Morin, who had come from Le Mans, and Fr Segrétain,[584] the parish priest of Le Tassillé; he was a respectable priest whom I had got to know on a journey six months earlier, and who had inspired me with great affection. From the beginning, he had thought of withdrawing to Solesmes and his presence that day was motivated by this desire that had already got a grip on him. We did not talk about it at all that day.

---

[583] The custom of the Solesmes Congregation, which prevailed until the Second Vatican Council, was for non-ordained choir monks to be addressed as 'Père' ('Father') even though they were not yet clerics. This custom has now been discontinued.

[584] Julien Segrétain (1796–1861), was one of four monastic professions received by Guéranger on 21 November 1837. He became sub-prior and then prior of Solesmes from 26 January 1853 until his death. See the archives of the abbey of Saint-Pierre de Solesmes.

When the bell had announced the ceremony, we assembled in the parish church wearing Roman surplices, but without bands. The vicar general, who was following the secular clergy and the processional cross, came to collect us. We left the church singing the psalm *In convertendo*,[585] which seemed to me to lend itself to the circumstances. This re-entry into the old eleventh-century priory was very much a return from captivity. The tears[586] and trials that God does not spare were awaiting us. As for sheaves of gladness,[587] they would not be lacking, if not in this world then at least in the next.

The Mass was sung in the monastery church by Canon Ménochet according to the Roman rite. Before this, he had installed the prior and the other brothers in the choir. The large congregation was obviously curious and even astonished. We could see that this crowd, clerical or otherwise, no longer knew who St Benedict was, whose translation we were celebrating. Nevertheless, God was watching over us attentively, and the Holy Patriarch approved of the tribute. After the Gospel at this Mass, in which Fr Morin and Fr Boulangé were fulfilling the function of sub-deacon and deacon, Canon Ménochet gave an address to the gathering that was marked by strong faith and kindness towards us. After Mass was over, a procession made its way towards the guest room, where the celebrant took the Blessed Sacrament to transfer it to the church. There he placed it in a mahogany tabernacle that was set up on the altar of Our Lord in the right transept. The blessing of the church and the regular places had taken place before Mass.

At lunch we read *The Life of St Benedict* by St Gregory, and at supper we began an abridged history of the order by

---

[585] That is, Psalm 125 [126], which begins, *In convertendo Dominus captivitatem Sion: facti sumus sicut consolati* ('When the Lord delivered Sion from bondage, we became like those who are comforted').

[586] *Euntes ibant et flebant, mittentes semina sua* ('They go forth weeping, sowing their seed').

[587] *Venientes autem venient cum exaltatione, portantes manipulos suos* ('They shall come again with rejoicing, bringing their sheaves with them').

Bulteau.[588] The serving at table was performed somewhat awkwardly, but Canon Ménochet was very indulgent to us. He left the following day, having shown us affectionate and cordial concern.

From Vespers of this great day, the divine office has never been broken off in our church. From the beginning, without deviation, we have observed the customary that is still kept today for singing or simple recitation, according to the rank of the feast. Mass and Vespers were sung every day, despite our small number. On feast days, the celebrant donned a cope for the *capitulum* and incensed the altar during the *Magnificat*. We could not have ministers at Solemn Mass, but on Assumption day Fr Le Boucher served at the altar as a deacon. This custom continued on high days until we became more numerous.

Regular abstinence from meat has also been kept from the beginning, as sanctioned in the constitutions approved by apostolic authority in 1837. The same goes for the times of offices and the daily round of conventual observances. The only exception to this was for Matins, which from All Saints' day until Easter I had thought of celebrating in the evening after Compline. We tried it on 1 November, or rather on 31 October. The office, including Lauds, lasted until beyond 11.00 p.m. In this arrangement, we did not rise until 5.00 a.m. After a week, the small community was so tired that we had to restore Matins to 4.00 a.m. throughout the year.

From the installation day, we thought of ourselves as novices. This novitiate would end with the taking of vows for one year on 11 July 1834. We had no habit other than the cassock without bands, and a Roman surplice in choir. From All Saints' day until Easter we wore over this a hooded cloak made of black cloth. This was while we were waiting to adopt the religious habit, which we still did not dare to wear for fear of alerting the police.

---

[588] Louis Bulteau (1625–1693), literary figure. The work to which Guéranger refers is his *Abrégé de l'histoire de l'ordre de Saint-Benoît et des moines d'Occident* (1684). Bulteau also published a translation of the *Dialogues* by St Gregory the Great in 1689, which may have been the version mentioned by Guéranger above. See Vapereau, *op. cit.*, p. 338.

As far as a means of subsistence was concerned, our only fixed revenue was from Mass offerings. The small sum of money we had saved to begin with amounted to about five hundred francs. This sum could not last for very long since it was being used to maintain eight (*sic*) people. Nevertheless, I was not worried since I was convinced that God would always come to our assistance; several modest contributions did in fact arrive. Madame Swetchine's efforts were not to yield anything until the winter. Small offerings would also arrive occasionally, and Father Cellarer would find something in the church collection box from time to time. I had had written on this box: 'For the needs of the establishment', not mentioning the word 'monastery' or 'community' in anticipation of a raid from the king's prosecutor. We had to get the better of the legal system without being imprudent. Within a few years we were accepted as we were, although this did not prevent the authorities from trying to threaten us at various times, but without result. On several occasions in the first few years, Madame Swetchine's correspondence testified to the danger of the situation. It would certainly have been difficult to form the establishment in Paris with the publicity that I had given it; in a country province, and in the absence of denouncement from the prefect and sub-prefect, Louis-Philippe's government turned a blind eye.

We were barely installed when the first opposition came our way. *L'Ami de la Religion,* which was still edited by Picot, continued to exercise supreme control over a considerable body of the clergy. The influence of Picot, a layman who lacked even the most elementary ideas about ecclesiastical matters, reigned over many bishoprics and seminaries. On the pretext of waging war against Fr de La Mennais and his school, he had ended up becoming the official oracle of the most narrow-minded and foolish Gallicanism. Solesmes had offended him straight away. He found my name on the list of the new Benedictines and, although he could not be unaware that nothing had been done without the agreement of our bishop, this consideration did not stop him. The edition for 30 July contained a critique of Solesmes, about which the journalist wanted to make French Catholics suspicious. The article began by praising the Congregation of Saint-Maur and then continued in these terms:

Several months ago, the newspapers advertised a new project to re-establish the Benedictines. They even published a sort of prospectus, which rightly sang the praises of the Congregation of Saint-Maur, and which appeared to want the revival of this learned body. To this end, a fund was opened and a letter from Monsieur de Chateaubriand, who took the title of 'honorary Benedictine of the new Congregation of Saint-Maur', praising this undertaking was quoted approvingly. This new sort of affiliation seemed rather singular, and many people felt that it was not in accord with the simplicity and gravity of monastic custom. We have never heard of honorary Benedictines, or of laymen attached to the Congregation of Saint-Maur. Be that as it may, it was advertised that some young clerics had bought the former priory of Solesmes, near Sablé in Le Maine. They were to assemble on 11 July, when the feast of St Benedict is generally celebrated in France. The house was to be composed of six (*sic*) choir religious and four lay brothers. The principal author of this project seemed to be Fr Guéranger, an honorary canon from Le Mans and author of a treatise about the election of bishops, which was reviewed in this paper, and also of several articles about the liturgy that were previously published in the *Mémorial catholique*. He and his associates were said to be linked to the opinions of the authors of *L'Avenir*.

It was expected that these men would try to join up with one of the former Benedictines. There are still several respectable members of the Congregation of Saint-Maur in France, whose assistance seems necessary for the new associates in order to give them a good understanding of the spirit of the Rule and inculcate in them the traditions of the order of St Benedict. This help would be all the more natural since the future Benedictines are all rather young; the experience of some former monks would be both agreeable and useful to them. Nevertheless, they have not felt the need for this advice and support, and have started their undertaking alone. It is said that they have not even concealed their wish not to have any Benedictine from Saint-Maur with them, since the Congregation was sullied by Jansenism and Gallicanism; they were afraid of perpetuating this spirit among themselves.

This judgement is harsh and unjust. There were Jansenists in the Congregation of Saint-Maur but they were very few, especially towards the end. Their Gallicanism was no more dangerous than that of so many priests against whom this charge has been made in the *Mémorial* or in *L'Avenir,* and who have nevertheless given spectacular proof of their devotion to the Holy See.

In all honesty, we are amazed that men who wish to become Benedictines are rejecting all contact with the surviving Benedictines in France. They had advertised in their prospectus that they were longing to raise this ancient Congregation of Saint-Maur from its ruins; but then they sideline it completely, avoiding all dealings with it. They are abandoning their initial devotion to the great names of Mabillon and Montfaucon, whose renown would have protected them. What does the new association stand for? What sort of Benedictines are they who refuse the traditional initiation? Who will guide them during their novitiate? Will there even be a novitiate? It is said that on the 11 July they appointed a prior; but have novices ever appointed a prior? Moreover, this prior is just as much of a novice as the others. Whatever his talents, spirit, virtue and learning, he cannot yet have a very good understanding of the spirit of the Rule, and it is hard to see how he can form others.

These are the thoughts that occur to us regarding an undertaking to which we regret being unable to give exclusive praise. Everything leads us to believe that the new associates have good intentions, but it is to be feared that they have not fully worked out the direction that must be followed to ensure the success of their work. The first founders of the order did not start like this, and neither did the Congregation of Saint-Maur. What would happen if the novices at Solesmes, instead of being formed in recollection and silence in the virtues proper to their state, were to throw themselves immediately into a literary career, publishing books and devoting themselves to scholarly research? This would be to put the finishing touches to the building before laying its foundations. This is not all, however, and one newspaper has implied that the young Benedictines may be about to produce a journal. Why shouldn't they, this newspaper said? This idea would certainly have seemed very strange to St Benedict and his first disciples. Novices producing a journal and thus being formed in the religious life; this must be a joke.

Nevertheless, we understand very well that some pious men could be taken in by the hope of resurrecting a body that is famous in the Church for its virtues and services. We understand that the clergy as a whole would welcome such an idea to form a house of recollection, prayer and study.

As we have said, 11 July had been chosen for the opening of the house of Solesmes. One newspaper said it was the bishop of Le Mans who had presided over the ceremony. This is a mistake; the prelate was temporarily absent from his diocese. It was Fr Ménochet, a canon and vicar general of Le Mans, who presided over the ceremony. First, the priory church was blessed. A solemn procession went to the parish church to collect the assembled associates, and they were led to their new home singing psalms. Fr Ménochet gave them a talk about their vocation and exhorted them to persevere. Then Mass began, after which there was a procession in the cloister and the Blessed Sacrament was deposited in the tabernacle. There was great satisfaction at restoring Catholic worship in a church that was of interest, due to its ancient features and contents. The priory church of Solesmes, built towards the end of the fourteenth century, is decorated with statues and bas-reliefs made in the fifteenth and sixteenth centuries. In the right chapel there is a group of six statues, which depict the death of Our Saviour. René the Pious,[589] the duc d'Anjou, had them made. The statues in the left chapel are more modern, being attributed to Germain Pilon.[590] One can see Jesus among the doctors, the dying Holy Virgin and her sepulchre; each of these groups is made up of several statues. This church is a veritable museum; it is a surviving

[589] René I (1409-1480), king of Naples, duc de Lorraine and Bar, duc d'Anjou, comte de Provence. He was renowned for his literary and artistic taste, and commissioned many paintings, books, sculptures and plays. For further information, see Voisin, *op. cit.,* p. 895.

[590] Germain Pilon (c.1515–1590), sculptor. The collection of about forty statues known as the 'Saints de Solesmes' is often attributed to him. His father, however, was also a sculptor, and had taught his son. Furthermore, he shared the same name as his son and had also worked in the region of Le Mans. It therefore seems likely that they worked together on this collection. For further information, see Larousse, *op. cit.,* v. 12, pp. 1016–17.

monument to the devotion of those times when it was an honour for princes and lords to adorn and embellish churches.

To come back to Solesmes, ensuing events will tell us the spirit in which it is to be directed, and if it is to be an edifying, useful community, where there is no place for attachment to novelties. In this past century, attachment to novelties has ruined several Congregations, and further novelties would be even more fatal to an emerging body that does not offer every guarantee of enduring stability.

It was difficult to be more gratuitously spiteful, but from that day onwards the enmity between Solesmes and the serpent was never to calm. This attack had come not only from Picot but also from the Gallican camp for which he was the spokesman, and it had been expressed in such a way as to cause us real harm. I had had some warning of it before the outburst and had started to write to Picot in my defence, hoping that this would ward off what could be a fatal blow for us. He included my letter in his edition for 8 August. This letter, which crossed the article of 30 July in the post, ran as follows:

Priory of Solesmes, diocese of Le Mans, 1 August 1833

Sir,

Having been appointed head of the establishment that has just formed at Solesmes in the diocese of Le Mans, under the Rule of St Benedict and the statutes of the Congregation of Saint-Maur, I ask you to give space in your newspaper, which is one of the mouthpieces for the clergy, to the following complaints that I send you as much in my own name as in the name of my brethren.

The establishment at Solesmes was formed only with the authorization and encouragement of the bishop of Le Mans. We receive all that we are from him, and a single act of his will could dissolve our association without there being any question of the slightest resistance on our part.

Our principal aim in assembling at Solesmes has been to establish a house of recollection and prayer, where some shadow of the former virtues of the cloister may flourish once again. We also wish to provide a refuge for souls who are called to religious life, but who do not find in France the necessary assistance to pursue their vocation.

Our secondary aim has been to devote ourselves to ecclesiastical studies, considered as much in themselves as in their connection with the branches of other human sciences. Sacred Scripture, Christian antiquity, canon law and history will be the principal areas of our work. Furthermore, we are far from encouraging pretensions that are incompatible with the weakness of an institution that has only just come into being. We wish only to consecrate ourselves to the faithful service of the Church, in the time remaining free to us after the celebration of the divine office.

We are not a faction and we do not belong to any party. Before admitting a man to our society, we do not make enquiries as to what he thinks about matters that the sovereign authority of the Church has felt should be left free.

Nevertheless, we do ask for complete submission from all our brothers to all of the decisions and teachings of the apostolic see, and in particular to the encyclical letter of our Holy Father Pope Gregory XVI, dated 18 September 1832. The intention of this encyclical is explained fully by the apostolic brief sent recently to the archbishop of Toulouse.[591]

As far as current affairs and personal political questions are concerned, we do not intend to take part in them. To our mind, this pretension seems ridiculous for monks, and culpable in men who should give all their time to prayer and study.

We are confident in placing this objection in your newspaper, dear editor, and hope that via this medium it may reach those people who, so we are told, have found our association a cause for scandal. We forgive them completely, and ask them to believe that we, no more than they, know of no other party than Jesus Christ and his Church, and no infallible doctor other than the one for whom the prayer of the Son of God alone has won unfailing faith.

Yours respectfully,
Fr Guéranger, priest.

---

[591] Paul-Thérèse d'Astros (1772–1851), appointed archbishop of Toulouse in 1830. See footnote 209, p. 54. He published his *Censure de 56 propositions de Monsieur de La Mennais* in 1832.

Fr Bouvier had been very annoyed about the article of 30 July. His concern for us led him to write a letter of complaint to Picot on 3 August. This letter made too many concessions to the journalist, conceding that several of us had been indiscriminately favourable to the doctrines of *L'Avenir*. Fr Bouvier sought clumsily to appease Picot with regard to my articles against him in the *Mémorial,* articles that I had acknowledged to be too harsh. Yet the editor of *L'Ami de la Religion* still hesitated to include Fr Bouvier's letter, and did not do so until 15 August. Even then, he still tried to win the upper hand for his own position in the gloss that accompanied the letter, which took advantage of what Fr Bouvier had said about the articles in the *Mémorial,* and passed over their real content in silence. He took the liberty of ridiculing the letter from Chateaubriand, and again criticized with the same banality the title of 'prior', which he thought premature. Apart from this, and with much ill will, he accepted the letter, the content of which was as follows:

New letter about the establishment at Solesmes

Apart from Fr Guéranger's letter, which we included last week, we have received a letter from Fr Bouvier, the vicar general of Le Mans, about the same subject. Perhaps the inclusion of this letter is not necessary after the first one, but we are very pleased to give Fr Bouvier proof of deference to his wishes. Here is his letter:

Le Mans, 3 August 1833

Sir,
    The leading article in your edition of 30 July 1833, dealing with the emerging community of Solesmes, has upset us. I feel bound to correct several assertions that are liable to cast disapproval on an establishment that could be useful on more than one count, and which should in any case be encouraged rather than criticized.

1. If several of the associates have been favourable to the doctrines of *L'Avenir,* they have given them up quite explicitly enough to fully satisfy the bishop of Le Mans,

who had some initial misgivings in this respect and who for this reason hesitated to give his approval. They have formally stated that they would not embrace any system, and that they would never form a separate party. On several occasions, Fr Guéranger has spoken to me of his regret at having written certain articles in the *Mémorial* in the way that he did; his ideas on this subject have changed significantly.

2. These good men are not seeking to isolate themselves from the former Benedictines. On the contrary, they would have been delighted to find some of them who truly wanted to be in charge of them, and who were not prevented by age or infirmity from taking up and living the Rule once again. They could not find such men, and they did not want to give up their plans simply because of this.

3. They are well aware that they are not yet true Bene-dictines, but only priests living in common under a rule modelled on St Benedict's rule and approved by the local bishop, to whom they continue to submit in all matters. They intend only to lead the life of Benedictine regulars, and hope to be canonically approved later on if their undertaking prospers.

4. They are not thinking about publishing books, and still less of producing a journal. This is a joke or an invention that can only come from a spiteful mind. Above all, they want to be excellent priests, to live as good religious, to use the time remaining after the choir office and their other devout observances for studying, and to abandon to providence any success that may come of it.

A house like this could be very useful for clerics who love the common life, who are attracted to study, and who have an extreme repugnance for the social side of sacred ministry. For this reason, we all wish prosperity on the house that has just been established at Solesmes. Appealing to your honesty and love for truth, I expect you to include these observations in one of your next editions.

Yours etc.,
Fr Bouvier, vicar general

It seems to us that this letter could be used to prove that we were not too severe in our first article about Solesmes. It will be noted that Fr Bouvier is well aware that the members of this association at Solesmes are not true Benedictines, which is also our opinion. He considers it a joke to imagine that they wanted to produce a journal, but we did not think this up; it was some friends of these men who told us this in a newspaper that we could quote. We thought that they were well-informed, and there was certainly no maliciousness in their account. It is true that these writers have done more harm than good to the undertaking by means of their exaggerated eulogies. Everyone agreed that the letter from Monsieur de Chateaubriand was quite ridiculous, and they also seem to agree that the title of 'prior' given to Fr Guéranger is premature to say the least. Therefore, we were not wrong to criticize all these things.

Fr Bouvier gives us to understand that the bishop of Le Mans had some initial misgivings about the sentiments of the associates at Solesmes towards the opinions of *L'Avenir*. It is, therefore, not surprising that we have had some suspicions in this respect. These men have made satisfactory statements to their bishop, but since we had no knowledge of these statements, which have remained secret, our unfavourable predispositions could not have been dispelled. The last letter from Fr Guéranger is the first sign that we have had of his current views regarding the opinions with which he had been associated. Our eagerness to include his letter is proof of our goodwill. Moreover, we are delighted to see from Fr Bouvier's letter that this young cleric has on several occasions expressed regret to the venerable vicar general at having written certain articles in the *Mémorial*.

These explanations will perhaps prove that we did not act thoughtlessly, and still less under the influence of our passions, in our article about Solesmes. We are ready to welcome every work whose aim is to glorify God, and we will not be the last to praise this one if it enjoys all of its expected success.

Picot's reproach to us for not bringing in the former Benedictines leads me to say a word about the dealings we had with some of them when we were founded. The former Benedictines were already very sparse since the last professions dated back to 1790. I have spoken about Dom Le Comte, whom I had known in Nantes and who had been about to bring the benefit of his virtue and experience to Solesmes. Dom Groult was not uninterested in us, but there was no hope that he would leave Vaugirard for Solesmes. Dom Chabert,[592] a canon of the city of Tours and a highly esteemed man, sent me a most gracious and kind letter, and later supplied us with various liturgical books of the order. In Le Mans, Dom Fréart,[593] an honorary canon whose naïve devotion made people forget his unfortunate weaknesses during the Revolution, welcomed the foundation of Solesmes with all his heart, and it was he who gave us our first martyrology. His former colleague, Dom Dubreuil,[594] who lived in Normandy, sent us affectionate encouragement through him from time to time. I have forgotten some of them, but I must not fail to mention Dom Debroise,[595] a canon of the Church in Rennes. When he later had the opportunity, he did not fail to express his fraternal support.

The divine providence that did not allow the name of the Congregation of Saint-Maur to be conferred on our monastic family did nevertheless procure for us a token of our union with this famous body, and in a very moving way. Dom Ambroise-Augustin Chevreux[596] had lived at Saint-

---

[592] Bernard-Étienne Chabert (1761–1847), professed at Saint-Melaine in 1785. See *Matricula*, p. 180.

[593] Pierre-Bernard Fréart (1758–1835), professed at Saint-Germer in 1779. He took the constitutional oath of the clergy and became parish priest *intrus* and episcopal vicar. He resigned these functions in 1794 and became director then inspector of mail, a position which he held until 1820. He was made an honorary canon of Le Mans in 1803. See *Le Chapitre*, pp. 16–17. See also *Matricula*, p. 174.

[594] The *Matricula* lists just one monk of this name who made profession in the Congregation of Saint-Maur: Pierre-Jean Dubreuil (1718–1791), professed at Saint-Wandrille in 1735. Guéranger would thus appear to have made a mistake in recalling the name of this monk.

[595] Jean-Elisabeth Debroise (1766–1859), professed at Saint-Serge in 1787. See *Matricula*, p. 181.

[596] Blessed Ambroise-Augustin Chevreux (1728–1792), professed at Saumur in 1744. He was ordained priest in 1752 and was appointed novice master and later prior at the abbey of Saint-Vincent in Le Mans,

Vincent in Le Mans, and later became the superior general of the Congregation of Saint-Maur. After refusing to take the oath to the civil constitution of the clergy, he was imprisoned and killed at the Paris Carmel in September 1792. In this way, he redeemed by his own blood the faults committed by the many members of this body who were sullied by Jansenism, Gallicanism and later on even by Philosophism.[597] One day during the first ten years of our Congregation (I cannot remember this year with any precision), the niece of a lady to whose home Dom Chevreux had withdrawn in Paris when he was arrested, came to Solesmes to offer us (free of charge) the pastel portrait of this venerable monk, the seal of the Congregation of Saint-Maur, the superior general's everyday stamp and an antiphonary for Vespers of second-class feasts, which was made of vellum manuscript and was formerly used by the celebrant in the choir of Saint-Germain-des-Prés. These objects had been carefully preserved by the lady whom I have just mentioned, and when her niece heard about the re-establishment of the order at Solesmes she thought that she could do no better than deposit this precious store into our hands. In this way, the Congregation of Saint-Maur appeared to be placing its succession into our hands by means of a third party, entrusting us with the portrait (which is probably unique) of its martyr superior general, and with the seals of his administration.

Surely it was significant that this attempt to restore the order of St Benedict in France appeared in this region of Maine, from where a mission had left to visit the Holy Patriarch so as to obtain from him his rule and his disciples?

---

which was later Guéranger's major seminary. He served as prior, cellarer and visitor in various houses of the Congregation before being elected superior general in 1783; he was re-elected in 1788. At the Revolution, he opposed the civil constitution of the clergy and tried to continue his monastic life. He was arrested and martyred on 2 September 1792 and was beatified in 1926. See Prevost et d'Amat, *op. cit.*, v. 8, pp. 1116–17.

[597] In the eighteenth century, the term 'philosophism' described a system of thought that recognized no other authority than human reason.

Surely St Maur,[598] who had been the principal instigator of the rule in the West via the Gauls, would protect this humble attempt at a monastery where, four years later, the apostolic see would recognize and approve the re-establishment of the Benedictine order in France? Surely the dove of Plombariola[599] (St Scholastica), who chose this region of Maine as the resting place for her sacred bones,[600] had some affection for Solesmes, where shortly afterwards she prepared a nest for those chaste doves who would call her their mother?

Mary watched over us so as to strengthen our weakness. News of our association had reached 'Notre-Dame des Ermites' in Einsiedeln,[601] and on 11 July a French monk, Dom Claude Perrot,[602] sent us the following letter from this Benedictine sanctuary of the Queen of Angels. We rightly considered it as a token of the maternal protection of Mary, whose love and power always comes to the assistance of those who trust in her.

---

[598] St Maurus (6th century), became at monk at Monte Cassino. He later became identified with another Maurus (d. 584), who founded the Benedictine abbey of Glanfeuil (also known as St-Maur-sur-Loire) in Gaul. Although this identification has now been discredited, its acceptance in the seventeenth century led to St Maurus being adopted as the patron of the Congregation of Saint-Maur. See Farmer, *op. cit.,* p. 360.

[599] St Scholastica's nunnery was situated at Plombariola, about five miles from Monte Cassino.

[600] Around 650, Bishop Béraire founded the monastery of Saint-Pierre in Le Mans, which he wanted to place under the Benedictine Rule. He is said to have had the relics of St Scholastica placed there at the same time as those of St Benedict were allegedly transferred to Fleury in the seventh century. St Scholastica later became the patron saint of Le Mans.

[601] The hermitage of Einsiedeln, Switzerland was founded by St Meinrad (d. 863) in 838. It was replaced by a Benedictine monastery, which was founded in the tenth century. For further information, see Cottineau, *op. cit.,* v. 1, pp. 1034-9.

[602] Claude Perrot (1803-1881), professed in 1822; ordained priest in 1827; chaplain to the nuns at Einsiedeln (1839-1853); master of lay brothers (1842-1846); master of choir brothers (1853-1868); he wrote extensively to promote perpetual adoration of the Blessed Sacrament. See the archives of the abbey of Einsiedeln, Switzerland.

Benedictine Monastery of Notre-Dame des Ermites
Einsiedeln, Switzerland
11 July 1833

My dear superior,
My dear and very reverend brothers,

The Church in France, always rich in salutary institutions even when her enemies seem to have rendered her sterile, today rejoices in an event that recalls her golden age, and which has rekindled her most beautiful hopes. This event is your association into a Congregation under the rule of our Patriarch and founder, St Benedict, on the very day dedicated to his solemn commemoration. The happy, delightful news has reached the depths of Switzerland and has filled with joy the Benedictines of the monastery of 'Notre-Dame des Ermites'. They could not fail to look upon this new seed of the ancient and famous Congregation of Saint-Maur without feeling the deepest gratitude towards divine providence, which is so wonderful in its ways, so rich in its gifts and so admirable in the means it employs to carry out its divine decrees: *A Domino factum est istud, et est mirabile in occulis nostris.*[603]

As the only Frenchman living in our holy house, it is especially fitting that I should take a keen interest in your new life and in everything that may henceforth influence your future. It is a pleasure for me to assure you that today, 11 July, the very day of your installation, all of my thoughts, prayers and good wishes have been focused on you alone. May it please the God of mercies to be generous in bestowing his divine blessings on your holy community, and to make it a place of refuge for many such sublime souls whom Catholic France continues to beget, and whom God calls into the desert. May it also be a place of peace and fraternal union for sacred studies, which seem to have been repudiated by our frivolous age. Above all, may it please the Queen of Heaven to extend her protective hand over you; may she be a refuge for you against all the powers of hell, which never fail to incite persecution of all who are called to glorify God and console his Church. Considered under this last aspect, your new career may give rise to misgivings for the future. Unfortunately, it no

---

[603] 'The Lord has done this thing, and it is wonderful to our eyes'.

longer belongs to kings and the great men of this world to establish pious foundations, to endow the servants of God and to assist the efforts of his Holy Church, as in former times. All they can now give is a feeble glimmer of tolerance accorded to pagan and Christian alike. The true sons of the Church, however, being better instructed than ever by the experience of our own time, wish for no other support than the Lord who made heaven and earth: *Bonum est sperare in Domino, quam sperare in principibus.*[604]

How happy I would be if I could witness your offerings and sacrifices on this day and share in the joy of the faithful of Le Mans, who are witnessing new servants of God consecrate themselves in their midst to the holy rigours of penance and service of the Church. At least I am present in spirit at these moving ceremonies, and I am united in intention to all holy souls whose fervent prayers will strengthen the work, which is so clearly inspired from heaven. Dear brethren, if we are ever in a position to be of service to you in any way then please do not hesitate to ask. Accept, dear brothers, the sincere congratulations of our whole community, and especially of its unworthy spokesman.

Your very humble servant and brother,
Dom Claude Perrot

The bishop soon returned from the waters, and went back to Le Mans towards the end of the month. His health was far from encouraging, but he bravely resumed his ministry. I soon wrote to him to give an account of our establishment. Wanting to establish in this monastery a sign of our trust in the Sacred Heart of Jesus, to which I had dedicated the work, I asked the prelate for permission for Benediction of the Blessed Sacrament on the first Friday of every month, which is especially devoted to the divine mystery of the heart of the man-God. I also asked for Benediction on various feasts. Everything was granted, but I only received the right for the concession after the prelate's death. He also wanted to grant in perpetuity an indulgence of forty days to all the faithful who would pray in our church for the success of the project

---

[604] 'It is better to hope in the Lord than to hope in princes'.

during the octave of the translation of St Benedict. The protection of this good bishop was essentially our only support in the face of the expected opposition, as much from within as outside the diocese. God soon removed from us even this support, to teach us to rely on no one but him alone. On 27 August the bishop died suddenly, without even having had time to receive the last rites. Such a loss was felt by us very keenly at a time like this. The diocese might now have as its bishop a man who was hostile to us, who could have been influenced by *L'Ami de la Religion*. Moreover, the interim administration of the Chapter was sufficiently opposed to us for Fr Bouvier to write and tell me that henceforth he felt forced to conceal his interest in us. He encouraged us to keep as low a profile as possible, and to wait patiently for the choice of successor to Bishop Carron.[605]

In fact, our situation in the region was not wonderful. No one knew what a monk was anymore, and the name 'Benedictine' had been completely forgotten. The result of this was fundamental indifference, accompanied by hostility in many people. This was because we were unfortunate enough to be prophets in our own country, and also because we were taken to be Mennaisians. Naturally, I bore the responsibility for this accusation on behalf of everyone, and those who were kicking up the greatest fuss would have been hard pushed to quote a single line from me in support of Fr de La Mennais' philosophical system. They had never read my book, *De l'élection et de la nomination des évêques*, which Fr Lacordaire had attacked in *L'Avenir* as not squaring with the liberal Catholicism that this newspaper had founded. I was known to be an Ultramontane, and the political aversion for the Orléans dynasty professed by most of the clergy lured them into a Gallican reaction against those who, following Rome's example, were accepting the government *de facto*.

Nevertheless, it was not correct to accuse us of flattering the power that stemmed from the July Revolution. Firstly,

---

[605] Jean-Baptiste Bouvier himself became the bishop of Le Mans (1834–1854).

we had decided that in the event of being attacked by the administration, we would use all possible means of defence offered to us by the *Charte* of 1830. Furthermore, we were resolved never to sing the *Domine, salvum fac regem nostrum Ludovicum Philippum*[606] in our church, since this practice was contrary to the norms of the Roman liturgy. For the same reason, we did not say the *pro rege nostro*[607] in the canon of the Mass. Despite their professed Legitimism, the secular clergy used to sing the *Domine salvum* at both Mass and Benediction in their churches, and they accused those of us who did not sing it of making trouble for the July government. Perhaps it was of some merit for us in our precarious situation to proclaim the freedom of the Church in this way. On more than one occasion, our abstention was noticed by people from whom we could have expected some benefit or feared in some way. We never deviated from our practice, but the Legitimists did not warm to us for this very reason.

The Legitimist camp, which was then much larger than it is today, professed a violent disdain for everything that did not share its sorrows and hatred. Our establishment was in its eyes a protest in support of the new regime, for the sole reason that we kept out of every political alliance. In the county chateaus, our establishment was said to be doubly annoying; if it was unsuccessful it would be detrimental to religion, and if it was successful it would give reason to believe that something good could be established under the July government. Therefore, we could not rely on either the friendship or the assistance of the local aristocracy.

As for the bourgeoisie who had won in July, they dismissed us instinctively. Particularly in Sablé, they were famous for their ignorance and intellectual vacuity, and they considered us to be Chouans or at least Legitimists. We were thus obliged to live in this region without relying on anyone. Moreover, there was no shortage of people for whom we did not even exist.

---

[606] 'Lord, save our king Louis-Philippe'.
[607] 'For our King'.

We received proof of this during the seminary holidays. One afternoon, several professors from this establishment came to visit us. As these good men were walking in the garden, one of them, Fr Chevereau,[608] let slip this significant remark while he was looking at the buildings: 'What a beautiful house. And what a shame that it is not inhabited!' This naivety embarrassed the others. We remained silent, but it was clear that two or three months after our installation by a vicar general in the name of the bishop, the people of Le Mans were not aware of our existence.

The parish priest of Sablé was secretly hostile to us, but at least we could rely on the kindness of the parish priest of Solesmes, who crossed swords with some of his colleagues on our account. The good Fr Jousse only fell out with us in 1839, but he held firm to his opposition until the end. He was not well-read and sometimes lapsed into a naivety that we found delightful. One day I was in the garden with him; it seems that I could not understand some preposterous question or other about horticulture. He interrupted me, saying: 'So, you haven't read *Le Bon Jardinier*?'[609] 'Never,' I replied. He changed the topic of conversation, but I had fallen in his esteem and a few days later he said to someone: 'Would you believe it? This Fr Guéranger who is said to have read so many books has not even read *Le Bon Jardinier*.' Another time, he was questioning me about the etymology of the word 'Solesmes'. After enumerating the various Latin names of the village as found on certificates and other documents, I finished by telling him that, properly speaking, the etymology seemed almost impossible to discover. 'Really,' he said with a satisfied look, 'well, I'll tell you. Solesmes comes from

[608] Hippolyte Chevereau (1806–1880), ordained priest in 1828; became a professor at the minor seminary of the Tessé, and then at the major seminary of Saint-Vincent. In 1840 he became rector of the major seminary, as well as a titular canon and honorary vicar general of Le Mans. He was vicar general of Le Mans from 1842 until 1855, and again from 1867. For further information, see Prevost et d'Amat, *op. cit.,* v. 8, pp. 1088–9.

[609] *Le Bon Jardinier* ('The Good Gardener') was an annual almanac of ornamental plants and trees. It would have been well known to horticultural enthusiasts at the time.

Saladin.[610] You know that Saladin was a Huguenot[611] who declared war in this region during the time of the Huguenots. That's why my parish is called Solesmes.' This will give the measure of the character who was to play some role in this account. Apart from him, we hardly received any visits from priests except from Fr Coquereau,[612] who had replaced Dom Fonteinne in the Sablé curacy. He was spiritual, kindly and courteous; he was later raised to military honours and died a chaplain of the fleet.

Translators' note
Dom Guéranger's account of his life ends abruptly at this point. It is clear from the text that he intended to complete his account, but this intention was never fulfilled. For further details of Guéranger's life, the reader should refer to the several biographies that have been written about him in French, to his published letters and to other publications dealing with his life and work. Especially noteworthy are Guéranger's personal diary, which covers the period 1852–1874,[613] and also various chronicles by monks of Solesmes covering the years 1831–1846 and Guéranger's three main visits to Rome (1837, 1843, 1851–1852).[614]

---

[610] Saladin (Yousouf-ben-Ayoub Salah-Eddyn) (1137–1193), the Kurdish Sultan of Egypt (1171–1193) and Muslim hero of the third crusade (1189–1192). For further information, see Voisin, *op. cit.,* p. 931.

[611] The term 'Huguenot' was coined in sixteenth-century France and was used to refer to the Protestants. In no sense at all was Saladin a Huguenot, and neither did he fight a battle in France.

[612] Félix Coquereau (1808–1866), ordained priest 1833 and became a curate in Sablé; he moved to Le Mans and then Paris, where he found greater scope for his vocation as a preacher. In 1840 he was appointed chaplain of the *Belle-Poule*, which went to St Helen's on an expedition to collect Napoleon's ashes. After various voyages, he was appointed chaplain of the fleet in 1850. For further information, see Angot, *op. cit.,* v. 1, p. 714.

[613] *Diaire de Dom Guéranger, 1852–1874,* Archives Dom Guéranger, V/3, Solesmes, 2007.

[614] *Chroniques et Journaux de Voyage,* Archives Dom Guéranger, V/2, Solesmes, 2007.

Appendix

Letter of 18 January 1832
from Fr Prosper Guéranger
to Pope Gregory XVI

Beatissime Pater,

Licet terreat me Apostolici Culminis Majestas, attamen non amplius desiderium et totum cordis mei votum valeo cohibere. Audebo igitur, filiorum minimus et ultimus, orbis Parentem affari, eique jam a pluribus annis concepta, Magnorumque virorum aucta suffragio, humili mente aperire.

Duo sunt, Beatissime Pater, Eccelesiæ Christi cujus Caput divina clementia effectus es, permaxime necessaria, et sine quibus velut utroque lumine orbæ, non est ei species neque decor; monasticæ vitæ professio scilicet, et ecclesiasticarum scientiarum cultus. Luget, eheu, quadraginta abhinc annis impie depopulata, Ecclesia Gallicana cui vix, a tanto tempore, umbram institutionum monasticarum, rarissimis in locis et quasi furtim conspicere datum est; luget et non vult consolari, illa quæ olim apud exteras gentes incomparabilis doctrinæ habebatur, nunc autem, multis de causis et doctrina et doctis miserrime destituta. Interim grande animarum exitium quærentium solitudinem in qua Deus ad cor loquitur et non invenientium; necnon ingens sacerdotii nostri dedecus, ob veterum traditionem, sanique juris oblivionem, ob exilem doctrinam junioribus clericis suppeditatam, eo quod jam non sint qui ingratis difficillimisque studiis incumbere curent. Undique jam a pluribus annis clamor desolatus exsurgit; omnes tantam malorum abyssum norunt, confitenturque. Nullus est, fere nullus, qui de utriusque plagae remedio, efficaci modo, recogitaverit. Plures attamen sacerdotes postquam ingemuissent coram Deo qui consolatur omnes ruinas Israel propria infirmitate non fracti, plurimumque confidentes in Domino, eo usque audaciæ devenerunt ut censerent se non penitus Ecclesiæ Dei inutiles fore, si pro tantis malis præcidendis, et impenderent sua, et se ipsos superimpenderent. Hi sunt, Beatissime Pater, qui mihi fide generosa adhæserent, et quorum vox, nunc apostolatus tui concutit aures. Hæc quidem sibi exsequenda proponunt. Occidentalium monachorum Patriarchæ Beati Benedicti regulam amplectentes; veterem monasticam disciplinam instaurare; præhabito propriæ perfectionis studio, scientiæ ecclesasticæ totis viribus incumbere, sacris litteris, catholicis traditionibus, pontificioque juri totam vitam impendendo; uno verbo, clarissimæ congregationis Sancti Mauri premere vestigia, humili certe gressu, sed forte feliciori. Longe enim abierunt a nobis deploranda illa adversaque apostolicæ dignitati et potentiæ systemata, sæpissime eximiis aliunde operibus, infauste permixta. Jam nobis non sunt Alpes; et nos Romani sumus, Romanam in omnibus doctrinam propugnare parati.

Itaque, Beatissime Pater, ego hodie, nomine proprio, sociorumque personam gerens, quæso Sanctitatem tuam quatenus dignetur ad nos respicere, rem tanti momenti considerare, filiosque quid agere debeant edocere. Memineris, Beatissme Pater, te quoque Beati Benedicti discipulum, et proinde augendæ Sancti Patriarchæ familiæ studiosum. Numerosi coetus affulget nobis spes fundatissimam; huic arridere digneris, et nulla novos Benedictinos terrere poterunt.

Illud, Beatissime Pater, humillimi postulo ut mihi supplicanti Sanctitas Vestra velit consilium cordis sui, super hoc notum facere, testorque me paratum ad obediendum in omnibus, sive carissimum opus derelinquere oporteret, sive, ut spero, ad illud exequendum satagendum esse judices.

Quod si invenerit gratiam coram oculis tuis illa ordinis Sancti Benedicti instauratio, dignare, Beatissime Pater, ordinarium nostrum, Episcopum videlicet Cenomanensem, certiorem facere, Sanctitati Tuae nostrum gratum esse propositum. Illud enim Apostolicum testimonium reverentur suscipiet eximius Præsul, et quodam modo expectat, cum scilicet mihi dixerit se nobis propitium fore, si nobis propitia fuerit apostolica sedes.

Tunc ad Romanum Ecclesiam citissimi mittemus, canonicam confirmationem exspectantes, statuta specialia quibus regulam Sancti Patriarchæ Benedicti ad scopum nostram aptabimus, et ea quæ a constitutionibus Apostolicis ordinata sunt circa regularium domorum erectionem ad unum verbum adimplebimus. Sed prius nobis a te dicendum est, Beatissime Pater, an existere, quam quomodo debeamus.

Pusillo gregi benedictionem Apostolicam digneris tandem impertiri cujus nomine, nec non pro seipso, tam pretiosum pignus efflagitat, Beatissime Pater, Sanctitatis tuae, humillimus devotissimus obedientissimus servus et in Christo filius,

Prosper Guéranger, presbyter
Canonicus honorarius Ecclesiæ cathedralis
Sancti Juliani Cenomanensis in Gallia
Cenomani in Gallia die 18 januarii 1832

Most Holy Father,

When I consider the majesty belonging to the Chief of the Apostles, I am filled with fear; nevertheless I find myself no longer able to restrain the desire and longing that fills my whole heart. So I, who am the least and the last of his sons, hereby make bold to address the Father of the whole world, and humbly to make known to him a project which was conceived several years ago now, and which has the active support of men of high standing.

Most Holy Father, two things especially are necessary to the Church of Christ, whose head by divine clemency you are. Without these two, which are like the two lights of the firmament, the Church has neither form nor beauty (Is 55:2). They are the profession of monastic life and the cultivation of ecclesiastical studies. Alas! The Church in France is in mourning: she who was sacrilegiously despoiled forty years ago now, and who in all that time has scarcely been able to glimpse even a shadow of monastic life, and that, as it were, furtively and in very scattered places. She is in mourning, and refuses to be consoled (Jer 31:15; Mt 2:18): she who was once esteemed among the nations for the incomparable quality of her teaching, and who now, under various pretexts, has become unhappily destitute of both teaching and teachers.

Meanwhile great harm is suffered by those souls who seek and do not find that desert in which God speaks to their heart (Hos 2:14). Our priesthood also is brought into low repute for its abandonment of former ways, its forgetfulness of sound law, and the shallowness of formation given in its seminaries, so that there is now scarcely anyone capable of devoting himself to the necessary studies, extremely difficult and thankless as they are. For many years now, and from all sides, the same desolate cry rises up: everyone is aware of and acknowledges this deep abyss of every ill. But there is no one, or almost no one, who has come up with an effective means to remedy this double affliction.

Yet there is a group of priests who have wept before that Lord who gives consolation to the ruins of Israel (Is 51:3). These men are not disheartened by their own weakness, but trust very much in the Lord: indeed so much so that they have come to that point of audacity, whereby they reckon that even they themselves will not be entirely useless to the Church of God if they devote all they have, and even more so if they devote all they are, to the cause of putting an end to these great evils. It is these men, most Holy Father, who with generous fidelity have attached themselves to me, and whose plea is herewith coming to your apostolic notice.

This is what they propose to do. They wish to embrace the Rule of St Benedict, Patriarch of the monks of the West. They wish to restore the ancient monastic discipline; and while keeping the pursuit of their own perfection as their first priority, they wish to devote all their energies to ecclesiastical studies, spending their whole life in the study of sacred letters, Catholic traditions and the rights of the Roman Pontiff. In a word, they mean to pursue the path formerly trodden by the famous Congregation of Saint-Maur; certainly in all humility, but also perhaps somewhat more fruitfully. Far from us, indeed, that deplorable school of thought, inimical to the dignity and power of the apostolic see, subscribed to in general by the Maurists. What a sadness it is that such opinions were so often insinuated into otherwise truly excellent works. As for us, the Alps do not exist.[615] We are Romans, and we are ready to fight for the Roman doctrine in all matters.

And so today, most Holy Father, in my own name, and also on behalf of my companions, I ask Your Holiness to deign to turn your attention towards us. Consider this matter, which is of such great moment, and teach your sons what they should do about it. Remember, most Holy Father, that you too are a disciple of St Benedict, and consequently must be anxious to increase the family of the Holy Patriarch. The fixed hope of a numerous throng shines on us. Deign to look favourably on this project, and nothing will be able to terrify the new Benedictines.

This is what I ask, most Holy Father: that Your Holiness might choose to make known to me, who is most humbly beseeching him, the counsel of his heart regarding this matter. I solemnly declare myself ready to obey you in all things: whether it should be necessary for me to abandon this work so close to my heart; or, as I hope, whether you judge that we should set to work with a will to bring it all to fulfilment.

If this restoration of the order of Saint Benedict finds favour in your sight, deign, most Holy Father, to inform our Ordinary, the bishop of Le Mans, that our proposal is pleasing to Your Holiness. This excellent prelate will reverently receive the apostolic decision. Indeed he is, as it were, waiting for it, since he has told me that he will be favourable to us if the apostolic see is also favourable.

Once this permission has been obtained, we will send to

---

[615] Guéranger means by this that the physical barrier of the Alps mountain range, which separates France from Italy, is no barrier to the unity of heart with Roman doctrines pledged by him and his companions.

the Roman Church with the utmost haste the special statutes by which we propose to adapt the Rule of the holy Patriarch St Benedict in accordance with our intended goals. We will then await canonical confirmation. Whatever the apostolic constitutions ordain concerning the regular erection of our houses, we will fulfil to the letter. But we first need to be told by you, most Holy Father, whether these houses should exist at all before we can go on to decide how they should exist.

Finally, most Holy Father, graciously deign to bestow as a precious pledge the apostolic blessing on the little flock (Lk 12:32) in whose name, and also very much for himself, he earnestly entreats Your Holiness – he, your most humble, most devoted and most obedient servant and son in Christ.

Prosper Guéranger
Priest and honorary canon of the cathedral church of
Saint-Julian in Le Mans, France
18 January 1832

Index

Printed in the United Kingdom by
Lightning Source UK Ltd., Milton Keynes
140177UK00001B/13/P